THIRD EDITION

The Complete Job Search Book for College Students

by Richard Walsh

Foreword by Michelle Soltwedel

A Step-by-Step Guide to Finding the Right Job

Adams Media
Avon, Massachusetts

Published by
Adams Media, an F+W Publications Company
57 Littlefield Street, Avon, MA 02322. U.S.A.
www.adamsmedia.com

ISBN 10: 1-59869-321-2
ISBN 13: 978-1-59869-321-8

Printed in United States.
**Library of Congress Cataloging-in-Publication Data
is available from the publisher.**

Many of the designations used by manufacturers and sellers to distinguish their product are claimed as trademarks. Where those designations appear in this book and Adams Media was aware of a trademark claim, the designations have been printed with initial capital letters.

This publication is designed to provide accurate and authoritative information with regard to the subject matter covered. It is sold with the understanding that the publisher is not engaged in rendering legal, accounting, or other professional advice. If legal advice or other expert assistance is required, the services of a competent professional person should be sought.
—From a *Declaration of Principles* jointly adopted by a Committee of the American Bar Association and a Committee of Publishers and Associations

*This book is available at quantity discounts for bulk purchases.
For information, call 1-800-289-0963.*

Contents

Part I: Gearing Up for the Hunt

Part II: Tools of the Trade, Resumes and Cover Letters

Part III: Making the Right Impression

Part IV: Landing the Job

Why You Need This Book

I'm pleased that I was asked to write the foreword for *The Complete Job Search Book for College Students*. This job search guide is different and very much needed.

As a professional recruiter with more than a decade of experience interviewing hundreds of entry-level candidates, I can honestly say that I've pretty much seen it all: Cover letters littered with grammatical errors, and resumes that look nice but lack substance; highly educated applicants with little or no clue about the skills employers want, or how to get them; college graduates with solid credentials, but with no clear career focus. I wish every candidate had read a copy of *The Complete Job Search Book for College Students* before they came into my office, or, better yet, before they even started looking for a job.

Now in its third edition, *The Complete Job Search Book for College Students* is the definitive guide for serious first-time job seekers. Newly revised to address the unique challenges college graduates face as they approach today's competitive workplace, this book is more than a collection of sample resumes and interview questions. It's a complete handbook for landing your first professional job, including tips on how to:

- Establish a timetable for job search success
- Develop the key qualities and skills employers want most
- Gain valuable experience through academic and extracurricular activities
- Build resumes and create cover letters for the electronic age
- Use the World Wide Web to research careers and job opportunities
- Handle tough interview questions with confidence
- Evaluate multiple job offers and negotiate better pay and benefits from a position of strength

Perhaps no other choice you will make in life is more important than your choice of a career, and no other job is more important than your first one. So why leave either one to chance, when you have *The Complete Job Search Book for College Students* at your disposal?

If your goal is to one day land a job that will lead to a satisfying career—and it should be—I encourage you to read and follow the advice contained on the pages of this book. No matter where you are in your college experience—entering freshman or recent graduate—it's never too early or too late to start living your future.

Michelle Soltwedel
Champaign, Illinois

Read This First

When you first arrive on campus as a freshman, the prospect of hunting for your first post-college professional job probably seems an incredibly long way off. After all, you have four years of study to get through between your first day of class and the day you don your cap and gown. Why should you be thinking now about something that lies so far ahead?

Because, compared to the time you'll spend working for a living, your college years are just a tiny blip on the radar screen of your life. And because the four years you spend on a college campus are going to fly by a whole lot quicker than you think. Before you know it, you'll be collecting your diploma and heading off to work.

You want your first job to be a good one, right? You want it to provide a decent living and, at the same time, to be challenging, fun, and the beginning of even better things to come, don't you? Well then, what are you waiting for?

Finding satisfaction in the workplace doesn't happen by accident. You plan for it. And no matter where you are in your college career—just buying your first textbooks, struggling to decide on a major, getting ready to graduate in a few weeks—the time to start searching for your first job is now.

A Timetable for Job Search Success

It's never too early to begin looking for your first post-college job. This may come as a surprise if you think of a job search as little more than sending your resume to a list of prospective employers. Getting your resume out is only one aspect of your overall job search game plan, and that can wait until your senior year. In the meantime, however, there are plenty of other career-planning tasks you can undertake right now. The following list is by no means complete, but it does offer some ideas for where you might jump into the job search pool at any level in your college career.

The sooner you get started, of course, the better your chances of landing the job you want. Ideally, you'll want to launch your job search as a freshman. But even if you're a senior who has given little thought to post-college career planning until now, you can still follow this timetable; you'll just have to condense it.

Freshman Year

- Get to know yourself. Pay attention to the activities and classes you especially enjoy; what is it about each one that intrigues you?
- Enroll in a variety of classes so that you have exposure to many different potential careers.
- Concentrate on your studies. Good grades won't guarantee you a job, but they sure can't hurt your prospects either.
- Pay a visit to your campus career center or placement office. Talk to a counselor about the resources and services available to students.
- Explore various career options and learn the requirements and aptitudes necessary. (Appendix A, "Great Jobs for College Grads," contains a list of careers with strong growth potential to get you started.)
- Begin developing your first professional resume and cover letters.
- Attend your first career fair.
- Look for a summer job in an industry that interests you.

Sophomore Year

- Identify your career focus and select your major accordingly.
- With the help of an academic advisor, develop a coursework plan that includes the appropriate requirements and electives for your major.
- Begin building a personal network of contacts.
- Join campus organizations and/or the student chapter of a professional association related to your career goals.
- Identify the marketable skills you will need to secure a job in your chosen field; determine which ones you already have and which ones you will need to acquire before graduation.
- Continue to refine the resume you began last year; practice your interviewing skills.
- Continue attending career fairs; collect literature and talk to company representatives.
- Secure a summer internship or paid position in your chosen career field.

Junior Year

- Continue concentrating on your studies, with special emphasis on classes related directly to your major.
- Continue attending job fairs, both on and off campus; look for internship opportunities.
- Seek leadership positions in the campus organizations you belong to.
- Develop relationships with key professors in your major field of study or the head of your academic department.

- Continue building your network of personal and professional contacts.
- Conduct informational interviews with professionals in your chosen career field.
- Refine your resume, cover letters, interviewing skills based on the new experience and skills you have acquired.
- Secure a summer internship or paid position related to your chosen career.

Senior Year

- Set a goal for when you will have a job and concentrate every possible effort on meeting it.
- Continue to keep your grades high, especially in courses related to your major.
- If you have not yet acquired work experience in your chosen field, find a volunteer opportunity to do so.
- Assemble and polish all of the materials you will need for your job search—resume, cover letter, letters of recommendation, transcripts, etc.
- Find out when recruiters are coming to campus and sign up for interviews as soon as possible.
- Begin interviewing early; many entry-level, post-graduation jobs are filled in the fall.
- Meet with your academic advisor to make sure you have met all the requirements for graduation.
- Attend job fairs both on and off campus; meet face-to-face with recruiters, collect business cards, and follow up.
- Use every possible source—networking contacts, directories, newspaper ads, career Web sites, etc.—to begin seriously seeking job opportunities.
- Stay in touch with your campus career center or placement office with regard to interview opportunities and your employment status.

Resume Building

A good share of this book is devoted to putting together an effective resume aimed at securing your first post-college job. In subsequent chapters, you'll find general tips on resume writing and worksheets you can use to create a resume that is uniquely your own. You'll also find plenty of resume makeovers and samples to spark ideas for format and content.

But if you think you should wait until your senior year to develop your resume or that once you complete the document, it's done for good, think again. A resume is never truly finished. Because you are (or should be) continually improving your skills and adding to your experience, your resume is always going to be a work in progress.

You can begin building your professional resume as early as your freshman year. Start with the skills and work experience you already have, then add and subtract the details as you progress along your chosen career path. And don't be afraid to tailor your resume to a particular industry or job. One of the beauties of living in the computer age is that you're never stuck with multiple copies of a resume whose content doesn't quite fit the job you're applying for at the moment. With word-processing software and a high-quality printer, you can easily generate a resume that is individually tailored to a specific job description as needed.

Gaining Experience

No prospective employer expects that a student coming into the workplace directly from college is going to have a great deal of work experience in his or her chosen field. They do like to know, however, that you have at least some employment experience. That's why it's important to list the summer and part-time jobs you held during your high school and college years on your resume. Even positions completely unrelated to your chosen career path—camp counselor, lifeguard, retail clerk, ice cream scooper, etc.—show that you have initiative, a strong work ethic, and the ability to hold down a paying job.

If you want to get a leg up on the competition, however, it helps even more if you can show that you have some work experience, however menial, in your chosen field.

Paid summer employment

Ideally, as long as you're out of school for the summer, you'd like to earn some money. Summer jobs waiting tables and clerking in stores are pretty easy to come by; professional positions are a little harder to snag.

Let's suppose you are considering a career in public relations and set out to find a summer job in the field. It's unlikely that a public relations firm will take you on as a full-time junior publicist for only a couple of months. But the agency might need temporary support staff—someone to answer the phones, format press releases, update media lists, address invitations to a special event, and so forth.

It's not terribly glamorous, but if you're willing to do the "grunt" work, a paid position can give you great exposure to work in a particular field. While you might not get the hands-on professional experience you're looking for, you will at least earn some money and make important contacts while you observe what really goes on day-to-day in a professional working environment.

Volunteering

Nobody ever said you have to get paid before the work experience you list on your resume will count with a prospective employer. Volunteer positions are equally legitimate and sometimes afford you the opportunity to try things a traditional employer might not allow you to try because you lack a proven track record.

Find a not-for-profit agency or cause you care about. Then volunteer to teach a class, create a program, develop a marketing plan, design a promotional campaign—whatever you can think of that will help you build your skills and broaden your experience.

Internships

Listing an internship on your resume is one of the best ways you can prove your competence in and commitment to any career field; in fact, some employers put so much stock in internships, they refuse to hire an entry-level employee without one. Most internships are unpaid positions; some, but not all, may earn college credit. But what you lose in dollars, you more than make up for in opportunities to work side-by-side with professionals in real companies, on real projects.

Not only can an internship in your chosen field make you an especially attractive candidate for available jobs after graduation, an internship can actually lead directly to a full-time job. Let's face it, you're a known quantity at the company where you intern; if you've done a good job, you easily have a leg up on someone who's coming in cold.

Developing Personal Skills

While many job functions call for a specific set of technical skills, almost all employers, regardless of industry, look for similar personal qualities in the entry-level employees they hire. Your odds of landing a job will be greatly improved if you begin building competence now in the following three areas:

- **Leadership.** Employers in every field are looking for people who can think creatively and inspire others to do the same. Your college years are a great time to build your leadership skills. Become involved in campus and professional organizations early on; volunteer to serve on committees, then work your way up to leadership positions.
- **Teamwork.** Book smarts are important, but employers want people skills, too. So even if the job you're seeking requires that you function independently for much of the day—if you aspire to be a computer programmer or systems analyst, for example—there will still be times when you must work as part of a team. Seek out opportunities to develop your people skills through classroom projects and extra-curricular activities that require you to work closely with others. Be

prepared to demonstrate how, as part of a team, you have been able to accomplish a challenging task

- **Communication.** The ability to communicate effectively on the job can make or break your career. Now, while you're still in college, is a good time to hone your written and verbal communication skills. Class assignments—term papers, essay tests, oral presentations, and the like—will provide plenty of practice. Make note of your successes on class projects and look for additional opportunities to demonstrate your competence, such as joining the debate team or submitting articles to the campus newspaper.

A Special Message for Graduates

We've devoted a lot of space so far to the importance of early planning and the steps you need to take throughout your college years to ensure a successful career later on. If you've just graduated from college or will soon do so, you may be feeling as though you've missed the mark. You attended a good school and worked hard to earn your degree. And perhaps you've been thinking that's all it takes. "I'll get a good job now, right?" Unfortunately, the answer is no. More than 1.4 million students will be graduating from college this year and almost all of them will be looking for jobs. The competition is fierce, but that's no reason to lose hope. If you carefully follow the advice in this book, you can be the one who gets a good job—even if you're not a straight-A student and you didn't plan ahead.

It wasn't too long ago that simply getting a college degree set you apart from the vast majority of the competition and almost guaranteed you a good entry-level position in a professional career. Sadly, those days are past. Not only are some companies curtailing or even eliminating altogether their traditional on-campus recruiting programs, many continue to downsize by cutting back on managerial and middle-level positions. At the same time, however, more and more people are earning baccalaureate degrees, making the competition even tougher for those jobs that are available.

The majority of today's college students will not have a job when they graduate. Worse yet, some still won't have a job several months or even a full year later. Yet many students who graduate from college will land a terrific job—although it may not be the job they initially sought.

How can you make sure you're among those who land the best job possible? Is it the grades you earned in college, the extracurricular activities you participated in, or the school you went to that will guarantee you a career? Absolutely not! At this stage of the game, the quality of the position you obtain after graduation—in fact, your ability to obtain a position at all—will be much more dependent on how much effort and energy you expend on a well-executed job-search strategy.

You may be wondering if it's really worth your while to put a great deal of time and effort into finding a good entry-level position. After all, how important could that first job after graduation be? Most college students don't consider it important at all—but they should. More than half of college grads don't even stay with their first job for a full year, largely because they're dissatisfied with a position that typically leads nowhere. We're here to tell you that if you start out with the right job, a job you actually like, it can be the launching pad for a terrific career and the foundation for a lifetime of satisfying work experiences.

The time, effort and energy you put into your job search campaign will come back to reward you many times more than the extra hours you may have spent studying or participating in extracurricular activities during your college years. In a sense, your job search is a lot like a final exam—but the consequences of this exam could very well affect your happiness for decades to come. This is one test you can't afford to fail.

Throughout this book, you'll discover the essential aspects of a successful job search campaign and the actions you need to take to secure your first professional job. If you really want to make sure that your first "real" job is a positive first step toward a satisfying and rewarding career, then you need to put all of your effort into following the advice outlined on the pages ahead. We encourage you to examine this book thoroughly, review it again and again, and use it as a reference tool throughout your job search campaign.

So keep reading, and remember—no matter how early or late you start, you're on your way to a fabulous career!

Quick Tips: Searching for a Job Is a Job Itself

As you get ready to launch your job search campaign, remember these helpful hints:

- Stay focused—don't get sidetracked.
- Be positive—it may take many months to get an interview.
- Don't settle—No matter how inviting that first job offer looks, examine it closely; the offer may not be as good as it seems.

Gearing Up for the Hunt

Chapter One

What Every College Student Needs to Know *Now* about Job Hunting

Here's a piece of news that may surprise you: As a rule, the best jobs do not go to the best qualified individuals; they generally go to the best job-hunters. And no matter where you are in the job-hunting cycle—just entering college as a freshman and considering what classes to take or fresh out of college and competing for an entry-level position—this is a vitally important point. Because even though you may be up against people with stronger credentials than yours, you can still get the job you want, but only if you're willing to put in the extra effort and energy necessary to outshine the competition.

What to Expect

The job market today is more competitive than ever before, thanks in large part to the proliferation of career-oriented Web sites and increasing opportunities for job seekers to post their resumes online. It's not unusual for a company to consider hundreds of individuals for the typical entry-level position. Clearly, then, it is in your best interest to unearth every imaginable employment opportunity. In order to turn the odds in your favor, you will need to dig up many, many companies at which to apply.

But be forewarned: getting even one job offer will be tough. Many graduating students enter the job market thinking that getting a job will be easy, not all that much different from applying to college. Perhaps you were one of those who applied to only two or three top schools, the ones you especially wanted to get into, plus a couple of others that you considered "safety schools" or easy bets. If such efforts were successful in securing a spot at the college of your choice, congratulations!

Just don't expect landing a job to be quite so easy. You might have to apply to a hundred companies just to get a single interview. And just because you do get an offer, that doesn't mean you have to accept it. Sadly, too many people study in school for seventeen years only to graduate from college and accept the first job offer that comes their way. You shouldn't need to do that, especially if you are willing to put plenty of work into your job search campaign—and to begin doing so as soon as possible.

If you're really serious about job searching—and if you're serious about your career—you'll have to be diligent about making applications to as many companies as possible so that you can win multiple job offers. Only then will you have your pick of the very best positions.

Success will not go to the job searcher who invests little effort, becomes discouraged, and accepts the first job offer that comes along. Remember, the time you put into your job search will be time well spent if you make sure all your efforts and energy are going in the right direction.

Standing Out from the Pack

You can increase your chances of landing a great job by standing out from the pack. Most college students—regardless of their grades—have all of the basic requirements for the typical entry-level job. But to get the job, you must show why you stand out from the competition. You must demonstrate that in addition to fulfilling the basic requirements, there are some special reasons *you* deserve that extra consideration. And don't wait until you have your college diploma in hand to begin doing so. Regardless of whether you're about to graduate or still have several semesters of study ahead of you, the best time to begin your quest for a post-college position is now.

In all likelihood, your college or university has a wealth of job-hunting resources available for students. Don't think you must wait until it's time to begin researching companies and mailing out resumes to take advantage of them. Here's a few suggested activities you can pursue at any time during your college career—and the sooner the better—to begin getting a leg up on the competition for future jobs:

Visit your college placement office. Sit down with a counselor and discover firsthand what services are available to help students land summer internships and full-time jobs following graduation. Get a list of the companies that recruit on campus each year and find out what kinds of jobs they are seeking to fill so that you can prepare yourself for interviews well in advance. And don't forget to peruse the directories, job guides, sample resumes and other career resources that are available.

Stop by the alumni affairs office. Find out which alumni are pursuing careers in fields or with companies in which you are interested. Explore ways you might connect with them and begin to build a list of contacts.

Join a professional organization. Many professional associations have student chapters that meet on college campuses. Since they are typically sponsored by a local professional chapter, these student organizations provide excellent opportunities for direct contact with working professionals in the field. Visit the dean's office in your academic department to find out if there's a student chapter of the professional association in your industry of interest. If there's no student chapter, ask about attending the meetings of the professional chapter instead; most are open to students as guests.

Attend campus-sponsored career and job fairs. Campus-sponsored career fairs are largely informational and typically draw company representatives who are not actively recruiting. At campus-sponsored job fairs, on the other hand, recruiters come looking for entry-level job candidates. Even if you are undecided about a career and not ready to begin interviewing, career and job fairs can still be worthwhile. Any opportunity to meet company representatives and gather literature that may be useful at some later date in your job quest is an opportunity you can't afford to pass up. When it finally comes time to interview with job fair recruiters, your previous experience at these events will put you that much further ahead of the competition.

Go online. In addition to job postings, career Web sites offer a variety of information for job seekers on such topics as resumes, cover letters, interviewing, career fairs, "hot jobs," and more. Some sites even offer tips on how to choose a college major and find an internship. Most companies have Web sites, too. Don't forget to check the sites of companies in your field of interest for general corporate information and specific job postings.

Chapter Two

What Are Employers Really Looking For?

Although having a college degree will get your foot in the door, it's no magic ticket to landing your first job. In making hiring decisions, employers look for more than a high grade point average, club memberships, or athletic letters earned. They look at your work ethic and personality, too. So here, briefly, are six qualities every successful job applicant coming straight out of college should have.

Commitment

Employers want to know: How long will you stay with the company?

Believe it or not, the average college grad only stays with his or her first employer for nine months. And remember, we're only talking averages here; half of the grads who are hired stay for less than nine months! As a result, many employers have simply resigned themselves to the idea that most new young hires are unrealistic about what entry-level jobs entail and will soon leave in search of something "better." And they're right, of course.

Unfortunately, this cycle costs companies a lot of money, because training a new hire is very expensive. Some companies, large corporations in particular, spend as much as $60,000 per new employee for training programs over the first six months. If you leave after just nine months on the job, the firm stands to lose a good deal on its investment. No wonder, then, that most companies—especially those with training programs—will be very interested in whether you are likely to remain in a particular position for a period of time.

How can you show a company that you won't move on too soon? Your grades and your athletic letters probably won't offer much proof in this regard. Instead, you must display a true interest in the industry, in the job itself, and in that particular employer. Being able to intelligently discuss current trends in the industry and to show, through your words and actions, that you are genuinely interested in the job are two great ways to communicate to an interviewer that you're a low-risk hire.

Another way to demonstrate your commitment is to stress only a small number of extracurricular activities that you have pursued for an extended period of time. This shows that you didn't just jump from one activity to the next; you were actively involved in and committed to a few. Although downplaying the numbers may seem a surprising approach, the fact that you participated in only one or two activities during your college career may, in fact, look better to an employer than if you experimented with many. It demonstrates a "stick-with-it" attitude and a willingness to learn. As long as the activity you highlight was one to which you devoted a lot of time and energy and in which you made progress over the years, it will carry more weight than a list of many activities in which you were only nominally involved. Remember, consistency is a more important indicator to employers of your potential to commit to a job than good grades or a long list of extracurricular activities.

Additionally, you should be prepared to show the employer that you are likely to stay with the firm by making it clear that you know what you want. Although at this stage of the game you may not know the precise title of the job you are seeking, you must show the employer that you have some specific interests and a career direction in mind. You should also show that you have a feeling for what the job actually entails, that you understand the pluses and minuses of the position you are considering, and that you have decided, after making a realistic assessment of the job, that this is something you would enjoy doing for a substantial period of time.

Maturity

Another factor that employers weigh heavily in their hiring decisions is maturity. Many young graduates, in one-on-one situations with older adults, simply don't come across as confident enough to handle themselves in the professional world. Unfortunately, such judgments are often made based on only a brief job interview. Your references may help you in some cases, but your interview is going to matter much more, and first impressions do count. Later on in this book, we'll talk about how you can prepare for your interviews, and how you can make sure that you project yourself as a candidate who is mature and ready to enter the business community.

Professionalism

Employers will also be looking for a professional demeanor. Professionalism is a difficult quality to define, but is perhaps best understood as the ability to "fit in with others" in a given work group—i.e., adhering to their standards of communication, dress, and conduct. You can begin demonstrating this vital quality as soon as you contact a particular firm. You can show your professionalism, for example, by following an accepted format for your resume and cover letter. (We'll review all the details later in the book.) When preparing for your interview, be sure to choose appropriate clothing so that you create the right first impression. Likewise, your overall presentation, as well as your answers to specific questions at the job interview, should convey that you know how to conduct yourself properly in a business setting.

Adaptability

Proving you can perform the duties required for a particular job is not enough. Prospective employers also want to know that you are capable of growing within the company. Employers who hire new college grads for management training programs are generally looking to groom potential future senior managers. From the outset, you must assure a prospective employer that you can readily adapt to new positions within the company and that you can handle a good deal of responsibility.

Preparation

To land a job, you will need to project the image of a business-oriented person during your interview by showing your interest in the industry and in the business world at large. Employers want to see that you can perform the job function with a reasonably high degree of certainty, of course. But since most students applying for entry-level positions can't prove their capabilities by citing previous professional work experience, demonstrating a business orientation is absolutely crucial. Do your homework ahead of time so that, if asked, you are able to discuss your career direction and show that you are interested not only in the job itself, but in the company and industry as well.

Punctuality

Showing up late for a job interview is the kiss of death. Punctuality is a sign of responsibility. To have any hope of securing a job, you simply must be on time for your interview. If you are running late—and let's face it, through no fault of your own, that can happen sometimes—pick up the phone and alert the prospective employer to your situation. It's the courteous thing to do.

Putting It All Together

Recruiters seek applicants who are both knowledgeable and realistic about the job for which they are applying. They welcome applicants who appear mature, confident, responsible, and professional. If you can demonstrate that you are ready and eager to enter the business world and that you are capable of growing within a particular company and contributing to its success, you will most certainly stand out from the crowd.

So now that you have a better idea of the qualities companies are looking for, you may feel tempted to take action right away. But before you start picking up the phone or shooting off letters in hopes of securing the interview at which you can project these qualities, you will need to focus your search and take a good look at the specific "package" you will offer the employer.

Quick Tips: Do's and Don'ts

If you want to project yourself as a mature, professional candidate, follow these pointers:

- Always project a positive attitude and smile.
- Make sure your cover letter and resume are error free.
- Bring extra, wrinkle-free copies of your resume to interviews.
- Arrive on time for the interview.
- Look the part of a professional; don't show up in jeans and a T-shirt.
- Focus on your successes; never bad mouth previous employers.

Chapter Three

Getting Started

In an ideal world, your job search would have begun well ahead of the day you registered for your first college class. Your choice of a particular college or university would have been based on the school's reputation for offering a curriculum that would best meet your career goals. Then, from the moment you first arrived on campus as a freshman, every decision you made over the next four years—from the classes you chose and the extracurricular activities you pursued to the summer jobs you sought and the major you ultimately decided on—would have been directed toward a specific job goal.

Realistically speaking, of course, only a relatively few entering college freshmen know with any certainty the career direction they want to take, and even those who do quite frequently change their minds—sometimes more than once   as they make new friends and discover new interests over the course of their college careers.

Meanwhile, however, the semesters fly by until now, here you are—a recent college graduate or about to become one—facing the prospect of finding your first "real" job. What's the first thing you should do? It's not posting your resume online and sitting back to wait while the job offers flow in. It's not answering every interesting ad you see online or in the newspaper either. Before you actually apply for a job—in fact, before you even put your resume together in order to apply for a job—you must first focus your job search and formulate a plan. You must decide on the industry, job function, and geographic location of greatest interest to you. Why? Because this will make your job search more manageable and a whole lot less frightening. If you try to pursue too many different avenues, you are likely to become frustrated and unproductive; what's more, you are likely to reduce your chances of landing a job. Employers prefer job candidates who have real interests and a clear career direction. Recruiters know from experience that a job applicant who is truly interested in a particular industry, company, or job is more likely to enjoy that position, excel in it, and stay with the company for a reasonable period of time; so do your homework and narrow your focus. Recruiters do *not* like to hear that you aren't at all discriminating, that you'll take whatever job they have available.

Taking Inventory of Your Interests and Abilities

Let's suppose that you weren't one of those who had a clear career direction in mind from the get-go. You didn't choose classes that would look especially good on your resume or opt for one of the majors that career pundits say will likely offer the best career opportunities in the years ahead. Don't be discouraged; all is not lost. By creatively working with the skills you have, you can still land a good job. The key lies in knowing what you want and then determining how your abilities, interests, and experience can help you get it.

Formal assessment tools

One way to focus your interests and choose the field in which you would like to work is to take advantage of the many formal assessment tools available. One such tool is the multiple-choice interest-inventory test. Although called by different names depending on the test developer, all interest-inventory tests are quite similar; they are essentially personality tests that are designed to assess your likes and dislikes, interpersonal style, and career/lifestyle preferences in order to determine which jobs might be best for you. (Your college placement office probably has just such a test that you can review, or you may find several examples online.) If you don't have a clue about the type of career you might be best suited for, an interest-inventory test can point you in the right direction. And even if you are pretty sure about what you want to do, taking such a test can still be worthwhile. Because it is an objective vehicle, the test might reveal some interesting things you didn't know about yourself and identify significant personality traits that could be helpful in making decisions about the direction of your career.

But do be careful; these tests are not infallible. In fact, we heard one horror story about a business major whose test results showed he should be either an army general or a store clerk. The difference between these two as potential career choices was extreme enough to cast serious doubt on the whole exercise. This is not to say that an interest-inventory test can't be helpful. Just keep in mind that it is only one of many different tools you can use in your decision-making process. Regardless of what the test results tell you, the ultimate choice of careers is still up to you.

Self-assessment exercises

Self-assessment is another effective way to decide on a direction for your career and to identify the specific kinds of jobs you might seek. This method doesn't require you to complete a written exam; it does, however, require you to spend some uninterrupted time reflecting on your life to date as it relates to three distinct areas: skills, interests, and values. Once you determine the abilities you already have, the subjects in which you would like to delve more deeply, and the triggers that motivate you to act in one way or another, you can zero in on the jobs for which you are best suited. To accomplish this exercise, you'll need a quiet place to concentrate. So shut off your cell phone, disconnect your iPod. Spend some time asking questions and really getting to know yourself using the following three-step approach:

Step 1: Assess your skills. Even though you are still young and just fresh out of college, you have probably already amassed more experience than you think. Take a serious look at the classes you have completed and the jobs you have already held. What tasks were you called upon to perform? What skills did you acquire in the process? Did you work as part of a team? Did you take a leadership role? Were you able to assume positions of increasing responsibility based on work performance or good grades? Which subjects did you excel at? What projects or accomplishments are you particularly proud of? Answers to these and similar questions will help you zero in on the skills you bring to the workplace.

Step 2: Identify your interests. As anyone who's been out in the workplace for a while can tell you, there's nothing worse than working day after day at a job you don't like. Sure, the money may be nice, but if the job doesn't match your interests, you probably won't do it very well and you'll be downright miserable to boot. Before you get yourself into just such a position, take some time to think about what really interests you. A good place to start is with the skills you assessed in Step 1. Which skills do you especially enjoy and would you like to develop further? What do you want to achieve long-term? Do you want to be in a leadership position one day? What type of setting do you want to work in—outdoors or indoors, large corporation or family-owned business, in a small town or big city? Do you prefer to work alone or with other people? Are you a "big-picture" person or are you more comfortable with nitty-gritty details? What would inspire you to be your best? Truthful answers to these questions and more will likely lead you to an industry or job that is the right match for you.

Step 3: Articulate your values. Finally, after your have explored the skills you already have and considered the interests you would like to further pursue, your choice of a career comes down to determining what really matters to you. What do you value most? A sizeable paycheck? The opportunity to grow your knowledge or experience? The chance to make a difference in society or for even just one person? Are you materialistic or altruistic? Are you a homebody or someone who wants to see the world? Do you prefer a traditional 40-hour week or are you willing to work nights and weekends to climb the corporate ladder? Examine your values carefully. Knowing what's really important to you can make a huge difference in assessing whatever job opportunities may come your way.

Making a Good Match

Once you have decided on an industry and have begun making applications for specific positions, you can further refine this whole issue of interests and abilities by examining the daily tasks of the actual jobs you are considering. Look at what you may be called upon to do for each entry-level position as well as for any positions the entry-level job might subsequently lead to. Ask yourself if you really find the duties of these jobs interesting and if you would enjoy performing them on a daily basis.

Keep in mind that, on any given day, you will spend about as much time—maybe even more!—at your job as you do sleeping, so it's important to know that you'll enjoy the actual work before you decide on a particular type of employment. For instance, if you are seriously considering a career as an elementary school teacher, you better be sure that you enjoy spending a great deal of time with small children. If you want to be an accountant, ask yourself if you are a meticulous person who likes detail-oriented work. If you want to work as a reporter for a daily newspaper, be sure that you can handle a fast-paced, high-pressure, deadline-oriented environment. You get the idea.

In your quest for career information, do take advantage of the many books and other resources, including career-oriented Web sites, that detail what it's like to work in a particular career on a day-to-day basis. Talk to people who are already working in those careers to find out what a typical day on the job is like. You may also wish to contact the companies you are considering, in advance of making a formal application, simply to request a written job description. (Also, see Appendix A for a detailed listing and descriptions of great job options for this year's college class and beyond.)

Bear in mind, too, that you are choosing not just a job but a lifestyle. If you decide, for example, that your goal is to be a management consultant for an international firm, chances are you will be spending a great deal of your time in airplanes—so you'd better like to fly! Similarly, you should think about geography. Do you want a career that would require you to live in a large city, such as an urban engineer? Or would you rather live in a less populated, rural area? Are you a people person? A team player or a lone wolf? Go back and look at the skills, interests, and values you previously identified. Consider closely what you know about yourself before you commit to any one profession.

Think, too, about the compensation possibilities, not necessarily for the entry-level position, but for the subsequent positions to which it might lead. Which do you feel is more important: to make a lot of money or to be fulfilled by your work? Is it possible to have both? Think about your work schedule. If you want a job with a flexible schedule, your choices may be limited to certain types of industries. If you are very ambitious and achievement-oriented, that's likely to mean you will spend some time "burning the midnight oil." Are you prepared to do that? How fast do you want to advance to the next level in your chosen profession? Some careers, and even some companies, offer greater chances for quick advancement than others. The opportunities for advancement may be virtually nonexistent in some fields. Can you deal with that?

Other Important Considerations

You must also ask yourself whether the industry that you have identified as your focus is flourishing or dying. This isn't to say that you should jump into a particular field simply because it's hot right now. However, the potential for growth in a given field is worth considering because it may have a major impact on your career prospects some years down the road. If your industry of choice is flourishing, it could mean one of two things: that many more exciting challenges and better opportunities will be available to you, or that you have chosen a much less stable profession, and may have to jump from one company to another throughout your career just to stay employed. Sometimes careers in industries that are slowing down or maturing may be better choices, as they are more likely to offer greater opportunities for advancement over the years than industries that are booming and flooded with talented, young applicants.

Consider, too, whether the job function itself is flourishing or dying. Will the demand be increasing for your particular position in the years ahead or will it be slowing down? Once again, you need to consider not only the competition you face now to get the job, but also the competition you will likely face in the future to advance.

Today's job market is not the same one your parents faced when they graduated from college. Technology is advancing at such a rapid pace that some jobs are becoming obsolete. What is hot today may not be hot tomorrow, so spend some time researching career prospects and choose wisely.

To help you get started on your career planning, we've compiled a list of 36 occupations that have especially strong growth outlooks for the next decade or so. In Appendix A, "Great Jobs for College Grads," you'll find a brief description of what each job entails, information about the educational background and qualifications you will need to enter and advance in the field, and an indication of working conditions. The outlook for employment in each industry is also provided.

To learn more about the careers we've listed, as well as prospects for employment in other industries you may be considering, refer to the *Occupational Outlook Handbook*, which is published annually by the U.S. Bureau of Labor Statistics; it's available online at *www.bls.gov/oco*.

Being Realistic

Most importantly, make sure that your career plans are realistic. Accept that most entry-level positions are lower-paying, less-than-glamorous jobs and that it will likely take you many years to achieve your career goals and advance to your ideal job. That is why it is so important to set realistic goals, particularly in a constantly changing economic climate.

Today's job market is fiercely competitive, and as a job seeker you face many challenges. However, if you recognize this fact and keep putting sufficient effort and energy into your job search day after day, you will greatly increase the number of opportunities that are open to you and you will ultimately find the top-notch job you deserve. Your job search is your first full-time, professional assignment. Treat it as such, and you will reap the rewards.

Quick Tips:

Informational interviews are a great way to find out more about what it's *really* like to work in a particular field. Start by asking friends or relatives if they know anyone who works in the industry in which you are interested. And don't rule out alumni associations or even cold calls. The possibilities for setting up informational interviews are widely available, but you may have to seek them out.

Internships are another strong way to get good information about a field, and they come with a built-in bonus. If you end up liking the job and the employer, in turn, likes you, an internship can be a terrific stepping stone to a full-time position!

Chapter Four

The Best and Worst Ways to Find Jobs

Some of the most popular job-search methods are, surprisingly, quite unsuccessful for most of the people who use them. In this chapter, you'll have a chance to take a look at the real value of the major techniques at your disposal.

On-Campus Recruiters

Many college students (and their parents) assume they can focus their job-hunting plans solely on companies that recruit on campus. Approaching a job search campaign in this way is a bad idea; there simply aren't enough companies recruiting on college campuses these days to provide an ample source of jobs for all interested students. Those companies that do recruit on campus typically visit a large number of colleges and universities and receive many more job inquiries than they are able to interview, let alone hire, for. It is not uncommon for firms to receive hundreds of applications for every job opening. The competition is so fierce that a typical student's chances of actually landing a job through the on-campus recruitment process are about equal to his or her chances of winning a state lottery; it's not *impossible*, but it sure is tough.

Nevertheless, it is still true that some of the very best positions for recent college grads are offered by companies that recruit on campus. At first glance, the starting positions at these companies might not seem that much better than jobs you could find by using other job-search methods until you consider that many of these companies offer fast-track management training programs, which may lead to promotion and other job opportunities. By all means, do pursue on-campus recruiting opportunities, but make sure you don't spend all of your time and effort in this one area.

One of the most frequently overlooked avenues for landing a job straight out of college can be found on the nearest bulletin board. Companies that don't actually visit college campuses often post notices indicating their interest in receiving applications from job candidates. In an effort to keep overhead costs down, they limit or eliminate recruiting visits, yet they are still interested in hiring new grads. Check bulletin boards around campus and be on the lookout for job postings. These companies are not as visible to college students as the firms that actually visit campuses, but they can be an even better source of job opportunities due to decreased competition for the openings they have available.

Internships

Among the many benefits to snagging an internship, the most important is that internships sometimes lead directly to full-time jobs. When a company needs to fill an entry-level position, it will most likely consider its interns before any outside applicants because (1) the intern is already familiar with the company, its products, staff, and general operations, and (2) the company already knows whether the intern would be a good hire based on previous work.

In addition to giving you a leg up on the competition, internships offer several other advantages. If you aren't sure about a career path, an internship will give you first-hand knowledge of what it would be like to work in a particular field. Internships also strengthen your resume and can provide you with some valuable business contacts.

College Career Planning and Placement Offices

Your college placement office can help you find a job by matching your qualifications with appropriate job openings. Here, too, you can get counseling, testing, and job search advice—and you can take advantage of your school's career resource library. If you are uncertain about the direction you should take, your college placement office can help you identify and evaluate your interests, work values, and skills. In addition, your placement office may offer helpful workshops on such topics as job search strategy, resume writing, letter writing, and effective interviewing as well as job fairs that will put you directly in touch with prospective employers.

Job Fairs

Job fairs are becoming an increasingly popular element of the job hunt, and no wonder. Recruiters like them because they offer the chance to talk with the largest number of applicants in the least amount of time; job seekers appreciate job fairs for the opportunities they provide to "size up" prospective employers in a relatively nonthreatening environment.

Job fairs come in many shapes and sizes these days and, in order to make the most of these events with regard to your individual job search, it is important to understand the differences. In all likelihood, your first exposure to a job fair will be on campus;

most large universities have at least one such event every year. Campus-wide job fairs are typically sponsored by the university's career planning and placement office; they may cover a broad base of disciplines or be targeted to a specific one, such as communications, engineering, technology, business, and so forth. For some employers, job fairs serve as a prelude to their on-campus interviews; for others, job fairs represent the one time all year they will visit your campus. Since recruiters come to college job fairs specifically looking for entry-level employees, these events are usually a good way for students to learn about specific employers and to make important contacts.

In contrast, commercial job fairs are staged by independent companies in centralized locations, usually at convention centers or hotels in large metropolitan areas. They are heavily advertised and tend to draw hundreds of job seekers at all educational and experience levels. Consequently, the lines of applicants wanting to speak with recruiters are often long and the competition can be quite fierce. These events are not particularly useful for college students or recent grads, unless a particular company you have your heart set on working for is represented and you are willing to wait in line for a couple of hours to meet the recruiter.

From the standpoint of networking and information gathering, either type of job fair can be useful. Just don't expect to land a job from one; there simply isn't enough time and the competition is too stiff. At any given company site, you will likely be one of at least a hundred applicants the recruiter will see that day and you'll be lucky to snag even five minutes of his or her undivided attention. That's not to say that job fairs are a waste of your time or energy. Any opportunity you have to speak with a hiring employer—even if it's only for a few minutes—is an opportunity you have to present your credentials and possibly make enough of an impression that you will be invited to interview one-on-one at a later date.

Job fairs can be a little intimidating, especially for first-timers, so it helps to have a game plan in mind before you go. Well ahead of job fair day, do a little homework to determine which companies will be represented and, if possible, what positions they have available. When you arrive at the fair, don't just head for the nearest table or step into the first line you see. Spend the first half hour or so walking around. Scope out the recruiters and the other job seekers, collect some of the literature companies have made available on their tables, even eavesdrop on a few conversations between recruiters and other applicants, then begin your rounds of the recruiters you want to meet. If there's a long line of applicants waiting to see a particular recruiter, don't waste time just standing around; head for another table and return later when the crowd has decreased.

At the completion of your allotted time with a recruiter, he or she will probably hand you a business card; if not, ask for one. Then be sure to follow up with a thank-you note and a request for a one-on-one meeting to further discuss your qualifications.

As you make your rounds throughout the day, keep in mind that even though you are one of several hundred applicants in the room, you are essentially under a microscope. At any given time, someone could be watching, so be careful about what you say and how you act throughout the day; making the right first impression is as important here as in a private, face-to-face interview with a recruiter.

One final reminder—go dressed to the job fair as you would for a job interview and carry a briefcase. You can use it to hold the stack of resumes you'll need to bring along and the company literature you will surely pick up throughout the day.

Job Counseling Services

The job counseling services offered in your city or town may be another useful option. You can find them listed in your local phone directory or by writing:

National Board for Certified Counselors
3 Terrace Way, Suite D
Greensboro, NC 27403
(336) 547-0607
www.nbcc.org

Professional Employment Agencies

Should you work with a professional employment agency? Probably not at this stage of the game. The bulk of these agencies tend to focus either on secretarial or administrative positions or on highly specialized professional openings intended for job seekers with a great deal of professional experience. Since you don't fit into either one of those categories, chances are an employment agency won't be able to help you find the professional position you want. While an agency could possibly have a few jobs appropriate for recent college grads, it isn't very likely.

What's more, many people who use employment agencies wind up in a job they really didn't want in the first place. Employment agencies are commissioned by employers to find qualified candidates for job openings. As a job seeker, you should know that the agency's main responsibility is to meet the needs of the employer—not to find a suitable job for you.

Bottom line—very few recent college grads find professional positions through employment agencies; your time would be better spent pursuing other, more productive avenues.

Nonprofit Agencies

Many nonprofit organizations offer counseling, career development, and job placement services. In many cases, these services are targeted to specific groups, such as women, minorities, and persons with disabilities. Check your local phone directory for the agencies providing services for special groups in your geographic area. You might also contact the national organizations listed below for information on career planning, job training, and public policy support.

For women:
U.S. Department of Labor
Women's Bureau
200 Constitution Avenue NW
Washington, DC 20210
Phone: (202) 693-6710, (800)
827-5335
www.dol.gov/wb/

Wider Opportunities for Women
1001 Connecticut Avenue SW
Suite 930
Washington, DC 20036
Phone: (202) 464-1596
www.wowonline.org

For minorities:
National Association for the
Advancement of Colored People
(NAACP)
Attn: Job Services
4805 Mount Hope Drive
Baltimore, MD 21215
Phone: (410) 580-5777, (877)
NAACP-98
www.naacp.org

National Urban League
Employment Department
120 Wall Street, 8th Floor
New York, NY 10005
Phone: (212) 558-5300
www.nul.org

For the blind:
Job Opportunities for the Blind
Program
National Federation of the Blind
1800 Johnson Street
Baltimore, MD 21230
Phone: (410) 659-9314
www.nfb.org

For the physically challenged:
President's Committee on
Employment of People with
Disabilities
1331 F Street NW
Suite 300
Washington, DC 20004
Phone: (202) 376-6200
www.pcepd.gov

Public Employment Services

Your state employment service, sometimes referred to as Job Service, maintains about 1,700 local offices (also called employment service centers), nationwide, that help match job seekers with appropriate job openings at no charge. The Job Service also offers counseling and testing to help you choose a career by determining your occupational aptitudes and interests. Check your local phone book for the office nearest you.

Newspaper Classified Ads

Are newspaper classified ads a good source of opportunities for those entering the job market after graduation? Unfortunately, no. In fact, for *anyone* trying to find a job at *any* point in his or her career, newspaper ads are not particularly effective. Department of Labor statistics show that few people find jobs through newspaper ads even though many job hunters spend a tremendous amount of time and effort combing through the classifieds.

One reason newspaper ads are not a good source for job opportunities is the sheer volume of responses they generate. Once a company advertises a job opening in a newspaper, it is likely to be deluged with hundreds of applications. This can be so disruptive to normal business operations that many companies will try anything and everything to fill a job opening before resorting to listing it in the classified section. Consequently, you can assume that the job openings listed in the newspaper at any given time represent only the tip of the iceberg in terms of the actual number of jobs available.

And there's more bad news. By the time a job does get listed in the classified ads, there's a good chance the position has already been filled or is close to being filled. Even if the position is still available by the time the company receives your resume, the competition will be so fierce that your chances of getting an interview will be quite small.

For all of these reasons, relying solely on newspaper ads is a very tough way to land a job. That is not to say that you should ignore promising opportunities you see advertised; you just shouldn't make scanning the want ads your primary research activity.

Think of your job search as a military campaign—in order to win, you should follow every avenue that is open to you, but always keep in mind that some avenues are likely to be more productive than others. Since it's hard to predict which avenue might pan out, you shouldn't rule out any possibilities. At the same time, however, you can't afford to spend too much time in any area that is unlikely to be productive. So for purposes of your job search, consider newspaper ads a secondary line of attack at best.

Direct Contact

Among the best ways for a college grad to find a job is through direct contact. Direct contact means introducing yourself to potential employers, usually by way of a resume and cover letter, without a prior referral. If done correctly, this type of "cold contact" can be very effective. This method of finding a job will be discussed in greater detail in Chapter 7.

Web-Based Resources

Little more than a decade ago, only a handful of college students and recent grads were using the Internet to find a job. Today, job seekers of all ages and experience levels routinely go online to look for career opportunities and apply for jobs.

Job hunting via the World Wide Web works two ways. You can either post your resume to the Web and wait for hiring managers with job openings to contact you, or you can respond to the online classified ads employers post for specific positions. If you elect to use the Web as part of your job search, you'll probably want to do both. In either case, your first step will be to find an appropriate career Web site, and there are dozens to choose from.

Thanks to an aggressive marketing campaign, Monster.com is perhaps the best known. But there are many others, including CareerBuilder.com, TrueCareers.com, Jobs.com, Jobs.net, BestJobsUSA.com, and HotJobsYahoo.com to name a few. (See Appendix B for a brief description of these and several other popular career Web sites.)

To create a comprehensive list of your own, go to *www.google.com* and type in the word "jobs." You'll be amazed at the number and variety of Web sites that pop up. Some are general—offering a wide range of services for job seekers in broad categories, such as banking and finance, health care, manufacturing, retail, sales and marketing, etc. But there are specialized sites, too, where you can browse job availabilities in narrower fields such as higher education, aerospace, or entertainment. You can refine your search even further by accessing sites dedicated to jobs in a specific location. For example, we spotted Web sites listed on Google that are specifically for job opportunities in Oregon and California, as well as the United Kingdom, Canada, and Japan.

Be sure to check company Web sites for job opportunities, too. More and more companies are posting jobs to their corporate Web sites, and surveys show that a larger percentage of the new hires coming from the Internet are coming through company Web sites rather than job boards at career Web sites, like Monster and CareerBuilder.

Putting together a resume for posting to the Web can be tricky business (we've outlined some of the basics in Chapter 10), but it's really not all that difficult. Most of the career-oriented Web sites will walk you through the process, step-by-step. They also provide a wealth of information on cover letters, resumes, interviews, and other topics of interest to job seekers.

Posting your resume one day doesn't mean you can expect to be fielding dozens of calls inviting you to interviews the next. While it is true that thousands of hiring managers now have 24/7 access to your credentials, not many of them will actually ever offer you a job. Statistics show that fewer than four percent of new hires originate from resumes posted to career Web sites.

Conversely, your chances of landing a job from an online classified ad you answer are about the same or maybe a little worse than the chances of securing a position from a classified ad in the newspaper. And if you think the competition was fierce in the print advertising realm, you're in for a major rude awakening here. Now instead of a few hundred applicants in your metropolitan area, you're up against thousands from all over the world! We're not saying it's impossible to find a job through an online classified, we're just saying it will be tough. If you choose to use this medium, be aware that the odds are stacked against you, and make it only a small component of your overall job search efforts.

Networking

Networking is perhaps the most effective job-hunting tool of all. It can be used by anyone, even those job-hunters who don't yet have an "insider network" of professional contacts in place. Networking takes many forms; with a little skill and a lot of effort, it can be a very productive tool. In Chapter 8, we'll take you through the networking process step-by-step.

Quick Tips for Answering Online Ads:

- Don't rely solely on Web-based resources or online classifieds for your job search.
- Do a little research on the company whose ad you are answering to give yourself that extra edge.
- Do be technologically savvy. Using the right key words will help your resume scan more effectively and grab the attention of prospective employers more often. (Read more about scannable resumes in Chapter 10.)
- Don't be afraid to apply to old ads, or reapply to companies where you have sent your resume before. The job search may have been reopened, or the position never filled in the first place.
- Should you answer a blind ad? By all means. Blind ads are often placed to avoid a deluge of phone calls or if the position to be filled has not been vacated yet! (Can you say "fired"?)

Chapter Five

Making a Job-Search Plan

Before you embark on a job search, it's vitally important to have a plan, preferably one you have committed to paper, so that you can pace yourself and monitor your progress against predetermined goals. Job-hunting is hard work and having a plan will help you maintain the vigorous pace of the job-search process and keep you from becoming frustrated or unmotivated. If your plan turns out to be not very effective, you will be able to see problems more clearly and tackle them head-on by changing direction or using different techniques.

Choose a Career Path

Your first step in creating a job search plan is to select an industry and job category to target. If you have trouble deciding on just one career path, do a little more research on the fields you are most interested in. Surf the Web, peruse the shelves of your local library, or make a visit to your college's career center; they're all great sources of information about many different professional occupations. Speak with people who work in the different industries in which you are interested, too. If, after consulting all of these sources, you still can't decide which career is the best for you, simply pick one field from your list of possibilities and focus your job-search efforts on it exclusively. If you don't find any job leads after an appropriate interval of time, try switching to a different field or a different position.

Narrow the scope

Once you've decided on a career path, it's time to consider where you might work—not a particular company just yet, but a geographic location. Do you want to stay where you are, or would you like to move somewhere else? Either way, you need to take a closer look at the field you've chosen and explore the prospects for securing a job in the place you'd most like to live. Some choices are pretty obvious. If you're aiming at a career in marine science, for example, your job prospects are not going to be particularly good in a land-locked state like Kansas; you'll want to concentrate your job search in coastal areas instead.

On the other hand, careers in more generalized fields like accounting, insurance, human resources, marketing, or sales are possible just about anywhere. Your challenge in this case is to determine which takes priority—the place you want to be or the prospect for employment in a particular area. Fortunately, you live in the computer age, so gathering the facts you need to make an informed decision is not difficult. Let's say you have a degree in computer technology and you want to live in a part of the country where the winters are warm. What are the job prospects for computer programmers in south Florida? You can easily find out online, along with information about the cost of living, average wages, opportunities for continuing education, and more.

Now that you've decided on a career path and narrowed your search to a specific location, you're ready to begin formulating your job-seeking plan.

Develop a strategy

Your job search plan should take into consideration many different job-finding strategies. Make a list of people with whom you might get in touch initially for networking; find out which sources of company listings will best suit your needs; determine whether you should participate in on-campus recruiting; decide which career Web sites and newspapers are worth monitoring regularly. Then predict how much time you are going to spend pursuing each avenue and set up a schedule for doing so. It's very important to set specific goals and plan out your job search on paper; you'll be less likely to fall behind. You'll also find that it's easier to put that extra bit of effort and energy into job hunting if you can actually see the progress you're making as you go along.

A Job-Hunting Plan for Your Senior Year

If at all possible, begin your job search campaign early in your senior year—it will give you a leg up on the competition. Here's a suggested month-by-month job-hunting plan for your senior year:

September/October

Decide on which industry or job function you are most interested in. After you've reviewed Chapters 10 through 15, put your resume together and practice writing cover letters. Buy any supplies that you will need, including high-quality paper and envelopes for your resume and cover letters.

November

Develop a comprehensive job search plan. If you determine that on-campus recruiting is a good option for you, decide which recruiters you'd like to meet and find out when they will be visiting your campus. Demonstrate your interest in the companies you choose by sending a letter prior to the interview and following it up with a phone call later.

December

Begin contacting companies that *won't* be coming to your campus, starting with those that have, through posted notices, expressed interest in receiving applications from college students. Next, begin contacting other companies that you learned about through your Internet or library research and the *JobBank* series of local employment guides (see Chapter 7 for more information about the *JobBank* series). If you plan to use your holiday vacation period for interviews, begin lining up appointments in early December.

January

Review Chapter 8, then begin networking.

February

Set aside time for interviews, both on- and off-campus.

March

Begin reviewing help-wanted advertisements in newspapers and posting your resume to career Web sites. Use your spring break from classes to schedule interviews and network with potential employers.

April

Assess your job-search efforts to date and zero in on the method that seems to be generating the best results for you so far. If you are not sure which technique to focus on, try networking and/or contacting companies on your own. These are generally the two most dependable methods for finding a job.

A Job-Hunting Plan for after Graduation

Can you expect to land a job before you graduate? Possibly, but only if you are persistent and dedicated to your job-search efforts. The reality is most college seniors won't have jobs by the time they graduate. If you fall into this category, do not be dismayed—you're not alone! And don't sell yourself short, either. After all, you went to school to get an education—and you achieved that goal. Finding a job is a whole different ballgame. With time and focus, you will reach that goal, too.

Ideally, for the first few months following graduation, you should make looking for a job your full-time job. If you have the resources to do this, you will want to work from a vigorous, intense plan that allows you to invest about 40 hours per week in your job-search efforts.

Vary your activities a little from day to day; otherwise, your job search may quickly become tedious. For example, you might spend your Sunday looking through the newspaper classified ads and surfing various career Web sites to determine which jobs are appealing and appropriate for you. On Monday, follow up on these ads by mailing your resume and cover letter or posting them online and perhaps making some phone calls as well. Over the rest of the week, spend your time on job-hunting activities other than following up on specific job openings. On Tuesday, for instance, you might focus on contacting companies directly. On Wednesday, you can do more research to find listings of additional companies you might contact. Thursday and Friday might be spent on networking, as you try to set up appointments to meet with people the following week and build your list of additional contacts.

Every few weeks, you should set aside some time to evaluate your progress and fine-tune your job search accordingly. If, after putting in a great deal of effort over a period of several weeks or months, you still aren't even close to landing a job, it may be time to reconsider your options. Is the job you want a realistic one for you? Are the opportunities for landing such a position greater in another city?

Depending on the answers to these and other pointed questions, you may want to think about changing your job search techniques, relocating to another city, or focusing on a different job or industry. But don't make any sudden moves. There is always the possibility that you simply need to ramp up your job-search efforts in your current location or within the industry you have decided on. The key is knowing when to persist in the current direction your job hunt is taking and when to give up what you're doing and start anew. And that's not always easy to determine. Talking with other job hunters and knowing the current state of the job market within your industry of interest will help you make better decisions about the future direction of your job search.

How Much Effort and Energy Should a Job Search Take?

Finding a job is not easy. It takes a good deal of energy and a tremendous amount of effort to land a job and there is no "one-size-fits-all" formula for doing so. If you are devoting full time, say 35 to 40 hours per week, to looking for a job, your job search will probably last from three to six months after graduation. If the economy is a little shaky, however, you should be prepared to search for up to a year or more.

Note: If you still don't seem close to finding a job after two or three months of searching full-time, you may want to consider a part-time position. (Financially, a part-time job may be necessary at this point; from a personal point of view, it may just provide a nice boost to your ego.) A part-time job will not only give you some much-needed income, it will help you gain a valuable sense of personal accomplishment.

After several months of tedious searching with little or no success, you are likely to feel pretty stressed-out; a part-time job will help break up your routine and keep you motivated and enthusiastic about your job search campaign. Working part-time also looks good on job applications. It displays initiative and a solid work ethic, both of which recruiters always like to see.

If you think that you might be having trouble finding a job because you have no experience in a particular field, consider doing some volunteer work in your area of interest or accepting an internship while you continue to look for full-time employment. Although internships are often unpaid positions, they can provide valuable experience and numerous business contacts; sometimes, they can even be stepping stones to full-time jobs.

Quick Tip:
Just because you have an appointment for an interview or even what you think is a solid job offer, don't stop looking for a job. We've heard horror stories about people who've shown up for the first day of work on their dream job only to find out that the position has been cut! Keep the job search process going until you've been in a new position for at least two weeks.

Chapter Six

Avoiding Common Pitfalls

Before looking at the specifics of contacting potential employers, let's examine some of the common pitfalls that can stall your job search.

Following the Pack

Tempting as it might be to take the easy route, don't let yourself get caught up in doing what everyone else is! If you know that a large number of people are trying to interview with just a few highly sought-after companies, for example, don't spend your time doing the same. Instead, try to interview with the companies others may have overlooked. Try something different, and you'll likely come across several job openings before your competition does.

Relying on Employment Agencies

Employment agencies are famous for trying to steer job seekers in directions they're not really interested in going simply because these agencies only have certain types of jobs available and, quite frankly, they want to fill them. That's why employment agencies often place college graduates in clerical positions. While clerical work can sometimes be an effective way to get your foot in the door at a company in which you are particularly interested, it's not the best path to a professional position. Unless you are having great difficulty securing something better, don't go this route.

Using Employment Marketing Services

Employment marketing services are different from employment agencies. Whereas the employer pays an agency to fill a particular position, *you* pay an employment marketing service (often thousands of dollars, in fact) to help you find a job. What do you get for your money? Not a lot. Mostly these companies simply send out letters, make copies of your resume, and initiate phone calls on your behalf, all of which you are likely doing anyway if you are serious at all about your job search. And since the results are usually nothing to write home about, our advice is don't pay someone else to help you find a job! Go out and get one yourself. Not only will you save a great deal of money, you'll gain some important experience and make valuable contacts in the process.

If you feel that you really need help finding a job but don't know where to turn, try your college placement office before signing on with a marketing service. (Most colleges will assist you in your job search even if you graduated several years ago, and what's more, they'll do it for free!)

Calling 900 Numbers

With the proliferation of Web-based resources for job seekers in recent years, job-hunting services with 900-prefix numbers are, thankfully, declining in popularity. There are still a few around, however, and most of them are scam operations. These companies advertise that they offer access to many terrific job openings, and that all you have to do is call to be on your way to a great career. Our advice is, *don't*! These services usually list only a few job leads, most of which are for positions that have, in fact, already been filled. In addition to the low quality of the leads available on 900 numbers, the calls themselves can be very expensive—as much as $10 to $20 each.

Relying Too Heavily on the Internet

There is no question that the Internet has had a significant impact on job-hunting in recent years. In fact, according to a Pew Research Center study, more than four million Americans go online every day to look for information about jobs. And no wonder. Hunting for a job online is quick, easy, convenient, and cheap; it's just not terribly effective.

Most of the people searching for jobs online focus their efforts on just a handful of the most popular career Web sites. Monster.com, for example, claims to have about 15 million resumes in its active database. That's a lot of competition. Which could explain why companies report that fewer than 10 percent of their new hires have come through job boards on specialty sites (colleges, trade associations, etc.) and all-purpose career sites (Monster, HotJobs, CareerBuilder, etc). The job seekers who visit company Web sites looking for job opportunities fare slightly better. A recent study showed that of all the hires coming through the Internet, about 13 percent came from company Web sites. Does this mean you should abandon your Internet job-searching efforts? Not necessarily; just don't spend an inordinate amount of time on them. Experts disagree on the exact percentage of time job seekers should devote to searching online, but they do agree on this: The leading source of new hires is personal referrals. Bottom line—networking remains the number one way to land a job. So put the bulk of your efforts on making those contacts.

Running Low on Energy

Another trap you will want to be wary of is letting yourself believe that job searching is easier for everyone else than it is for you. It's natural to become frustrated and discouraged when you aren't seeing immediate results from all your hard work. You will have self-doubts from time to time, but you mustn't let them overwhelm you. No matter what that little voice inside your head tries to tell you, job searching is *not* easy for everyone else!

Looking for a job is tough, whether you are a recent college grad or someone who's been out in the workplace for many years. Every time you do it, it will get easier, but job hunting will always be a challenge, particularly when it's your first time. You may be experiencing a level of rejection you have never felt before. Rest assured that if it's tough for you, it's equally tough for other people, and just about everyone who goes through the process is feeling the same way you are. Stay with it, work hard, have confidence. You *will* get the right job!

Chapter Seven

Contacting Companies Directly

Contacting companies on your own does not mean merely sending out mass mailings or making a barrage of hurried phone calls. Direct contact means making a professional, personal approach to a select group of companies. As we noted in Chapter 5, for your job search to be effective, you need to focus on a particular field, job function, or geographic locale, and nowhere is that piece of advice more true than in contacting potential employers directly.

What Kinds of Companies Should You Contact?

Aren't the largest, most successful companies the best places to look for a job? Don't they offer the most security? Not necessarily. Contrary to what many believe, when it comes to landing a job, big is not always better. In recent years, some of the largest and most successful companies in America have dramatically downsized their work forces. These companies are *not* secure places to work. Furthermore, these giants are the very companies that get deluged with resumes and job applications on a regular basis. Would you believe some of the largest banking corporations in the U.S. receive as many as 3,000 resumes every day? You can well imagine how easy it would be for your resume to get lost in that kind of shuffle.

By contrast, you can find many more moderately sized companies, ones that have only several hundred employees and are not well known to the general public, but are perfectly good places to work. These are the companies you should contact. They are large enough to have several job openings at any given time, yet small enough to often be overlooked by other job hunters. This means there will be less competition for openings and a greater chance that you will find a job. The best sources of job opportunities for recent college grads are actually small companies—especially those with fewer than fifty employees. These companies are not very visible and although they offer fewer job openings than larger firms, they also typically offer much less competition. Another significant advantage of zeroing in on small firms is that you are likely to find in them significant room for career growth. At the same time, however, smaller companies may be less stable than larger firms, and offer less job security and fewer benefits. Nevertheless, the bulk of the job openings available today exist within these small companies. Yet these are the opportunities that are most often overlooked by college students and recent graduates.

Sources of Company Information

How do you find out which companies you should contact? First, you must decide on the fields in which you are most interested. Do some research on the Internet or at the library and put together a list of the companies that might potentially be hiring in those fields. You should gather information about several companies; if you focus on only one at a time, you will slow down your job hunting process and soon become frustrated. It is not necessary to go into great detail about any one company at this point in your search; instead, gather just enough information about many different companies to have a pretty good understanding of what they do and how you might fit in.

Where can you find this kind of information? On the Internet, of course.

Your best source for the most reliable and up-to-date information about any company is its corporate Web site; almost every company—both small and large—has one these days. Some company Web sites are more detailed and sophisticated than others, with splashy graphics and links to pages on everything from corporate history, organizational structure, and staff to product descriptions, customer testimonials, and sometimes even career opportunities. But even if the company's Web site is only a home page with a couple of drop-down boxes, the information is free and readily available; it's worth your while to spend some time looking it over.

You're not likely to find any negative information about a company on its own Web site, of course, so if you're looking for the other side of the picture, you'll need to dig a little deeper. Use a search engine like Google or Yahoo! to comb the Internet for *any* information—good or bad—about the company in question. Something you find in your Internet search might just change your mind, one way or the other, about whether you want to pursue a career with this particular company.

Another place to gather company information is at job fairs. Most of the corporate recruiters that come to job fairs bring along a lot of printed materials—brochures, annual reports, press releases, sales literature, etc. Even if you don't get the opportunity to talk one-on-one with a recruiter, don't be hesitant to pick up some of his or her literature. That's what it's there for; and it's a sure bet the recruiter would rather you helped yourself to it than to have to carry it all back home.

Another obvious source for company information is *the JobBank* series from Adams Media (the publisher of this book). *JobBank* is a collection of employment directories listing almost all companies with 50 or more employees in large cities and metropolitan areas throughout the U.S. Each *JobBank* is a complete research tool for job-hunters, providing up-to-date information about potential employers in a particular geographic area, including:

- Full name, address, and telephone number of the firm
- Web sites and e-mail addresses
- Contact name for professional hiring
- A description of the company's business
- Listings of common positions
- The addresses of professional associations

The series covers 36 different industries, from Accounting to Utilities. The number of employers listed in each book ranges from hundreds for smaller cities to nearly 1,500 for metro New York and Los Angeles. These books are available for the following regions: Atlanta, Austin/San Antonio, Boston, the Carolinas, Chicago, Colorado, Connecticut, Dallas–Fort Worth, Florida, Houston, Los Angeles, New Jersey, New York City, Ohio, Philadelphia, Phoenix, San Francisco, Seattle, Virginia, and Washington, D.C. Your local library also may have a copy of *The National JobBank*. This 1,100-page reference, published annually, contains more than 20,000 employer profiles for the entire United States.

Many other resources exist that you may find helpful in pulling together your lists of potential employers. For example, you may want to check *Dun & Bradstreet's Million Dollar Directory* and *Standard & Poor's* investment guide, both of which list basic information about companies such as the name of the president and a brief description of the company's products and/or services. These directories, as well as many state manufacturer listings, may be found in your local library. The advantage that the *JobBank* series offers over these directories is that *JobBank* books list typical entry-level positions for each firm and include the name of the person you should contact.

You might also do some checking in your own backyard. In many academic disciplines, faculty members come to the campus only after years of experience in the corporate world. Ask around; perhaps one of your professors formerly worked at the company you aspire to join and would be willing to advise—maybe even mentor—you in your quest for a professional position there.

Remember, your aim is to learn a little about many companies. You do not need to know everything about a company before you make your first contact. Simply being able to demonstrate that you are up to speed with what's going on in a particular industry will go a long way.

The Best Way to Contact Small and Large Companies

How you go about contacting a company depends upon the size of the firm. At firms with fewer than 50 employees, you will want to contact the president directly.

Typically, out of the 50 people who might work at a small company, approximately five to seven will be professionals; the others will typically be classified as clerical or support staff. Small firms hire professional employees on an irregular basis and, in all likelihood, the president of the company will be directly involved in the recruitment and hiring process.

As a rule of thumb, you should always at least *try* to contact a department head or the president of a company—even in the case of both moderately sized companies with several hundred employees and large companies with more than 1,000. As you apply to larger and larger companies, you will, however, find it increasingly difficult to get through to top-level executives. Instead, you will often be "bumped" to the human resources office. Do not become discouraged by this. In large companies, most of the hiring takes place in the human resources office and it can turn out to be a valuable resource. Many books about job searching will tell you to avoid human resources offices like the plague, but, as a recent college grad looking for your first professional job, you'll find that you can't very well do that. Most company presidents and even many department heads are not likely to want to interview even a very strong candidate who has just graduated from college and has virtually no work experience.

The first step you should take in contacting a company directly is to send a copy of your resume with a cover letter. The letter should be addressed to a specific person and that is where your research comes in; simply addressing letters to "Human Resources Director" or "Company President" demonstrates that you haven't done your homework. (See Chapters 10 through 15 for tips on how to create a job-winning resume and write terrific cover letters.)

After you have sent your letter and allowed sufficient time for the person to receive and read it, you should follow up with a phone call. For best results, plan to call the recipient of your letter one or two days after your resume arrives so that it will be fresh in his or her mind and you will be more likely to be remembered.

Is it okay to call a company to determine if there are any job openings *before* you make the effort of sending your resume? Certainly. If you are unusually confident and articulate on the phone, you may have great success with this approach. Such calls are especially effective if you are contacting smaller companies since you are more likely to reach a key decision-maker directly, rather than being blocked by a secretary. At larger companies, on the other hand, you will probably find that simply sending a resume and cover letter, then following up with a phone call is a much more effective approach.

Following Up with a Phone Call

Never just send your resume and cover letter; always follow up with a phone call. What you say on the phone is important, of course, but even more important is *how* you say it. You should strive to always speak with an aura of confidence. Even though there may be no job openings available at a particular company, you need not be apologetic for making a call. All companies must hire at some point, and each has, at least in theory, a responsibility to be courteous when an outsider makes a call inquiring about potential job openings.

Will all of your calls be answered courteously? No. Some, in fact, will be answered quite abruptly; you may be calling somebody who is very busy or simply having a bad day. But you must not react in kind; always project confidence and courtesy. Remember, one of the top qualities companies look for in entry-level hires is maturity, and one of the ways you can demonstrate that you have it is by sounding self-assured (not pushy) on the phone.

It is extremely important that your conversation be succinct and to the point; you are calling a busy person who doesn't have time to listen to you beat around the bush. One good way to keep your conversation on track is to write out a short script in advance. Practice it several times until you are familiar with the words and can say them without sounding as though you are reading from a piece of paper. You are bound to be nervous when approaching a prospective employer; the written script will help you remember everything you want to say. You will need to make the following three points:

1. Why you're calling
2. Why you'd be a strong candidate for hiring
3. What type of position you're interested in

You should be able to say all of this in twenty seconds or less. At the same time, however, you must be sure to speak your words clearly and slowly enough so that you will be readily understood.

What Should You Say in a Follow-Up Phone Call?

Let's say you're calling a small bank, perhaps one with a single office and a staff of just thirty people. Because the bank is so small, you will want to speak with the president. Here is an example of what you might say:

Receptionist: Good morning, Main Street Bank. How can I help you?
You: Good morning! I'd like to speak with Mr. Smith, please.

(Mr. Smith is the president of the bank. Your call is then transferred to his office.)

Secretary: Mr. Smith's office.
You: Good morning! This is Bob Jones calling. Is Mr. Smith available?

Do not tell the secretary at this point that you are calling about a job; she might block your call. Instead, simply project a professional and businesslike manner, as if there is a good reason why you are calling Mr. Smith, which, in fact, there is. You may be asked to say why you would like to speak to Mr. Smith. In that case, the conversation might go something like this:

> *Secretary:* Mr. Smith is very busy. May I tell him what this is regarding?
> *You:* Yes, my name is Bob Jones. I just graduated with honors from City University with a degree in Finance. I am seeking an entry-level position at your bank as a loan officer.
> *Secretary:* We don't have any openings at this time.
> *You:* Well, I understand that might be the case. But I would like to have a few minutes to speak with Mr. Smith anyway, in case something might come up in the future. I know he's very busy—I only need to speak with him for a moment.

With a little luck, your courteous demeanor will prompt the secretary to put your call through to Mr. Smith. If applicable, this would be a good time to indicate that you already sent in a resume and that you live in the same town in which the company is located (local roots can often help your cause). Even if you are told that no jobs are available at this time, it is important that you still try to speak with Mr. Smith. Should a job opportunity arise within the next couple of months, there's a good chance Mr. Smith might remember you and call you in for an interview before the position is even advertised. Don't take "no openings at this time" to mean "no openings ever"—it doesn't!

Be polite but aggressive in your job search. Show that you are genuinely interested in the firm. Keep in mind that that the department head or company president to whom you are speaking may be in a position to create a job for you.

If your call gets rerouted through human resources, try to use this same strategy: get the decision-maker on the phone, briefly explain why you're calling, demonstrate that you're a strong candidate for hiring, and request an interview.

If you are successful in getting Mr. Smith (or any decision-maker) on the phone, your conversation might go something like this:

> *Mr. Smith:* Hello?
> *You:* Hi! Is this Mr. Smith?
> *Mr. Smith:* Yes, this is he.
> *You:* Mr. Smith, my name is Bob Jones and I've lived in this town for the last ten years (or: I'm a member of such-and-such local organization). I recently graduated from City University with a degree in Finance and I very much want to pursue a career in banking. I'm interested in becoming a loan officer and while I

understand that you may not have any openings at this time, I would like to come by and talk to you briefly about the opportunities that might be available in banking. I sent you a resume and cover letter last week. Did you receive my materials?

One of the reasons you want to ask Mr. Smith if he has received your letter and resume is to get a conversation started. Mr. Smith might respond by saying, "Yes, I read your letter, I saw that you've done such and such . . ." If he does not recall your letter, this is your opportunity to briefly summarize its contents. Avoid close-ended questions like, "Mr. Smith, do you have any job openings now?" It's too easy for Mr. Smith to simply say no—and end the conversation. Instead ask if he's received your letter, so that you can initiate a polite, upbeat conversation, and request an interview.

What if the call doesn't go so smoothly? Here is an example of one way to handle tougher calls:

Mr. Smith: Hello?

You: Mr. Smith?

Mr. Smith: Yes, this is he.

You: Mr. Smith, my name is Bob Jones. I recently graduated from City College and I . . .

Mr. Smith: Bob, I did get your letter and I want to thank you for thinking of our bank. You have some very strong credentials and I'm sure you're going to do very well, but we don't have any job openings at this time.

You: I understand that you may not have any job openings right now. But I've lived in this area for quite a while, and as I indicated in my cover letter, I very much want to pursue a career in banking here. I'd like to have a chance to meet with you for just a few minutes anyway, just to see if you could tell me a little bit about the banking industry in this town and about the opportunities one might expect at places that might be hiring. Would this be possible?

With this conversation, you're showing Mr. Smith some important things: That you're a confident, professional individual; that you're polite; that you're *not* demanding a job, but that you would like to have the opportunity to talk with him briefly; and that you respect his expertise and knowledge of the local banking industry. He will appreciate your courteous approach and, in all likelihood, will at least grant you a few minutes to discuss banking in general. Using this approach may not net you a job immediately, but it will almost certainly win you points with Mr. Smith, and who knows where that might eventually lead?

Chapter Eight

Networking Your Way to a Job

Networking is the process of exchanging information, contacts, and experience for professional purposes. One reason so many people use networking is that it's a great method for finding a brand new job or landing a better one.

Is Networking an Appropriate Tool for College Grads?

Traditionally, networking has been used by people with a great deal of work experience and many professional contacts. But even if you have little or no experience whatsoever, networking can still be an effective job-hunting tool.

Perhaps you're asking yourself, "Don't I have to know people who are in a position to hire in order to network? Don't I have to know a lot of people in general, or in a specific geographic area, to get a job through networking?" The answer to both questions is no. You don't have to know anybody at all—you just have to *get to know* people, and networking is one of the best ways to do it.

The Key to Networking

One of the secrets of networking is knowing what you want—or at least appearing to know what you want. For instance if you are trying to break into a field where you don't have any experience, tell your networking contacts that you are interested in the industry they work in and show them that you are knowledgeable about that industry. In this way, you will be perceived more or less as an "industry insider." If you can show that you intend to become part of the industry, that you are going to start an important career in their area of expertise, your contacts may conclude that you could one day be an important contact for them. Industries are social entities; once you've shown that you're an industry insider, you become part of that social circle. So—how do you start? First, keep up-to-date with your industry of choice by reading its trade publications. These are specialized journals and magazines that address the concerns of professionals in a given industry; virtually every business category has at least one. The motion picture and entertainment industry's chief trade publication is *Variety*; publishers subscribe to *Publishers Weekly* to keep track of the major events in their field. Go online or check your local library to find the magazine, journal, or newsletter that claims as its readers the people who work in the industry you have selected. Then read those publications regularly. Another great source of information about an industry is its professional or trade associations. Most industries have one or more associations established to promote its interests and foster the sharing of ideas; a quick online search or examination of *Encyclopedia of Associations* at your library will reveal the associations that exist in your field.

In addition, keep an eye out for information about your chosen industry that appears in the mainstream media: your daily newspaper and the *Wall Street Journal*, magazines like *Time* and *Business Week*, news broadcasts, books, and other sources. Lastly, you should make a point of getting out and talking to people about developments in your industry, even at social events such as parties or community gatherings where you would not expect to find "insiders." Before long, you will come across as someone genuinely interested in the field, and you will get much better results from your networking efforts.

Tracking Down Leads

Who should you contact? If you had experience in your industry of choice, you would need only scan your cell phone directory or pull out your Palm Pilot for a ready-made list of people with whom you have already established contact. But how do you network if you're just getting out of college and don't have that prior experience to draw from?

At first glance, your prospects for networking may look a little bleak, but, in reality, you probably have more options available than you think. Remember that job fair you attended last semester? If you followed our advice about job fairs in Chapter 4, you should have a stack of business cards to leaf through or, at the very least, a pile of company literature to peruse. Start your networking with the recruiters you've already met. And even if the follow-up letters you sent immediately after the event (you did send those follow-up letters, right?) did not result in a face-to-face interview, there's no harm in asking again. None of the recruiters may bite this time either, but you won't know unless you ask. One of them could know someone who's looking for a candidate with your qualifications, so it's worth checking out.

Alumni directories are another good place to look for leads, and every college, grad school, or prep school has one. There's a certain camaraderie that automatically exists between the alumni of any school; former grads who remember their college days with fondness are often eager to help future grads get off to a good start. Even a smaller college graduating only about 1,000 students yearly can be a significant source of industry contacts. Over the years, the numbers add up so that a small school could potentially have 50,000 graduates in the workplace, any one of whom might be very willing to talk with you about his or her industry and supply you with names of important contacts you can add to your list.

Friends, relatives, and neighbors can be important contacts, too. Even though they might not work in the industry in which you're interested, they could very well know someone who does. Someone who knows someone who . . . well, you get the idea. At first, you might not think you have many contacts at your disposal—but if you stop to think carefully you'll realize that in fact you do. Let's say that, between your friends, relatives, neighbors, and academic contacts, you come up with a list of thirty-five people you can contact. And let's assume none of them works in the industry you're interested in. As a group, however, they may know seventy people who do work in that industry, or who work in a related industry, or who are in a position to know someone who works in the industry. That's a lot of people . . . and a lot of connections. So, you see, you probably have access right now to many different potential contacts in your industry of choice.

Keep in mind that your goal in contacting so many people is not to win a job necessarily, but to get referrals. At this stage of the game, you want people to refer you to other people until you come across job leads. Contact your initial base of people; tell them you just graduated from college or are about to, that you want to pursue a career in such-and-such a field, and that you're eager to talk to anyone who could give you some background information. This is a much better approach than stating outright that you want a job; by using the "soft sell," you'll glean information, learn about the industry, and become more of an insider. If, in the process, you do come across someone who has a position available, you'll sound less threatening if you say you just want to come in and talk rather than if you say you're looking for a job.

Name-Dropping

When it comes to networking, there is nothing wrong with dropping names. In fact, we recommend it; name-dropping is one of the most important ways to get ahead in the business world. ("Jane Phillips suggested I call you.") As you continue networking, you will find yourself increasingly dropping the names of people you have met only by phone. If you are uncomfortable about this, you shouldn't be; it's the way the business world works. Someday you may be in a position to help other job-hunters, and your name may be the one that's dropped; in the meantime, you need to do everything you can, including dropping a few names, to increase *your* chances of finding a job.

What Does a Networking Conversation Sound Like?

Here's a sample of what your networking conversations might sound like:

You: Hi, Uncle Mike! It's Bob. As you may have heard, I just graduated from college and I want to pursue a career in banking. Is there anyone you can think of who might be willing to talk to me about the banking industry, to give me some good background information?

Relative: I really can't think of anyone in the banking industry—but why don't you call my attorney, Don Silva? I deal with him every month or so. He knows a lot of business people, not necessarily in the banking industry, but you never know. See if he can be of any help. His number is 555-1234.

You: Thanks a lot, Uncle Mike!

You then call the attorney, immediately identifying who referred you:

You: Mr. Silva, my name is Bob Jones and my uncle, Mike Jones, suggested I give you a call. I'm interested in a career in banking and I wondered if you might know anyone in that field who might be able to talk with me about the industry.

Attorney: Well, I'm not really sure. Let me think about it a little bit and I'll get back to you.

Keep the momentum on your side by offering to follow up yourself.

You: That would be great. Why don't you think about it for a couple of days and I'll call you back. If there's someone in the industry you can refer me to or someone who might know someone in the industry, I'd really appreciate it.

If a contact seems reluctant, you could redirect the conversation in this way:

Attorney: Gee, I do know a few people in the industry, but they're probably not hiring now . . .

You: That's no problem. I'm just gathering information. I just want to talk to someone for a few minutes to find out what's going on in banking. If you'd like, I can stop by for a few minutes at your convenience so we can meet, and in the meantime maybe you could think of some names you'd feel comfortable referring me to.

Your contact may be hesitant to give out any names without seeing in person that you're a polished, professional individual. Offering to stop by may help you overcome his reluctance. This technique also buys time and gives your contact the opportunity to think of some more names of people to whom he can refer you.

Even though you have expressed interest in a career in banking not law, the attorney example is still a good one; you should consider meeting with people who service others in your chosen industry. If a contact seems unwilling to meet with you face to face, don't be overly insistent. Instead, ask him or her to recommend someone else for you to call. Eventually, you should be able to network your way to someone who works within your chosen industry.

Remember, you don't want to scare your contacts off. Even if you suspect a particular contact is in a position to hire, *do not* specifically ask about a job; it might cause him to back away. Ask instead about the industry in general, relay that you are interested in pursing a career in that field, and try to set up a time to meet briefly for the purpose of obtaining background information only.

Let's suppose that you know for a fact that a certain contact has an opening available for which you would be suitable—perhaps you saw an ad in the classifieds. Should you mention it in your conversation with this person? Absolutely not. Remember, you earned this contact through networking, not by reading the classifieds. You want to position yourself as an industry insider who is networking, not as just another job seeker responding to an ad. Follow this advice and you'll be taken more seriously than other people who call simply in response to a newspaper ad. What's more, your contact will feel more comfortable talking to you. It's the rapport you build with your contacts over time that makes networking one of the best ways to learn about job openings.

Overcoming Your Initial Uneasiness

Many college students and recent grads are uneasy talking to strangers on the phone, and they're not alone. Most people are, at first, a little uncomfortable calling people they don't know to ask for contact names and appointments. But like anything you've never tried before, networking gets easier the more you do it.

You are bound to be nervous the first few times, but with practice you'll feel much more comfortable making calls. The key is to think about what you're going to say in advance, then pick up that phone and just do it. Remember, this is a job you must do yourself; no one else can network for you. Once you gain some confidence, the calls will get easier and you'll soon find that they make a big difference in your job search campaign.

The Informational Interview

Informational interviews are extremely important. Not only do they build your network of contacts, but they can lead to valuable information and additional contacts. Do not, however, approach an informational interview as though it were a job interview. Stick to gathering information and leads, then see what happens.

Here are some suggested questions you might want to ask during an informational interview:

- How did you get started in this business?
- What do you like most about your job, your company, your industry?
- What do you dislike most about your job, your company, your industry?
- What are the current career opportunities for college grads in the industry?
- What are the basic requirements for an entry-level position in the industry?
- Is there a trade association, trade publication, or Web site that might aid me in my job search?
- Where do you see the industry heading in the near future?
- What advice would you give a college grad looking for a job in the industry?
- Could you recommend someone else for me to contact in the industry?
- Is there anything else I should know about the industry?

If a networking contact has been particularly helpful to you, by all means send a thank-you note. And even if you didn't get everything you hoped to get from a meeting, it is still appropriate to drop your contact a line. Not only is this the courteous thing to do, it keeps your contacts current. You never know when this person might turn out to be an important business contact for you in the years to come—especially if he or she is active in your industry.

Networking Online

If you're one of those people who fears networking—you'd rather have a root canal than make a cold call, for instance—we have good news. You can build a network without ever even picking up the phone. The technique is called online networking, or "e-networking," for short. Anyone with a computer keyboard, Internet access, and an e-mail address can do it.

E-networking has lots of advantages, not the least of which are anonymity and immediacy. You have time to think about what you're going to say and how you'll respond, so there's no chance you'll get tongue-tied as you might during a first phone call or face-to-face meeting. Nor do you have to worry about taking notes during the encounter. You can simply print out the reply. And since everyone with an e-mail address is accessible by Internet, you won't have to work your way around gatekeepers or play telephone tag to get to the person you really want to talk to. While e-mail doesn't have quite the immediacy of a phone call, it comes in a close second. Most people check their e-mail pretty regularly throughout the day, so you're likely to get a swift reply to your requests for information and additional contacts.

The downside, of course, is that e-mail doesn't give you quite the give-and-take of conversation; you may have to send messages back and forth a few times as you get answers to questions that prompt more questions. Be careful how you phrase things, too. The tone of most e-mail messages is less like formal correspondence than a chat between friends, but without voice inflections and facial expressions. Consequently, a biting little quip that would sound clever face-to-face can sometimes come across in an e-mail as downright angry and sarcastic. Re-read what you've written carefully before you click "send."

Building an E-Network

Building a network online is a lot like building a network in the traditional way. You start from where you are . . . in this case, with e-mail. You probably already have a list of contacts with whom you regularly exchange e-mail (or at least should). Start using it to gather industry information and to increase your contact base. Dash off a message to close friends, relatives, teachers, past employers—in short anyone you know who might know someone who might know someone—asking for their help in your quest for career opportunities. Stay in touch on a regular basis, but be selective. Don't forward every funny joke that lands in your e-mail in box; if you do, you may soon discover that your contacts are so overwhelmed with the number of messages originating from your e-mail address, they've just quit opening them altogether. E-mail does you no good if your messages aren't getting through.

E-mailing a new contact for the first time is much like making a cold call—but without the fear and trepidation. You will need to introduce yourself to the new contact, tell how you found him or her, briefly describe your background and the purpose of your message, then ask for what you need—information, advice, a referral, and/or the names of additional contacts. Watch the tone of your message and always be courteous. Since you may be approaching someone you don't know, be especially careful about the subject line. Many people won't even open an e-mail if they don't recognize the sender. Instead of something vague like "Seeking your help re: career opportunities," try mentioning the name of the person who referred you in the first place. That should catch your contact's attention.

Going Beyond E-mail

There's more to building a network online than just beefing up your e-mail address book, of course. Consider the following options for tapping into informational resources and establishing helpful contacts you might otherwise miss:

Newsgroups. Newsgroups are components of the huge worldwide discussion forum known as Usenet. Remember those bulletin boards you saw around campus? You'd post a note, then someone walking by would add a note to your note or post a note of their own. Pretty soon the board would be littered with all kinds of articles, notes, and notices. That's how newsgroups work. People with common interests come together in a newsgroup to post articles pertaining to a particular subject and to comment on the articles others have posted. There are thousands of newsgroups in operation, each devoted to a specific topic. You can join newsgroups about everything from the serious to the sublime to the just downright silly. There's undoubtedly at least one newsgroup devoted to your industry where you can glean interesting information and possibly make useful contacts. Be aware, however, that newsgroups are not regulated and most aren't even moderated. Whatever someone wants to post, they can. Don't accept everything you see as the truth. For information and instructions on using newsgroups, as well as lists of Usenet groups, go to Usenet Info Center Launch Pad at *www.ibiblio.org/usenet-i/*.

Chat rooms. You probably already know how chat rooms work; you may even participate in some regularly for personal information and social interaction. Now, consider joining chats for the purpose of advancing your job search. Many career Web sites offer the opportunity for real-time chats with other job seekers and sometimes even with hiring managers. You may be able to pick up some job-hunting tips as well as information about new developments and trends in your industry; if you're lucky, you could even learn about job openings before they're widely advertised.

Networking Web sites. Believe it or not, there are Web sites specifically devoted to networking. Some have been established for the purpose of making professional contacts, others are more socially focused—that is, on some sites you may be more likely to find a new boyfriend or girlfriend than a new business contact. Most are open to all, but, in some cases, you will have to pay a fee to participate. Monster.com operates a networking Web site at *http://net work.monster.com*. Others include *www.linkedin.com* and *www.friendster.com*.

Chapter Nine

Getting an Edge on the Competition

The difference between finding a terrific job in a relatively short period of time and suffering through a prolonged job-hunting campaign lies in your willingness to expend a little extra effort. It's a jungle out there all right and if you want to land a job, you'll have to find a way to stand out from the crowd. In this chapter, we'll examine some of the ways you can get that "extra edge" and outshine the competition.

Start Early

One important way to get the "extra edge" in your job-hunting campaign is to start as soon as you can. It bears repeating that the beginning of your senior year is the best time to begin your job hunt. By the time graduation rolls around, you will then be well along in your search and may even be closing in on several firm job offers. If you have already graduated and are just getting started with your job search, don't panic—there are plenty of other steps you can take to distinguish yourself.

Read the Trade Literature

Make it a habit to read the trade literature of the industry you intend to focus on, as well as a variety of background books and periodicals about the field. Remember, your aim is to come across as an industry insider; to do so, you'll need to be familiar with industry-related topics so that you can network and interview more effectively.

Stick to Your Plan, but Reevaluate When Appropriate

Another key to effective job searching is sticking with the plan you made. Although it may not at first seem to be working, give it time. Of course you will probably need to reevaluate every so often to make sure that your chances of getting the job you want are realistic. If everyone you speak to tells you that the industry is in bad shape, that there are layoffs at companies of all sizes, that the outlook for newcomers is bleak—maybe you should look into a different field. If the majority of people you speak to say you are underqualified, perhaps you need to look into firms where the competition for positions is not as fierce—or consider a position for which your qualifications are better suited. At some point, you may even decide to try another field entirely.

Getting Tips from Other Job-Hunters

From time to time, you may find it helpful to meet and talk with other job-hunters. Seek out job-hunters who, like you, are creative and innovative in their search, who are willing to share leads, insights, and techniques with one another. Interacting with other job-hunters on a regular basis will yield fresh ideas and help boost your morale.

Using Ads for Older Job Openings

Instead of answering only employment ads you see in the most recent newspaper or in a current Web posting, try responding to older ads too. It's possible that the person hired to fill a position that was advertised six months ago didn't work out. If that's the case, you probably won't face a lot of competition this time around because few other people will think to respond to that ad. By the same token, a company that had a job opening six months ago may have a different position open that hasn't been advertised yet, so you'll have a jump on the competition if you make contact now. As a rule of thumb, there is often a long interval between when a manager first starts thinking about filling a position and when a position opening is publicized. You may even find older ads to be more useful than new ones in terms of unearthing realistic job opportunities.

You can also use older ads as a source of information on which companies are hiring in your field, even if the particular jobs posted are not ones you are suited for. You may find when you contact a company that has advertised jobs in the past that it is now considering hiring for an upcoming (and still unadvertised) position that is right for you.

More Networking?

Absolutely. Networking is a job-hunting skill you can never spend too much time on. Go back to your list of contacts and call once again those people you already contacted for leads several months ago. Your conversation might go something like this:

> *You:* You know, I'm still interested in a career in banking. I know that we talked a few months ago, but I wondered if any other names might have possibly come to mind, names of people with banking experience or contacts that I might call.

You may be pleasantly surprised by the responses you receive. You'll likely be catching a contact in a different frame of mind and it is not uncommon to learn of someone new. It could be, too, that since the last time you spoke with your contact, he or she has become aware of new leads that you might not otherwise hear about due to your contact's hectic schedule.

Contacting the Same Firms Twice

Don't be afraid to call some of the firms you contacted a few months previously. You could say:

> *You:* My name is Bob Jones, and I contacted your firm several months ago about an entry-level position in banking. I'm particularly interested in working for your company. I've been talking with other firms and I'm very much committed to this industry. I recently saw your firm mentioned in the paper, and I'm more convinced than ever that this would be a terrific place to work. I feel I have a lot to offer you. I know you didn't have a position available the last time I contacted you, but I'm hoping you'll reconsider my application now.

This approach shows that you are persistent and genuinely interested in the firm, qualities that are likely to make you stand out in the contact's mind.

The technique works especially well when you contact firms with whom you have actually interviewed. Only a fraction of those applying for a position get to the interview stage; if you were one of them, the firm was obviously impressed with your qualifications, so the chances are good that you will be remembered and may be considered for another position within that company. If you feel uncomfortable about telephoning, write a letter instead. At the end of this chapter, you'll find a sample of a letter you could send to a company with whom you interviewed but which did not offer you a position.

When All Else Fails

If, as time goes by, you find you aren't making any headway in your job search, consider trying another type of position, a different industry, and/or another city. The ideal way to apply for a job in another city is to move there first and then begin applying at local companies. Of course, this is not always a viable option. It is possible to conduct your job search long-distance, but you should be prepared to point out immediately your willingness to relocate to a particular area.

What's Next?

By now, you have a pretty good idea of what your job-search battle plan looks like. Before you head for the trenches, however, you'll need plenty of top-notch ammunition—and that means developing the best possible resume and cover letter. In the next few chapters, we'll show you how to do just that.

Sample Letter for Contacting the Same Firm Twice

81 Sandypine Road
Joppa, MD 20707
(410) 555-1551

October 27, 2007

Mr. Henry Stanhope
Personnel Manager
Lisa Fleischman Associates
2125 Wisconsin Avenue NW
Suite 202
Washington, DC 25507

Dear Mr. Stanhope:

As you may recall, I interviewed with you back in March for a position as an Advertising Assistant. I very much enjoyed meeting with you and was impressed with your organization.

I realize that you have probably filled the opening for which I interviewed, but I am taking the liberty of contacting you now because I am still very interested in obtaining a position with Lisa Fleischman Associates. Perhaps you have an appropriate position available currently or anticipate an opening soon?

In case you no longer have my resume on file, I am enclosing another copy for your consideration. As you can see, I graduated from Colgate University this past May with a Bachelor of Science in Marketing. In addition to my degree, I have experience working in both marketing and sales.

I would like to be considered for any appropriate job openings that may arise. I may be reached at the above listed phone number between 9 a.m. and 5 p.m. weekdays for an interview at your convenience. Again, thank you for your time. I look forward to hearing from you.

Sincerely,

Rosemary L. Brandenburg

Rosemary L. Brandenburg
Enc.: Resume

Tools of the Trade—
Resumes and Cover Letters

Chapter Ten

Writing Your Resume

If you think your resume is not important, consider this: The average recruiter receives 100 or more resumes for every available position, but has time to interview only the five or ten most promising applicants. The choice of which applicants to reject is generally made after only a brief skimming of their resumes. It could easily be said, then, that the resume is more the recruiter's tool for eliminating a candidate than the candidate's tool for gaining consideration.

Unless you have phoned in advance or talked one-on-one with a recruiter—which you should try to do whenever possible—you will be selected or rejected for an interview solely on the basis of your resume. So it must be outstanding. While a resume is certainly no substitute for a comprehensive, well-planned job search campaign, it is one of the most important tools you will need in order to find a job. Since your resume is likely to be the first impression you make on a prospective employer, you will want to make sure that it represents you well.

Resumes in the Electronic Age

Technology plays an integral role in today's recruitment and hiring process, which for you, the modern-day job seeker, is both good news and bad. On the upside, word processing software makes it easier to draft and revise resumes and, thanks to online databases, thousands of prospective employers can have access to your credentials 24/7. But herein lies the rub: your resume must stand up to the challenges of various technological environments. If you don't recognize terms like ASCII and scannability, or why they matter as you put together your resume, then you better start boning up. These days, it's not so much what you say, but how you say it and show it off. When it comes to creating a resume for the electronic era, the presentation and format are as important as the content.

You can get by in most technological environments with just one resume, if it's done right. But to cover your bases with regard to delivery, you will need to be able to generate your resume in two basic formats: one that is e-mailable and one that is scannable. Since your scannable resume will become the prototype for all formats—the hard copies you mail with your cover letter to prospects and carry to interviews, the documents you attach to e-mails, and the electronic resumes you post yourself to online databases—let's start there.

The Scannable Resume

A single newspaper classified ad or online job posting these days is likely to generate hundreds of applications. At the same time, however, more and more companies are slashing their recruiting budgets and trimming their hiring staffs to the bone, which means there just aren't enough people to read all of the resumes that arrive on a weekly basis. Consequently, many hiring managers, especially those in large companies that receive thousands of resumes each month, have turned to computerized scanning systems to speed the sorting and processing of job applications.

When a resume arrives in the human resources department by mail or fax these days, the only human being who's likely to touch it is the clerk who feeds it through the scanner. From that point on, machines pretty much take over. If your hard copy resume is in a stack to be processed, here's what happens: the scanner sends an image of your document to a computer. The computer "reads" it, looking for key words, then files it accordingly in a database. When the employer has an opening to fill, he or she searches that database for resumes containing key words associated with the requirements for a particular position. If your resume contains key words that match those requirements, it will pop up and a human being will have the opportunity to finally read it, and possibly give you a call to schedule an interview. But if there are no key-word matches, your resume remains tucked deep inside the database doing absolutely nothing but sitting there until another opening with another set of key words comes along and the whole process begins again.

Not every company uses this scanning technology, of course. Small and midsized firms still employ the human touch, and many companies with an Internet presence and online databases prefer to receive resumes by e-mail. Still, enough large corporations rely on scanners that you will definitely want to make "scannability" a consideration in finalizing your resume. If the chances are better than average that your document will be read by more computers than people, then you must make sure it exists in a format that is easy for a computer to recognize, read, and understand.

Your ultimate goal is to get your resume out of the database and into the hands of the hiring manager. The trick for doing this is twofold: (1) you must choose the right key words to describe your educational background and experience, and (2) you must format your resume so a scanner can read it. If it's incorrectly formatted, it will scan poorly or not at all and you've probably lost your shot at a job with this company.

Choosing the Right Key Words

Key words are the nouns or short phrases that the computer searches for when scanning your resume and deciding whether to select it for further consideration. Using the right key words or key phrases is absolutely critical to your resume's ultimate success—or lack thereof. Key words usually refer to experience, training, skills, abilities, and achievements. For example, an employer searching an employment database for a sales representative might use the following key word criteria:

- sales representative
- exceeded quota
- cold calls
- high energy
- willing to travel

If your resume contains all of these key words and phrases, it will be among the first resumes selected. If it lacks just one key word, it will be in the next bunch, and so forth. Sadly, however, even if you have the right qualifications for the position of sales representative, if none of these key words appears in your resume, the computer will pass right over your document and the employer will never see it.

To complicate matters even further, different employers search for different key words, sometimes even for the same positions. Whenever possible, use the buzzwords common to your field or industry to describe your experience, education, skills, and abilities (this is where your research to become an "industry insider" comes in handy). Though there is no way to know for sure which key words employers are most likely to search for, you can make educated guesses. Check the classified ads for job openings in your field. What terms do employers commonly use to describe their requirements? Executive recruiters who specialize in your field are also a good source of this kind of information. To maximize your resume's chances of being selected in the search, use as many key words as possible. Remember, too, you only have to use a key word once in your document for it to be selected; to cover all bases and improve your chances, use synonyms wherever possible.

Resume Format

A resume is every job seeker's primary sales tool for describing the education, experience, and skills he or she brings to the workplace. In that regard, every resume is unique. At the same time, however, all resumes have certain commonalities. In order to be seriously considered for a job in today's technological environment, your resume must conform to the widely accepted formatting rules described below. If incorrectly formatted, your resume will scan poorly or not at all and you could lose the chance of landing your dream job as a result.

Length

As a rule of thumb, college students or recent grads should never submit a resume of more than one page in length. Considering how little professional experience you have likely accrued up to this point, you simply don't have that much to say. Be sure that what you do say, however, includes as many key words as possible to increase the likelihood that your resume will be selected in a key-word search.

Paper Size

Always use standard 8½" x 11" paper. Recruiters handle hundreds of resumes; if yours is on a smaller sheet, it is likely to be lost in the pile, and if it is oversized, it won't fit easily into a standard file folder and may simply be tossed out. Odd paper sizes are also more difficult to scan.

Paper Color

While it may be true that resumes printed on hot pink or electric green paper will get noticed, they don't scan well and they probably won't result in an interview. This is not the time to stand out from the crowd. White and ivory are still the only acceptable paper colors for resumes and cover letters.

Paper Quality

Standard, 20-pound office paper is perfectly acceptable; it actually scans better than more expensive papers such as ivory laid. To ensure a clear scan, your resume needs to be as sharp and legible as possible, black ink on white paper works best.

Type and Graphics

Word-processing and desktop-publishing software make it easy for you to manipulate the appearance of your resume by switching fonts and adding graphics. But that is not necessarily a good thing. To help ensure that your resume is both easy on the eyes and readily scannable, pay attention to the following rules:

- **Font.** Choose a nondecorative font (typeface) with clear, distinct characters, such as Arial (Helvetica) or Times New Roman. Stay away from script-like fonts and never use a reverse box to print white type on a black or gray shaded background. Scanners can't read reverse type.
- **Font Size.** A font size of 12 points is ideal. Don't go below 10 or above 14 points for body text, as type that is too small or too large is difficult for the scanner to read. Your name should be larger than the largest font in the text of your resume, but no larger than 20 points.

- **Font Style.** Most scanners will accept boldface, but if you are unsure, substitute capital letters instead for emphasis. Boldfacing and all caps should be reserved for elements you especially want to emphasize, such as your name or major section headings.
- **Graphics, Lines, and Shading.** A resume scanner will try to "read" graphics, lines, and shading as text, but the end result will be computer chaos. Avoid these elements. And do stick to traditional layouts for your resume. Scanners read from left to write; they are easily confused by multicolumn formats.

Printing Your Resume

The end result—your final resume—will be largely determined by the quality of the printer you use. Laser printers generally provide the best quality, but inkjet systems are also acceptable. Do not use typewriters or dot-matrix printers; the quality of type they produce is inadequate for most scanners. Your resume needs to be as sharp and legible as possible, so you should always send originals, not photocopies. For the same reason, you should mail, not fax, your resume. The only exceptions to this last rule would be if a potential employer has requested that resumes be sent only by fax, or if your cover letter and resume needs to arrive before an immediate deadline.

Proofreading Is Essential

Whether you key in the words yourself or pay someone else to do it for you, be sure to proofread the final product carefully. Mistakes on resumes are not only embarrassing, they can sink your chances of landing a job, particularly when something as critical as your name is misspelled. No matter how much money you may have paid to have your resume prepared, you are the only one who stands to lose if a mistake has been made. Proofread every word, every letter, as carefully as possible. The eye has a way of seeing what it expects to see, so get a friend to help you. Read your draft aloud as your friend checks the proof copy, then switch places. Have your friend read aloud while you check. Finally, go over it a third time—reading word by word, letter by letter, to triple-check spelling and punctuation.

If you are having your resume prepared and printed by a resume service and you can't bring a friend along to proof it, ask to take it home. Proof it with a friend, then bring it back later for corrections and final printing.

If you wrote and typed your own resume you may use your word processing program's built-in spelling checker to look for spelling errors. But beware—a computer spelling checker is not a substitute for proofreading. You still must proofread your resume with a friend to ensure that there are no errors. (Bear in mind that a spelling checker only recognizes words that are misspelled; it won't flag word-usage errors such as "to" for "two," or "belt" for "bell.")

The Two Basic Types of Resumes: Chronological and Functional

There are two basic types of resumes. The most common is the chronological resume; the other is the functional resume.

The Chronological Resume

A chronological resume is, in fact, a reverse chronological resume—items are listed in reverse chronological order, with your most recent schooling or job first. On a chronological resume, education and work experience are always grouped separately.

The Functional Resume

A functional resume lists your capabilities and qualifications, but does not include a list of work history or education in chronological order.

Functional resumes are generally used by candidates who have accrued a significant amount of experience over the years, but not necessarily in the field for which they are currently applying; chronological resumes could actually make such candidates, many of whom are making significant career changes, appear weak. For example, an army officer, teacher or homemaker seeking a position at a large corporation for the first time might choose a functional resume in order to emphasize life experience and skills acquired rather than specific jobs held or lack thereof.

Which Type of Resume Is Best for Recent Grads?

Corporate recruiters don't expect recent grads to have a lot of experience, so chronological resumes are perfectly acceptable. In fact, even though your chronological resume may be sparse on details, it is the better choice. Many corporate recruiters would immediately assume that a candidate fresh out of college who elects to submit a functional resume must be trying to hide some negative aspect of his work or school history. Bottom line—use a chronological resume.

Resume Content: Do's and Don'ts

If you think of your resume as a tool for selling yourself—and you should—then you recognize the importance of content. The educational achievements and on-the-job experiences you choose to highlight are what will set you apart from your competition. And don't forget those all-important key words and phrases!

What Comes First?

When you are coming to the workplace fresh out of college, your education should appear first—and should be outlined in detail. Experience should be listed first on a resume only after you have at least two years of full-time career work experience. After your education, list your job experience in reverse order, with your most recent job first and the rest going back in time.

Show Dates and Locations

Clearly show the dates and locations of your education and employment on your resume. List the dates of your employment and education on the left of the page; put the names of the companies you worked for and the schools you attended a few spaces to the right of the date. Lastly, align the city and state where you studied or worked with the right margin.

Avoid Sentences and Large Blocks of Type

Recruiters receive hundreds of resumes and they don't have time to carefully read them all, which is why short, concise phrases are much more effective than long-winded sentences. Consider the difference between these two examples, and note the use in the second of important key words and phrases such as "designed," "implemented," "cost savings," and "employee efficiency."

Long-Winded

Over the course of the months of December 2006 and January 2007, I completely redid the inventory system at my place of employment, which ended up resulting in a final savings of a great deal of money—perhaps $10,000. It was also considerably easier to perform office tasks efficiently under the new arrangement, not only for myself, but also for others who worked with me at the store.

Clear and Concise

Winter 2006: Designed and implemented new inventory system, resulting in a cost savings of approximately $10,000 and increased employee efficiency.

Make sure that everything on your resume is easy to read, every detail easy to find. Avoid paragraphs longer than six lines; never go to ten or more. If you have a strong story to tell and want to include more than six lines of information about one job or school, reformat the material into two or more paragraphs.

Highlight Relevant Skills and Responsibilities

Be specific. Slant your past accomplishments toward the type of position that you hope to obtain. Do you want to supervise people? If so, state how many people you have supervised in the past and the functions they performed. Highlight accomplishments that have saved money or improved productivity.

Education

Mention degrees received and any honors or special awards. Note individual courses or research projects that might be relevant for employers. For instance, if you are a liberal arts major, be sure to mention any courses you may have taken in such areas as accounting, marketing, statistics, computer programming, or mathematics. Even if these do not reflect your main interests at school, they demonstrate your knowledge of relevant workplace skills.

Personal Data

It is not imperative that you include personal data, but if you do, keep it very brief—two lines maximum. A concise reference to commonly practiced activities such as golf, skiing, sailing, chess, bridge, tennis, etc. may generate some interesting conversation during an interview. However, do not include your age, weight, height, marital status, or any similar details on your resume.

References

Do not list references on your resume. If you want to mention the subject, simply write "References available upon request." This enables you to update or change your references and to know when they are going to be contacted. If you are pressed for space, simply write nothing at all. Most employers assume that every applicant has references and will ask you to supply them at an appropriate time. It is better to use the limited space you have to detail your experience and accomplishments than tell the employer that you have references available, something he or she already knows.

Should You Include a Job Objective?

Probably not. Even if you are certain of exactly the type of job you want, including a job objective on your resume might actually eliminate you from consideration for a position simply because it doesn't quite match the goals you have specified. In all likelihood, you will end up with a job that is quite different from the one you initially wanted (most recent college grads do!), and that's not necessarily a bad thing. Just imagine the opportunities you might miss out on if you limit your options from the get-go with an objective that is too specific.

You might opt to use a job-objective heading at the top of your resume to express a general interest in the industry you have selected, but you should not designate a particular job. Even if you have made up your mind to settle for only one job function, it could appear presumptuous to specify this on your resume.

If you feel you must list a job objective, do so in general terms. For example, "Objective: an entry-level position in the banking industry" or "Objective: to pursue a career in book publishing."

The E-mailable Resume

A resume that is scannable is also e-mailable. But if want to add some special touches, like italics or boldfacing to a resume you'll be e-mailing as an attachment, you need not be so worried about whether these formatting elements will survive their journey to another computer; your word processing software has implanted the appropriate codes to make that possible.

Suppose, for example, that you created your resume in Microsoft Word and saved it to your hard drive as a Word document (.doc). The minute you clicked "Save," your software automatically retained any special formatting codes, such as fonts, margins, tabs, etc., right along with the actual words you typed. To send your resume as e-mail, simply attach the .doc file to your e-mail message; anyone with Word will be able to read it just as you created it.

Let's suppose, however, that your recipient doesn't use Microsoft Word. In that case, you will need to save a second copy of your resume, this time as a Rich Text File (.rtf). Rich Text Files are the universal donors of the computer world. When in doubt about the recipient computer's ability to read a particular word-processing program, attach the .rtf version of your resume to your e-mail; now anyone should be able to read it in its original format regardless of the word-processing software they use.

From time to time you may run across prospective employers who ask for your resume by e-mail, but specifically request that you not send it as an attachment. In such cases, you will have to remove the formatting codes and paste your resume into your e-mail message. This is not as difficult as it sounds.

E-mail messages are typically sent in ASCII format, which stands for American Standard Code for Information Interchange. ASCII files are generic and because no special formatting codes are added, they can be read by pretty much any computer. The resume you paste into your e-mail message will need to be in ASCII form. Sorry, but all those codes that make your Word document look so inviting by telling your software when to center a line, indent a paragraph, or italicize a word will have to go. To take them out, you must save your resume a third time, as an ASCII file. Simply select "Save As" from your File menu and, depending on which Word version you're using, choose "ASCII Text," "Plain Text," or "MS-DOS Text" as your file type. The resulting resume won't be quite so pretty, but it will be the right format for pasting into an e-mail message.

Five Tips for More Effective Resumes

Some more things to keep in mind when putting together your resume:

1. *Be factual.* In many companies, providing inaccurate information on a resume or job application is grounds for dismissal as soon as the inaccuracy is discovered. Protect yourself; don't say anything that isn't true.
2. *Be positive.* Your resume is a tool for selling your skills and accomplishments. If you have achieved something, say so, and put it in the best possible light. This is not the time to hold back or be modest—your competition won't be. At the same time, however, don't exaggerate to the point of misrepresentation.

3. *Be brief.* Include the relevant and important accomplishments, but do so in as few words as possible. A vigorous, concise resume will be examined more carefully than a long-winded one.

4. *Emphasize relevant experience.* Highlight continued experience in a particular job function or continued interest in a particular industry. De-emphasize any irrelevant positions.

5. *Stress your results.* Elaborate on how you contributed to your past employers. Did you increase sales, reduce costs, improve a product, implement a new program? Were you promoted? Use action verbs and, if possible, dollar figures and other numbers.

Quick Tip: Don't Lie!

One applicant wrote on his resume that he could type 60 wpm, but when confronted in an interview he confessed, "Well, I can't really type that fast. My girlfriend thought it would look good on my resume." Wrong! Can you say "end of interview"?

Chapter Eleven

The Resume Worksheet

Now that you have the basics, it's time to begin putting your resume together. This chapter will take you step-by-step through the resume writing process. You will need a quiet place to work and plenty of paper. Feel free to develop your resume right on your computer or to handwrite your answers. You may keep notes on separate pieces of paper or enter your responses on the worksheets provided.

Name

Write your name, in capital letters, as you wish it to appear on your resume. Center it horizontally on the page, about one inch from the top. Use your formal name, even if no one ever calls you by it. Use a middle name or initial if possible—it adds prestige.

Example
STEVEN M. PHILLIPS

Address/Phone

Space down two or three lines beneath your name and enter your school address and phone number on the left-hand margin and your permanent address on the right-hand margin.

Even if you have no plans to move back home, you should list your permanent address. It gives employers a place to leave a message for you if they are unable to reach you at your school number. In all likelihood, your parents will know where you can be found.

Note: If you live on campus and have a private phone, and you don't already have an answering machine, you may wish to buy or borrow one for accepting calls from prospective employers; you may also use your cell phone number. In either case, however, be sure that the greeting you record for potential employers to hear is serious and businesslike. This is no time to be cute.

School Address:

Street _____

Apartment, dormitory, or mail box # _____

Name of School (if living on-campus) _____

City, tate, Zip _____

Phone _____   _____

Permanent Address:

Street _____

Apartment # (if any) _____   _____

City, state, Zip _____

Phone _____

Example:

School Address
1015 Commonwealth Avenue
Apartment 16
Boston, Massachusetts 02145
Phone: 617/555-1483

Permanent Address:
507 North 6th Street
Houston, Texas 77024
Phone: 713/555-2341

Education

Next, list your education. (Note: If you have two or more years of full time relevant career experience, list experience ahead of your education.)

If you have not yet graduated and are currently working toward a degree (either full-time or part-time), begin with the phrase "Candidate for the degree of . . . "

If you have already graduated, begin with "Awarded a (degree name) . . ."

If you did not graduate and are not currently pursuing your degree, simply list the dates you attended and the courses studied. For example, "Studied mathematics, physics, chemistry, and statistics."

Not yet graduated:

Candidate for the degree of _____ in _____
(month/year), majoring in _____.

Already graduated:

Awarded a _____ in _____ (month,
year), majoring in _____.

Did not graduate, not currently pursuing degree:

Studied _____ (list key courses or subjects) and other courses (or subjects) from _____ (dates).

Courses

Then list from one to six courses, particularly emphasizing those that might be relevant to the positions for which you may be applying. If none seems relevant, list courses that might indicate your ability to excel at work assignments. If all else fails, list courses that simply sound impressive.

Courses include _____, _____, _____ _____, _____, and _____.

Grade Point Average

Next, you should list your grade point average (GPA)—but only if it will be viewed positively by recruiters. Grade point average will not make or break your application; it is only one aspect that recruiters evaluate. If an employer is extremely concerned about GPA, he or she will probably ask for a transcript anyway. How impressive your grade point average appears and whether or not you should include it on your resume may well depend upon the institution where you received your degree, the nature of your course load, and the competition for the particular position you are seeking. In any event, do not include a GPA below 3.0 on a 4.0 scale or a B- on a letter scale.

_____ grade point average.

If your GPA in your major field of study is much higher than your overall GPA, you should include this information with or without your overall GPA.

_____ grade point average in major.

Class Rank

If you ranked extremely high in your class (say within the top ten), you should include it on your resume.

I ranked _____ in a class of _____ students.

Academic Achievements, Special Projects, Thesis, Etc.

It's always a good idea to include notable academic honors, but if you are unable to list any, consider including a special project that you worked on instead. Even if the project required only a few days of your time, it could be important if it shows initiative in the academic area that has been the main focus of your college career.

Example:
Conducted an independent research study on the effect of television on pre-adolescent children.

If you weren't involved in any special projects, you may wish to list the title of your senior thesis or your minor field of study. The point here is to make it clear to the reader of your resume that even though you didn't necessarily graduate at the top of your class, you were a quick study and an eager participant in the academic process. The topic of your thesis might also appear ahead of your grade point average.

Example:
Thesis topic: "New Application of Co-Linear Coordinates."

List your academic achievements, awards, special projects, thesis topic, etc. here:

_____

_____

_____

Notable Academic Honors
List any special academic awards, honors, or competitive scholarships.

Example:
Education

2003–2007 **BOSTON UNIVERSITY**   **BOSTON, MASSACHUSETTS**
Candidate for the degree of Bachelor of Arts in May 2007, majoring in Mathematics. Courses include Statistics and Computer Programming. Thesis topic: "New Applications of Co-Linear Coordinates." 3.4 grade point average. Awarded the Elliot Smith Scholarship in 2005.

Extracurricular Activities
Even if you have glowing academic credentials, it is essential to list some extracurricular activities. They demonstrate that you are sociable, multidimensional—i.e., you did more than study during four years of school—get along well with people, and that you will easily adjust to the many different kinds of people you might encounter in the workplace. Extracurricular activities help a recruiter perceive you as a well-rounded person and desirable hire.

At the same time, by carefully choosing the extracurricular activities you list, you can help set yourself apart from the competition and move closer to the job you want.

Avoid simply listing many sports or clubs haphazardly. This might give the impression that you start many projects with enthusiasm but don't necessarily finish them. Furthermore, in the limited space available on your resume, you will only have room to describe a few items. If you include too many, you will give no indication of the depth of interest in any one activity. Instead, list only the activities on which you expended a considerable amount of time or in which you have a higher-than-average interest or ability. (Interests that you choose not to include under extracurricular activities may be included toward the bottom of your resume under the heading "Personal Background.")

Extracurricular activity #1: _____

Extracurricular activity #2 (optional): _____

Extracurricular activity #3 (optional): _____

Extracurricular activity #4 (optional): _____

Example:

Treasurer of the Mathematics Club. Responsible for $7,000 annual budget. Co-chairperson of Boston University's semi-annual symposium on "The Future of Mathematics." Exhibitor and prize-winner at local photography shows. Helped to establish university darkroom.

Should You Include High School Information?

Including high school information on your resume is optional. If you have made exceptional achievements in college and in your summer or part-time jobs, you should include these in your resume and omit your high school information. Most college graduates choose not to include high school information on their resumes, but there are sometimes good reasons to do so.

If you list your high school achievements on your resume, describe them more briefly than your college achievements. Even if they are very impressive, putting too much emphasis on your high school years may give the impression that your highest performance days were in the past.

Name of high school: _____

Location (city, state): _____

Date of high school graduation: _____

GPA: _____

Class Rank: _____

Academic achievements, special projects, etc. (list one to three):

_____

_____

_____

Notable academic honors (list one to three):

_____

_____

_____

Extracurricular activities (list one to three):

_____

_____

_____

Example:

1999–2003 **HOUSTON PUBLIC HIGH SCHOOL**   **HOUSTON, TEXAS**
Received diploma in June 2003. Achieved Advanced Placement
Standing in calculus and physics. Academic Honors all terms.
Assistant Editor of school yearbook.

Work Experience

Work experience, however limited, is an essential part of any resume. Recruiters want to see some kind of work history because it demonstrates that you have been able to land a job and have a good work ethic. Remember, volunteer work and unpaid internships are almost as important as paid work to recruiters. Be sure to include such activities on your resume in the same format as your work experience.

If, during college, you spent a summer traveling, studying, or performing some enlightening or substantive activity other than working for pay, be sure to include this information. Gaps in resumes raise red flags for recruiters. They might assume that you sat on the beach for an entire summer—or worse, that you were sidelined with a medical or other personal problem that could potentially interfere with your ability to work.

List your work experience in reverse chronological order. It is acceptable to group your summer positions together, listing them in reverse chronological order, followed by your part-time positions in reverse chronological order. Unless your part-time positions are significantly more impressive than your summer jobs, list your summer positions first. Full-time career-related internships should be listed ahead of summer positions, as they could be a significant advantage in getting the position you desire. While it is important to show jobs or other substantive activities for each summer during your college years, it is not necessary to list summer or part-time jobs that you held during your high school years unless they make a positive contribution to your resume. In fact, you should not list any jobs that you held for a very short duration. For example, if you held two different positions during a summer vacation, list only the job of longer duration. While you may be able to explain during a job interview why you switched jobs in the middle of the summer, the fact that you had two jobs of such short duration might prevent you from even getting to the interview stage in the first place.

Always be truthful on your resume. Not only is it the right thing to do, it can prevent problems down the road. More and more companies are checking facts on resumes these days; providing false information on a resume or job application is often considered grounds for dismissal, even if the falsehood is discovered years after you are hired. Remember, your resume is essentially an advertisement of yourself. Choosing which positions to list and highlight on your resume is an important part of creating a positive image. While you have every right to put your best foot forward and show your strongest points, you should never lie to do so.

How to List Your Previous Employment

On the left side of the page, list your dates of employment with each company. For summer positions, the word "Summer" followed by the year is sufficient. For part-time work, you may list the year(s) or starting and ending month and year.

In the center, list the company name. To the right, list the location (city and state). Be sure that you spell the company name correctly; the recruiter may recognize the firm or wish to verify your employment, and errors are likely to raise red flags.

Next, list your job title. In the case of a large corporation, list the department you worked for—but only if this is to your advantage. For example, if you are seeking a career position as a salesperson and you worked summers as a typist in a sales department, it would be a definite plus to spell that out. The assumption here is that even if you did not gain sales experience, you at least gained an understanding of the sales process at the company in question.

Describe the duties and responsibilities of your position. If you are listing several summer positions and several part-time positions, space constraints dictate that you either be very brief in describing each position or that you let the job titles for less significant positions speak for themselves.

Rather than list a perfunctory job description for each position, go into more detail on the more impressive, relevant, or interesting positions. Remember, the purpose of your resume is to open the door for an interview. This is not an exam or a play-by-play of your work history. You should focus on presenting those aspects of the position that speak most positively about your experience. Do not feel compelled to write a summary of your job or even to list your major duties as though you were putting together a formal job description.

Instead of listing job duties, you might focus on accomplishments or achievements, even if they are only small ones. For example, suppose you are describing your summer job as a lifeguard. A brief summary of your duties might read: "Supervised waterfront for busy public beach; responsible for safety of bathers, maintaining public order and cleanliness of the beach and parking areas." While this description might, at first glance, make the position of lifeguard sound more impressive than simply writing "Lifeguard at public beach," it does little to distinguish you from any other person who has ever worked as a lifeguard. It would be much more effective to list an on-the-job accomplishment or achievement—even a minor one. For example, if you set up a box beside the trash can to collect bottles and cans for recycling, you could replace the previous job description with, "Established recycling program for bottles and cans." This shows motivation, effort, and initiative beyond basic duties.

Summer Jobs During College Summers:

Date of employment (summer, year): _____

Company name: _____

Company location (city, state): _____

Job title (and department, if relevant): _____

Job description and/or accomplishments:

_____

_____

Date of employment (summer, year): _____

Company name: _____

Company location (city, state): _____

Job title (and department, if relevant): _____

Job description and/or accomplishments: _____

_____

_____

Date of employment (summer, year): _____

Company name: _____

Company location (city, state): _____

Job title (and department, if relevant): _____

Job description and/or accomplishments: _____

_____

_____

Example:

Summer 2006   **DATA PUNCH ASSOCIATES, INC.   NEW YORK, NEW YORK**
Mail Clerk and Courier for Accounting Department. Reorganized mail distribution and sorting system in the department. Delivered sensitive documents to the executive department.

Summer 2005 **TOWN OF FALMOUTH** **FALMOUTH, MASSACHUSETTS**
Lifeguard at busy public beach. Established recycling program for bottles and cans.

Summers 2004 **SAM'S BEEFBURGERS**   **CHICAGO, ILLINOIS**
Began work as dishwasher. Promoted to short-order cook.

Next, list summer jobs you held in high school, but only if *both* of the following apply: (1) your college summer work experiences are not particularly outstanding; and (2) you have no part-time work experience to list. (If after completing this process, you find you have too much material for a one-page resume, delete the summer jobs you held in high school.)

Summer Jobs During High School

Date of employment (summer, year): _____

Company location (city, state): _____

Job title (and department, if relevant): _____

Job description and/or accomplishments: _____

_____

_____

Date of employment (summer, year): _____

Company name: _____

Company location (city, state): _____

Job title (and department, if relevant): _____

Job description and/or accomplishments: _____

_____

Date of employment (summer, year): _____

Company name: _____

Company location (city, state): _____

Job title (and department, if relevant): _____

Job description and/or accomplishments: _____

_____

_____

Example:

Summer 2002 **TOWN OF LAKE FOREST** **LAKE FOREST, ILLINOIS**
Tutored emotionally disturbed grade schoolers for basic arithmetic in remedial summer school program.

Part-Time Jobs

Next, list your part-time positions. You should include only part-time jobs you held for at least six months. To avoid appearing like a job-hopper, do not list more than four part-time positions. It is not necessary to list a part-time position for each year; many students have no part-time positions to list at all.

Be selective in the part-time positions you list. Stress those that are the most relevant to your career: those that show initiative, are interesting, or that you held for the longest periods of time.

As a general rule, you should devote less space to part-time positions than to summer positions—unless your part-time positions represent unusually significant experiences, such as work in the industry in which you are now seeking full-time employment.

Your descriptions of part-time positions should be similar in format but briefer than those for summer positions. List the date of employment (on the left), the employer (in the center), and the city and state (on the right).

Part-Time Positions:

Date of employment (summer, year): _____

Company location (city, state): _____

Job title (and department, if relevant): _____

Job description and/or accomplishments: _____

_____

_____

Date of employment (summer, year): _____

Company name: _____

Company location (city, state): _____

Job title (and department, if relevant): _____

Job description and/or accomplishments: _____

_____

Date of employment (summer, year): _____

Company name: _____

Company location (city, state): _____

Job title (and department, if relevant): _____

Job description and/or accomplishments: _____

_____

_____

Example:
part-time
2004–2005   **BOSTON UNIVERSITY**   **BOSTON, MASSACHUSETTS**
University bookstore Floor and Stockroom Clerk. Responsibilities included arranging merchandise displays, customer service, and checking packing slips against shipments.

Alternative for Part-Time Jobs

If your summer jobs are fairly impressive, or if you are short on space, you may simply list several part-time positions you have held without providing individual job descriptions. You should list only those part-time jobs held for six months or more, and do not list more than four positions. For the jobs listed in this manner, you may also wish to add the name of the employer.

Part-time
(years covered)
Part-time positions include: _____, _____, and _____.

Example:
part-time
2003–2006   Part-time positions include Floor and Stockroom Clerk at University Bookstore, Short-order Cook, and Tutor in mathematics.

Alternatively, you may wish to list noteworthy part-time positions separately from other part-time positions. In this case, you would include the noteworthy positions with your other work experience under the heading "Experience." You would then simply list your other part-time jobs in the same format, under the heading "Other part-time positions."

Interim Jobs

It is not out of the realm of possibility that you may have to spend many months job hunting before you find a suitable career position. In the meantime, you may have to secure a temporary or "interim" job to generate some income while you search for a permanent professional position.

Should you list such positions on your resume? The answer depends on how strong your other work experiences are. If you have been out of school less than six months, it is not necessary to list an interim job on your resume. Otherwise, it's acceptable to include interim employment on your resume—but do not list more than one job.

Job Titles

When it comes to listing job titles, the best rule to follow is: simplify, simplify, simplify! It is better to use titles that are generic enough to be understood by all who read your resume than to use confusing terms that might be familiar only to your previous employer. If, at a particular job, you were called "First-level Pascal Programmer II," simply write this as "Computer Programmer" on your resume.

Do not exaggerate your job title. If you worked in an office greeting clients and answering phones, simply write "Receptionist" on your resume. Do not try to impress potential employers with a loftier sounding title such as "Inter-Communications Specialist." When the recruiter asks about your job experience at the interview, it will become immediately clear that you over-represented yourself and that could hurt your chances.

At the same time, you should not be afraid to use your resume as a way to put your best foot forward and "sell" yourself to the recruiter. The best way to do this is to keep the job title simple, then make the most of the job description that follows it. But remember: Keep your descriptions brief! You can always elaborate on your work experiences once you get to the interview.

Personal Background

If have room, be sure to include a section on personal background. While not the most important part of your resume, this section shows that you are an interesting person—and it gives the interviewer a possible conversation starter. Perhaps he or she will even share some of your interests.

List your areas of personal interest without embellishment—unless there is an unusually significant personal accomplishment in this category that might help you get a job. In any case, keep the details to a minimum. Don't list too many items. As we pointed out under extracurricular activities, it is better to list only a few in which you are particularly interested than to come across as someone who can't make up her mind. If the recruiter asks about a particular activity, you will have something to say. Also, keeping the list short implies more depth of interest and a higher level of expertise.

Three or four activities should be the maximum.

Personal Background

_____, _____, and _____,

Example:
Personal Background   Enjoy photography, reading science fiction, and playing bridge. Published two articles in mathematics journals.

References

If you decide to mention references on your item, it should be the last item included, and it should read:

References   References available upon request.

Do not list actual references on your resume for two reasons: it looks less professional, and it's good for you to know ahead of time when a reference will be called. Not listing them on your resume gives you greater flexibility, too. You can change your list of references based on the job for which you are applying. Do not feel you even have to mention references at all. If you are pressed for space and the choice comes down to including another relevant job experience or a line about references, opt for the experience. A recruiter automatically assumes that any job applicant has "references available upon request."

That's it! If you have completed all your worksheets, you have the basis for putting together a completed resume that looks great. (A sample resume is included at the end of this chapter to give you an idea of the proper overall format and arrangement.) Don't forget to check your resume for spelling errors and accuracy—then double- and triple-check it with a friend.

Quick Tip: Use Action Verbs

How you write your resume is just as important as what you write. The strongest resumes use short phrases beginning with action verbs. Below is a quick list.

achieved	founded	prepared
administered	generated	processed
analyzed	headed	published
assembled	identified	purchased
budgeted	installed	reduced
built	instructed	regulated
collected	integrated	revised
computed	interviewed	scheduled
coordinated	launched	sold
created	managed	streamlined
determined	monitored	studied
developed	negotiated	tested
devised	ordered	trained
discovered	organized	updated
evaluated	performed	upgraded
expanded	planned	wrote

Sample Resume

STEVEN M. PHILLIPS

School Address:
1015 Commonwealth Avenue, Apt. 16
Boston, Massachusetts 02145
Phone: 617/555-1483

Permanent Address:
507 North 6th Street
Houston, TX 77024
Phone: 713/555-2341

Education

2003–2007 | **BOSTON UNIVERSITY   BOSTON, MASSACHUSETTS**
Candidate for the degree of Bachelor of Arts in May 2007, majoring in mathematics. Courses include statistics and computer programming. Thesis topic: "New Applications of Co-Linear Coordinates." 3.4 grade point average. Awarded the Elliot Smith Scholarship in 2005.

Treasurer of the Mathematics Club. Responsible for $7,000 annual budget. Co-chairperson of Boston University's semi-annual symposium on "The Future of Mathematics." Exhibitor and prize-winner at local photography shows. Helped to establish university darkroom.

1999–2003 | **HOUSTON PUBLIC HIGH SCHOOL   HOUSTON, TEXAS**
Received diploma in June 2003. Achieved Advanced Placement Standing in calculus and physics. Academic Honors all terms. Assistant Editor of school yearbook.

Experience

Summer 2006 | **DATA PUNCH ASSOCIATES, INC.   NEW YORK, NEW YORK**
Mail Clerk and Courier for the Accounting Department. Reorganized mail distribution and sorting system in the department. Delivered sensitive documents to the executive branch.

Summers
2003, 2005 | **HARVEY'S BEEFBURGERS, INC.   HOUSTON, TEXAS**
Began work as a dishwasher. Promoted to short-order cook.

Part-time | **BOSTON UNIVERSITY   BOSTON, MASSACHUSETTS**
One of six students invited to tutor for the Department of Mathematics. Also graded student papers and worked as a Research Assistant in Theoretical Calculus.

Part-time
2004–2005 | **BOSTON UNIVERSITY   BOSTON, MASSACHUSETTS**
Bookstore Floor and Stockroom Clerk. Responsibilities included arranging merchandise displays, customer service, and checking invoices against shipments.

Personal Background | Enjoy photography, reading science fiction, and playing bridge. Published two articles in mathematics journals.

References | References available upon request.

Chapter Twelve

Resume Makeovers

While a good resume can open doors for you, a bad resume can just as easily slam them in your face.

In this chapter, we present five not-so-great resumes and point out some of their most glaring flaws. With a little rewriting and rearranging, we've managed to transform them into resumes that are more likely to land interviews. Study both versions carefully and you'll soon see the differences for yourself.

Quick Tips:

- Use caps, italics, and boldfacing effectively.
- Organize your resume so it's easy to read.
- Use action verbs and key words.
- Be brief and to the point.
- Use one typeface throughout your resume.
- Don't forget your phone number, both school and permanent, or cell.

✗ Resume lacks definition and is difficult to read at a glance.

Janet Dubois
1312 Liberty Street
Lowell, MA 01854
(617) 555-5208

EDUCATION

Brown University, Providence, RI
Bachelor of Arts degree received May 2006
Major: English Literature GPA: 3.10

Internship, Boston Literacy Program, Boston, MA
Assisted in reading program, teaching illiterate children and adults reading skills.

EXPERIENCE

Editorial Assistant, *The Bostonian Journal*
June 2006–August 2006
Edited articles, features, and illustrations for monthly publication.

Editor-in-Chief, Brown U. Newspaper
September 2005–May 2006
Selected submissions, edited and wrote headlines for submissions and columns, laid out pages, dealt with public, recruited columnists, trained associates.

Associate Editor, Brown U. Newspaper
January 2004–May 2005
Trained for Editor-in-Chief position; assisted in selecting submissions, edited and wrote headlines for submissions and columns, laid out pages, miscellaneous other tasks.

Copy Editor, Brown U. Newspaper
January 2003–December 2003
Edited news stories, wrote headlines, assisted with layout of pages, occasionally solicited advertising and helped with distribution.

COMPUTER
SKILLS

Word Processing—Working knowledge of WordPerfect and Microsoft Word.
Spreadsheets—Familiar with all aspects of creating and using a spreadsheet using Lotus 1-2-3 and Microsoft Excel.

ACTIVITIES

Senior Class Secretary, Dean's List

AFTER

✔ Note caps and bold.

JANET DUBOIS
1312 Liberty Street
Lowell, MA 01854
(617) 555-5208

✔ More visually appealing.

EDUCATION

Brown University, Providence, RI
Bachelor of Arts received May 2007
Major: English Literature
GPA: 3.10

Internship, Boston Literacy Program, Boston, MA
Assisted in reading program, taught reading skills to illiterate children and adults.

EXPERIENCE

Editorial Assistant, The Bostonian Journal
June 2007–August 2007
Edited articles, features, and illustrations for monthly publication.

Editor-in-Chief, Brown U. Newspaper
September 2006–May 2007
Selected submissions, edited and wrote headlines for submissions and columns, laid out pages, interfaced with public, recruited columnists, trained associates.

Associate Editor, Brown U. Newspaper
January 2005–May 2006
Trained for Editor-in-Chief position; assisted in selecting submissions, edited and wrote headlines for submissions and columns, laid out pages, performed miscellaneous other tasks as needed.

Copy Editor, Brown U. Newspaper
January 2004–December 2004
Edited news stories, wrote headlines, assisted with layout of pages, occasionally solicited advertising and helped with distribution.

COMPUTER SKILLS

Word Processing—Working knowledge of WordPerfect and Microsoft Word.
Spreadsheets—Strong familiarity with all aspects of creating and using a spreadsheet; hands-on experience with Lotus 1-2-3 and Microsoft Excel.

ACTIVITIES

Senior Class Secretary, Dean's List

✔ Note how reformatting helps to clarify this resume. Very little of the text has been changed.

> ✗ **Recruiters probably won't even read this resume.**

Frank Hamilburg
1334 23rd St., #104
New York, NY 10022
212/555-5512

EDUCATION
New York University, Manhattan
Bachelor of Science degree in Management
Date of Graduation: June 2006

> ✗ **Too long and wordy. Hard to read**

EXPERIENCE
John D. MacDougall, Inc., 55 East 10th St., New York, NY
Executive Assistant—Assistant to the President and Senior Vice President, responsible for providing extensive and highly confidential administrative assistance and support. Due to my highly visible and important role within the organization, I ensured that top company executives were constantly kept abreast of situations, problems, etc. that arose within the company, as well as within the industry. Responsible for the complete coordination of semi-annual company meetings consisting of 250 guests, which included the site selection, attainment of desired atmosphere, planning and arranging of speakers/guests, hotel accommodations and land and air transportation, as well as ensuring the successful attainment of budgeted costs. Also coordinated company social functions including dinners, parties, and holiday celebrations; which included initiating ideas for these functions, selection of the location of the function, coordination of all details such as reservations, transportation, etc., and also ensuring attainment of budgeted costs. Heavy involvement with the Young Executive Program; reviewed personnel reports for content, personal and professional objectives, kept records of job performance over time, and made recommendations of salary adjustments based on overall rating. Acted as the on-site computer resource with respect to the explanation and solving of all company computing problems. Working knowledge of WordPerfect, Microsoft Word, Excel and dBase programs. May 2005 to September 2005.

Tecchi Management Corporation, 833 Fifth Avenue, New York, NY
Administrative Assistant/Coordinator—Assistant to the President as well as the Accounting Manager. Constantly updated my supervisor on their employees' absenteeism, tardiness, performance appraisals and disciplinary actions needed to be taken. Responsible for the orientation of new employees on all company benefits and policies; taught employees company procedures for using technical equipment such as the fax machine, computers, copy machines, phone system, etc. Intense amount of communication with high-level staff and outside agencies. Performance of customer service functions, including the resolving of all consumer and agency complaints and problems. May 2004 to September 2004.

Avenue Investments, 1323 Avenue of the Americas, New York, NY
Administrative Assistant—In charge of confidential communications including typing company documents, correspondence, generation of charts and data, and filing. Associate in charge of outside communications via the telephone and switchboard. Completely responsible for the travel arrangements of ten company executives, including scheduling, coordination, and budgeting. Coordinated office supply inventory and responsible for maintaining and reordering supplies including letterhead stationery and computer disks. June 2003 to September 2003.

> ✗ **Too much detail about work experience, not enough detail about education.**

> ✔ **Easy and quick to read. Only relevant details are included; uses action verbs.**

Frank Hamilburg
1334 23rd St., #104
New York, NY 10022
212/555-5512

> ✔ **Expanded section on educational background.**

EDUCATION

New York University, Manhattan
Bachelor of Science awarded in June 2006, majoring in Management.
Courses included Physics, Biochemistry, Economics and Statistics. 3.4 grade point average in major. Honors: Dean's List.

Student member of the American Management Association. Props assistant for College Theatre. Co-captain of Intramural Volleyball Team. Actively involved in Students Against Drunk Driving.

EXPERIENCE

Executive Assistant
John D. MacDougall, Inc., 55 East 10th St., New York NY   (Summer 2005)
Provided extensive and highly confidential administrative assistance and support to the President and Senior Vice President
- Heavily involved with the Young Executive Program; reviewed personnel reports for content, personal and professional objectives; kept records of job performance over time; recommended salary adjustments based on overall rating
- Acted as the on-site computer resource manager with responsibility for troubleshooting and solving all company computing problems
- Coordinated company social functions and very large semi-annual company meetings

Administrative Assistant/Coordinator
Tecchi Management Corporation, 833 Fifth Avenue, New York, NY (Summer 2004)
- Assistant to the President and the Accounting Manager
- Responsible for new employee orientation; named go-to person for explaining all company benefits, policies, and procedures
- Involved in extensive communication with high-level staff and outside agencies
- Resolved all consumer and agency complaints and problems as customer service rep

Administrative Assistant
Avenue Investments, 1323 Avenue of the Americas, New York NY   (Summer 2003)
- In charge of typing, formatting, and filing of various confidential documents
- Generated charts and data
- Operated multiline telephone system
- Coordinated the travel arrangements of ten company executives, including scheduling and budgeting

COMPUTER SKILLS
- Hands-on experience with WordPerfect, Microsoft Word, Excel, and dBase programs

> ✗ **Too many different typefaces distract the reader.**

LINDA McFARLANE

School Address:
167 South Union Street
Burlington, VT 05401
Phone: 802/555-3354

Permanent Address:
756 Maple Street
Manchester, NH 03104
Phone: 603/555-0856

Education
2002–2006   **UNIVERSITY OF VERMONT   BURLINGTON, VERMONT**
Bachelor of Arts degree, May 2006. Major: Women's Studies. Minor: Art. 3.5 grade point average.

Experience
Summer 2005   **OFFICE OF THE PUBLIC DEFENDER BURLINGTON, VERMONT**
Summer Intern. Performed research, attended court sessions, posted bail for defendants. Liaison with District Attorney's Office.

Summers
2003–2004   **SWEETWATER'S RESTAURANT   BURLINGTON, VERMONT**
Began work as waitress, promoted to hostess. Also relief bartender.

Part-time
2003–2006   **ACADEMIC COMPUTING SERVICES UNIVERSITY OF VERMONT**
Computer counselor for campus computer lab. Hardware maintenance and software troubleshooting.

Part-time
2002–2003   **UNIVERSITY BOOKSTORE   UNIVERSITY OF VERMONT**
Cashier/Clerk. Acted as cashier, stocked shelves, and miscellaneous other duties.

Interests   Painting, sculpture, and aerobics.
References   Personal references available upon request.

> ✗ **Information is too brief.**

LINDA McFARLANE

School Address:
167 South Union Street
Burlington, VT 05401
Phone: 802/555-3354

Permanent Address:
756 Maple Street
Manchester, NH 03104
Phone: 603/555-0856

Education
2002–2006   **UNIVERSITY OF VERMONT   BURLINGTON, VERMONT**
Awarded Bachelor of Arts in May 2006, majoring in Women's Studies, minoring in Art. Courses included Economics, Statistics, Political Science, and Public Speaking. Thesis topic: The Political Economy of Our Domestic Health Care System. 3.5 grade point average. Awarded the Bailey-Howe Scholarship in 2004.

Contributing editor for campus newspaper, *The Cynic*. Member of the Outing Club and Varsity Crew Team. Designed and painted university-sponsored mural with the theme of cultural diversity.

✔ **Shows initiative and motivation.**

Experience
Summer 2005   **OFFICE OF THE PUBLIC DEFENDER   BURLINGTON, VERMONT**
Summer Intern working with five attorneys. Performed extensive research to support court cases and attended court sessions. Handled confidential documents and paperwork. Served as liaison with District Attorney's Office.

✔ **Emphasizes valuable experience**

Summers
2003–2004   **SWEETWATER'S RESTAURANT   BURLINGTON, VERMONT**
Began work as waitress, promoted to hostess. Also worked as relief bartender.

Part-time
2003–2006   **ACADEMIC COMPUTING SERVICES   UNIVERSITY OF VERMONT**
Computer counselor for campus computer lab. Maintained hardware; worked on network and mainframe. Performed extensive troubleshooting for students and faculty regarding software, hardware, and printer problems. Originated and conducted "Freshman Orientation Session" for new lab users.

✔ **Stresses accomplishments**

Part-time
2002–2003   **UNIVERSITY BOOKSTORE   UNIVERSITY OF VERMONT**
Cashier/Clerk. Acted as cashier, stocked shelves, and performed miscellaneous other duties as assigned.

Personal
Background   Enjoy painting, sculpture, aerobics, and camping. Member of the National Organization of Women.

References   References available upon request.

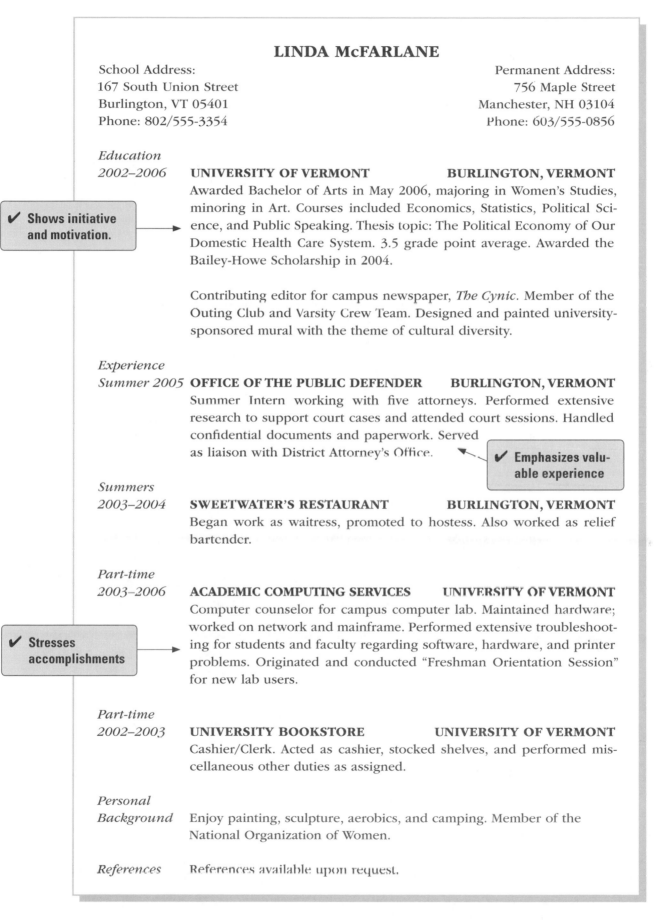

> ✗ Ho-hum . . . Drab language, needs action.

DANIEL R. PAPPAS

School Address:
121 University Terrace, Room 402
University of North Carolina
Chapel Hill, NC 27510
Phone: 919/555-5581

Permanent Address:
4 Squirrel Drive
Sarasota, FL 34234
Phone: 813/555-2955

Education

2004–2006 **UNIVERSITY OF NORTH CAROLINA   CHAPEL HILL, NORTH CAROLINA**
Bachelor's degree of Engineering; June 2006. Concentration in Mechanical Power Engineering Technology. Winner of the Newton Award for Engineers for research in magnetic fields in 2006.

Member of University Engineering Association. Member of cross-country track team.

2000–2004 **MEMORIAL HIGH SCHOOL   SARASOTA, FLORIDA**
High School Diploma in 2004. Got Advanced Placement Standing in Calculus and Physics. High Honor roll. Varsity member of spring, winter, and cross-country track.

Experience

Summer 2005 **QUEEN CITY ELECTRIC   SARASOTA, FLORIDA**
Intern for the power generation service division. Was helper in the overhaul, maintenance, and repair of large generators and auxiliary equipment. Worked to increase energy conservation by studying projects.

Summer 2004 **J. R. COLEMAN COMPANY   MEMPHIS, TENNESSEE**
Intern for production division. Helped make conveyors and elevators better. Helped to conduct study to make more profits. Resulting data was used to make group more efficient.

Part-time

2004–2006 **R & W NUCLEAR SERVICE COMPANY   CONCORD, NORTH CAROLINA**
Worked in tools division. Put on training sessions for fellow engineers so they could learn Computer Aided Design.

Skills Know Computer Aided Design (VERSACAD). Programming in GW Basic, Pascal, and Fortran.

References Personal references available upon request.

DANIEL R. PAPPAS

School Address:
121 University Terrace, Room 402
University of North Carolina
Chapel Hill, NC 27510
Phone: 919/555-5581

Permanent Address:
4 Squirrel Drive
Sarasota, FL 34234
Phone: 813/555-2955

Education

Education

2004–2006   **UNIVERSITY OF NORTH CAROLINA   CHAPEL HILL, NORTH CAROLINA**
Awarded a Bachelor of Science in Engineering in June 2006, with concentration in Mechanical Power Engineering Technology. 2006 winner of the Newton Award for Engineers for research in magnetic fields.

Member of University Engineering Association. Member of cross-country track team.

✔ Dynamic language

1998–2002   **MEMORIAL HIGH SCHOOL   SARASOTA, FLORIDA**
Awarded High School Diploma in 2002. Achieved Advanced Placement Standing in Calculus and Physics. High honor roll. Varsity member of spring/winter cross-country track team.

Experience

Summer 2005   **QUEEN CITY ELECTRIC   SARASOTA, FLORIDA**
Intern for the power generation service division. Assisted in the overhaul, maintenance, and repair of large generators and auxiliary equipment. Analyzed energy conservation projects for the maximization of energy management system and for interior lighting reduction.

Summer 2004   **J. R. COLEMAN COMPANY   MEMPHIS, TENNESSEE**
Intern for production division. Assisted in redesign of conveyors and elevators. Conducted study to reduce manufacturing labor while maintaining product quality. Modified and improved existing system using resulting data; increased group efficiency as measured by time and quantity parameters by 33 percent.

✔ Exciting action verbs

Part-time

2004–2006   **R & W NUCLEAR SERVICE COMPANY   CONCORD, NORTH CAROLINA**
Designed and tested tools used in nuclear power plants. Developed processes for using tools designed. Conducted computer training sessions for engineers using computer-aided design.

Skills
and Abilities   Hands-on experience with computer-aided design (VERSACAD), programming in GW Basic, Pascal, and Fortran.

References   References available upon request.

SHARON L. O'CONNELL
72 Oak Street, #3A
Seattle, Washington 92013

> ✗ Unecessary information. Better to specify "summer.,

> ✗ Phone number is missing.

Education 2003–2007	**BATES COLLEGE**	**LEWISTON, MAINE**

Candidate for the degree of Bachelor of Science, majoring in Biology, minoring in Horticulture. Courses include Biochemistry, Anatomy and Physiology, Chemistry, Physics, Computer Science, and Advanced Calculus. 3.77 grade point average. Awarded the Biological Sciences Society Award for Outstanding Students of Biology. I ranked 4 in a class of 276.

Experience

MAINE STATE PARKS AND RECREATION   MAINE STATE

May–August 2006

Volunteer for State of Maine Summer Clean-Up Program. Trash and litter removal, landscaping, repairs and maintenance of state buildings, signs, and benches.

June–August 2005

TUFTS UNIVERSITY   MEDFORD, MASSACHUSETTS

Assistant for the New England Environmental Newsletter. Provided administrative support to the Director of Environmental Affairs.

Part-time Sept.–May 2004–2007

BATES COLLEGE LIBRARY   LEWISTON, MAINE

Front desk clerk. Processed books, restacked shelves, answered phones, and assorted other duties.

Personal Background

Enjoy gardening, reading, and scuba diving.

References

References available upon request.

> ✗ Time gaps make a poor impression on recruiters.

> ✗ Failing to list extracurricular activities might result in your being labeled a high-risk hire.

SHARON L. O'CONNELL
72 Oak Street, #3A
Seattle, Washington 92013
703/555-9998

Education
2003–2007

BATES COLLEGE   **LEWISTON, MAINE**
Awarded a Bachelor of Science in May 2007, majoring in Biology, minoring in Horticulture. Courses included Biochemistry, Anatomy & Physiology, Chemistry, Physics, Computer Science, and Advanced Calculus. 3.77 grade point average. Awarded the Biological Sciences Society Award for Outstanding Students of Biology. Class rank: 4/276.

Founded the Bates College Greenhouse. Member of E.A.R.T.H. for Students. Weekend disc jockey for WBTS (college radio station). Created and hosted "Earth Talk," a radio program for discussing environmental issues.

Experience
Summer 2006

MAINE STATE PARKS AND RECREATION   **MAINE**
Volunteer for State of Maine Summer Clean-Up Program. Removed litter from state grounds; assisted with landscape maintenance at state and local parks; repaired and repainted state park buildings, signs, and benches. Promoted recycling and other environmental programs. Established new state garden at Old Orchard Beach.

Summer 2005

TUFTS UNIVERSITY   **MEDFORD, MASSACHUSETTS**
Staff Assistant for the New England Environmental Newsletter. Wrote and edited articles about environmental issues. Provided administrative support to the Director of Environmental Affairs.

Summer 2004

PURITAN ICE CREAM PARLOR   **SEATTLE, WASHINGTON**
Counter Person/Ice Cream Scooper. Invented new hit ice-cream flavor, Rain Forest Pecan.

Part-time
2004–2007

BATES COLLEGE LIBRARY   **LEWISTON, MAINE**
Front desk clerk. Processed books, restocked shelves, answered phones, and performed assorted other duties as needed.

Personal
Background

Enjoy gardening, reading, and scuba diving. Published bylined feature article in *American Horticulture*.

References

References available upon request.

> ✔ If you can't think of any major accomplishments, stress your small ones!

> ✔ Elimination of time gaps makes resume much stronger.

Chapter Thirteen

Cover Letters

Your resume is a summary of your credentials. Your cover letter, on the other hand, should essentially be a sales pitch. Your aim in these few short paragraphs is to demonstrate why you and your background are a perfect match for the position for which you are applying.

The cover letter is not the place to summarize your background. You have already done that on your resume. Remember, the corporate recruiter typically receives dozens, if not hundreds, of resumes and cover letters for each job opening. So you must find a positive way for yours to stand out from the crowd.

One of the best ways to distinguish your resume from others is to use your cover letter to highlight one or two of your accomplishments or abilities in order to demonstrate that you are an above-average candidate for this position. Stressing only one or two unique attributes will increase your chances of being remembered by the recruiter and getting to the interview stage, where you will be able to elaborate on the rest of your accomplishments.

To gain the extra edge, your cover letter must be worded in a way that your knowledge of the company and the industry becomes readily apparent. This shows that you are genuinely interested in the job for which you are applying and, more importantly, that you are not blindly sending out hundreds of resumes. The recruiter will view your interest as an indication that you are committed to the industry and, if hired, that you will likely stay with the company for a period of years.

Given that ours is an increasingly technological society, it should not surprise you to learn that your cover letters may not always travel by traditional routes. Employers are increasingly requesting that resumes be sent via e-mail. So, in addition to generating hard copies of your cover letters, you must also be prepared to generate electronic versions.

When to Send a Cover Letter

Never send a resume without a cover letter, regardless of whether you are using conventional modes of distribution or electronic ones. Even if you are answering an advertisement that reads simply "send resume," or you are following up on a phone conversation during which a hiring executive has asked you to "send a resume," be sure to include a cover letter. It is the professional thing to do.

Creating Hard Copy Cover Letters

Here are some issues to consider when writing and printing a cover letter on paper.

Length

Ideally, your cover letter should be no longer than four short paragraphs on one page. A letter any longer than that is unlikely to be read. Remember, the function of a cover letter is to grab the recruiter's attention so that you can sell yourself. Most recruiters have hectic schedules and prefer cover letters that are short and succinct.

Paper Size

Use standard 8½" x 11" paper for your cover letter. If you use a smaller size, the correspondence comes across as more personal than professional; a larger size not only looks odd, it won't fit neatly inside a standard file folder.

Paper Color

White and ivory are the only acceptable paper colors for resumes and cover letters. Don't be tempted into experimenting with unusual colors.

Paper Quality

As with resumes, standard, inexpensive office paper (20-pound bond) is perfectly acceptable. While you may be tempted to invest in a more expensive stationery paper such as ivory laid, it is not necessary and may, in fact, come across as too pretentious.

Preprinted Stationery

Avoid using stationery preprinted with your name and address—even if you already have a ready supply. Only a senior executive with many years of experience can get away with using preprinted letterhead. For a college student or recent graduate, pre-printed stationery might actually put you at a disadvantage.

Typing and Printing

Every cover letter should be an original. Even if you are sending out several letters at one time and the body of each is the same, they should be individually printed rather than photocopied. Use a standard font—this is not the time to get creative with typefaces—and personalize each letter, if possible, with the name of the recipient ("Dear

Mr. Smith," not "Dear Sir"). A laser or inkjet printer will generate crisp, clear letters. Sign each one by hand, individually, in blue or black ink.

The Envelope

Your cover letter and resume should always be mailed in a standard, business-sized (#10) envelope. The only exception to this rule is when you are enclosing an attachment, such as a writing or graphic arts sample or photographs, that cannot be folded to fit inside a #10 envelope. The address on the outside of your envelope should match the address on your cover letter; include the recipient's full name and title preceded by Mr. or Ms. Always type your envelopes using the same font as your cover letter; handwritten addresses are unprofessional.

Proofread and Correct Your Cover Letter

It's very easy to make mistakes on cover letters—particularly when you're writing many in succession. But it is just as easy for a corporate recruiter to reject out of hand *any* applicant whose cover letter contains errors. And with good reason. Would you want to hire someone who doesn't appear to take care with such an important piece of correspondence? As with your resume, you must proofread each cover letter carefully—and have a friend proofread each one as well.

If you spot a mistake, go back to the computer and correct it onscreen, then print a clean copy of the letter. Never use correction fluid or simply cross out the error and correct it by hand. That tells the recruiter you were too lazy to make any extra effort on his or her behalf.

Electronic Cover Letters

The majority of job opportunities posted on the Web, and even many that appear in traditional classified ads these days, ask for resumes by e-mail. When making your application electronically, you may be tempted to simply shoot off your resume and leave it at that. Don't. Just like a hard copy resume, which should never go in the mail without a cover letter, your electronic resume shouldn't travel solo either. And while the rules for electronic submissions are fewer—you don't have to worry about paper size, color, or quality, for example—there are still a few guidelines you should keep in mind.

Length

The primary purpose of e-mail is to communicate quickly and concisely. This is not the place to be verbose. Keep your sentences short, and limit your letter to no more than a paragraph or two. And by all means, do not even be tempted to use the abbreviations (LOL, IMHO, etc.), funky spellings, or smiley-face emoticons everyone seems to slip into their e-mail messages these days. Remember that the purpose of your letter is to land an interview and ultimately a job. If you want to appear serious and professional, save the "cutesy" stuff for e-mail messages to friends.

Typing

E-mail messages tend to be less formal than hard-copy correspondence, so you have a little more leeway with regard to selecting a font. Keep in mind that your recipient will be reading this letter on a screen, so the simpler the type style, the better. Sans serif fonts like Arial and Univers work well online. Courier New, a serif font which mimics the old pica typewriters, or Times New Roman may also be good choices. The body of your letter should be aligned flush left. Double space between paragraphs and do not indent the first line. Remember to re-read your message carefully before you hit "send." Believe it or not, your attention to grammatical details, or lack thereof, makes a strong statement to a prospective employer about your job worthiness.

To Attach or Not to Attach?

There are two schools of thought with regard to e-mail attachments. Some employers want to receive resumes as attachments; others, fearing viruses perhaps, prefer that you paste your resume into the actual e-mail message. The employer's preference will sometimes be stated in the ad or job posting, but when in doubt, paste. Cover letters are another matter altogether. They should never be sent as attachments. Why? Because, for the sake of simplicity and to avoid file corruption in downloading on the other end, you should attach only one file per e-mail. Make your cover letter the e-mail message and attach the resume to it.

Quick Tip: Proofread Your Cover Letter!

Don't rely solely on your computer's spell checker to spot mistakes. We've heard horror stories about candidates who did. One didn't notice this blunder: "I read about your advertisement in the *Boston Glove*." But he probably wasn't nearly as embarrassed as the college grad who majored in Pubic Relations! True story!

Chapter Fourteen

The Cover Letter Worksheet

Even before a potential employer reads a word of your cover letter, he or she has probably already made an assessment of your organizational skills and attention to detail simply by observing its appearance. How your hard-copy correspondence looks to a reader—its format, length, even the size, color, and quality of the paper on which your letter is printed—can mean the difference between serious consideration and automatic rejection. The same goes for electronic submissions, which have their own set of unique rules and standards.

Whether you are making your bid for consideration by "snail mail" or online, you simply cannot afford to offer a less than perfect presentation of your credentials. In the previous chapter, we discussed some basics concerning the overall appearance of your cover letters. Now we turn to content and formatting.

The Elements of a Cover Letter

Cover letters are generally more standardized than resumes, which can be done in a variety of formats. Here are the elements your cover letter should include.

Return Address and Date

Your return address should appear in the top right-hand corner, without your name, followed by the date. As a general rule, you should avoid abbreviations in the addresses on the cover letters. Spell out "Street," "Avenue," "Suite," etc. The exception to this rule is state names. It is perfectly acceptable—in fact, preferred—to write CA for California, IL for Illinois, MA for Massachusetts, etc.

Example:
(your street address)

(apartment #, if any)
(city/state/zip)
(date)
312 Main Street
Houston, TX 77031
January 3, 2007

The Addressee

Always try to find the name and proper title of the addressee before you send out a cover letter. Two lines beneath the date, list the full name of the addressee preceded by Mr. or Ms. (avoid using Miss or Mrs. unless you know the correct form for sure). On the next line, list the individual's formal title, then the name of the company on the line below it. Next, comes the company's address, which may take up more than one line. If a company name or address is particularly long, use your own judgment as to how much of it you should try to place on one line; if it spans too far across the page, break it up into two or more lines.

Mr./Ms. (full name of addressee): _____

Full title of addressee: _____

Full company name: _____

Street address, suite/floor number, (if appropriate): _____

City/state/Zip: _____

Example:

Ms. Suzanne Lee Waters
Vice President, Human Resources
Rockport Insurance Companies, Inc.
437 Coastal Highway, Suite 312
Boston, MA 02100

The Salutation

The salutation should be typed two lines beneath the company address. It should begin with "Dear Mr." or "Dear Ms." followed by the individual's last name and a colon. (Note: business letters use a colon rather than a comma following the salutation.)

Even if you have previously spoken with an addressee who has asked to be called by his or her first name, do not use a first name in the salutation of a formal business letter.

Dear Mr. (Ms.) _____:

Example:

Dear Ms. Waters:

Guidelines for the Body of the Letter

Since the purpose of a cover letter is to "sell" yourself to a prospective employer, you have considerably more latitude in terms of what is considered acceptable content for a cover letter than for a resume. Nevertheless, all cover letters from college students or recent graduates should adhere to the following basic principles:

- Use proper English; avoid abbreviations and slang. Use short sentences and commonly used words rather than stilted language or complicated sentence structure. Make your letter more interesting by using action verbs such as "designed," "implemented," and "increased."
- Personalize each letter. *Do not* send form letters or photocopies!
- In the first paragraph, state immediately and concisely the position or job function for which you wish to be considered.
- In the last paragraph, make a call for action either in the form of a specific request for an interview or the indication that you will be calling to request an interview.
- Keep the length of your letter to no more than a single page. Make every word count. And don't play games with type size or margins to squeeze a too-long letter into the space allowed. The most appealing cover letters are those that give the appearance of being half a page long.

First Paragraph

Immediately explain why your background makes you the best candidate for this particular position. Keep the first paragraph short and hard-hitting.

Example:

Having majored in Mathematics at Boston University, where I also worked as a Research Assistant, I am confident that I would make a very successful Research Trainee in your Economics Research Department.

Second Paragraph

Describe what you could contribute to this company. Show how your qualifications will benefit this firm. Remember, be brief! Few recruiters will read a cover letter longer than half a page.

Example:

In addition to my strong background in mathematics, I offer significant business experience, having worked in a data processing firm, a bookstore, and a restaurant. I am sure that my courses in statistics and computer programming would prove particularly useful in the position of Research Trainee.

Third Paragraph

Describe your interest in the corporation. Subtly emphasize your knowledge about this firm (the result of your research efforts) and your familiarity with the industry. It is common courtesy to act extremely eager to work for any company to which you are applying.

Example:

I am attracted to City Bank by your recent rapid growth and the superior reputation of your Economic Research Department. After studying several commercial banks, I have concluded that City Bank will be in a strong competitive position to benefit from upcoming changes in the industry and the increasingly competitive global marketplace.

Final Paragraph

The closing paragraph is your opportunity to call for action, so don't be afraid to specifically request an interview. Include your phone number and the hours when you may best be reached. Alternatively, you may indicate that you will follow up with a phone call within the next several days to arrange an interview at a mutually convenient time.

Example:

I would like to interview with you at your earliest convenience. I am best reached between 3 and 5 P.M. on weekdays at 555-1483.

The Closing

The closing should begin two lines beneath the body of the letter and should be aligned with your return address and the date (indented to the right of the page). Keep the closing simple—"Sincerely" suffices. Four lines beneath and aligned with the "Sincerely," type in your full name, preferably with a middle name or middle initial.

Sign above your typed name in blue or black ink. *Don't forget to sign the letter!* As silly as it sounds, people often do forget to sign their cover letters. This creates an impression that you don't take care with the details of your work.

Example:
Sincerely,

Jason R. Smith

Jason R. Smith

The Enclosure Line
You will come across as a meticulous, detail-oriented professional if you include an enclosure line at the bottom of the letter.

Example:
Enc.: Resume

SAMPLE COVER LETTER

1015 Commonwealth Avenue
Apartment 16
Boston, MA 01245

May 12, 2007

Mr. Clark T. Johnson
Vice-President/Human Resources
Boston City Bank Corporation
110 Milk Street
Boston, MA02114

Dear Mr. Johnson:

Having majored in Mathematics at Boston University, where I also worked as a Research Assistant, I am confident that I would make a very successful Research Trainee in your Economics Research Department.

In addition to my strong background in mathematics, I offer significant business experience, having worked in a data processing firm, a bookstore, and a restaurant. I am sure that my courses in statistics and computer programming would prove particularly useful in the position of Research Trainee.

I am attracted to City Bank by your recent rapid growth and the superior reputation of your Economic Research Department. After studying several different commercial banks, I have concluded that City Bank will be in a strong competitive position to benefit from upcoming changes in the industry and an increasingly competitive global marketplace.

I would like to interview with you at your earliest convenience. I am best reached between 3 and 5 P.M. on weekdays at 555-1483.

Sincerely,

Steven M. Phillips

Steven M. Phillips

Enc.: Resume

Electronic Cover Letters

The format for electronic cover letters is a little less formal than hard-copy correspondence demands. Since you'll be working within a framework dictated by your e-mail provider, you need not worry about typing in a return address or date at the top of the page. You do, however, need to be concerned about creating the best possible first impression. Here are a few basic guidelines you should follow when composing your electronic cover letter.

Your E-Mail Address

Even before a prospective employer reads your electronic cover letter, he or she has the chance to form a first impression. Make it a good one by selecting an appropriate e-mail address. If the screen name on your e-mail account is something like "sexychick" or "born2Bwild," the chances are good a prospective employer won't even open your message. Keep the cutesy names for personal e-mails, and come up with something that sounds more professional for your job search. Some combination of your first and last name or initials is probably your best bet.

Subject Line

Every e-mail message you write gives you an opportunity to spell out the subject of your message. With regard to electronic cover letters, the subject line is the place where you can let your recipient know that you are applying for a particular position, answering a specific ad, or updating information you may have sent previously. Do not be tempted to leave the subject line blank. That's what "spammers" do. So often in fact that many people never open any messages they receive that do not specify a subject, especially if they don't recognize the sender; they simply delete them. If you want your cover letter to be read, fill out the subject line.

The Salutation

Your salutation should be the first line of your actual e-mail message. You may begin with "Dear Mr." or "Dear Ms.," followed by the individual's last name and a colon. In cases where you do not know the name of your addressee, such as when you are responding to "blind" advertisements, it is perfectly acceptable to open with a generic salutation. "Dear Sir or Madam" or "To whom it may concern" may be a little formal for this medium; however, "Dear Hiring Manager" or "Good Morning" are perfectly acceptable. Beware of using salutations that are gender-specific. "Dear Gentlemen" or "Dear Sirs" might be offensive to some.

First Paragraph

State immediately and concisely the position for which you wish to be considered and why you are the best candidate to fill this particular job opening. If you are responding to a classified ad or Web-based job posting, be sure to reference the name of the publication or the number assigned to the posting. Keep your first paragraph short and hard-hitting.

Example:

I am responding to your posting for an advertising assistant (Job #45678), which recently appeared at monster.com. I will be graduating in May from Colgate University with a Bachelor of Science in Marketing. In addition to developing excellent research, communication, editing, and interpersonal skills during my college career, I gained experience in various facets of marketing (e.g., advertising, direct marketing, and market research) by completing a student-team project for Bagel Bakery, Inc. I have also had exposure to international marketing through a summer study program in Moscow as well as firsthand experience in retail sales.

Second Paragraph

In an electronic cover letter, the second paragraph is your close. This is where you reference your resume (either pasted below or attached) and suggest an interview, if appropriate.

Example:

The resume pasted below spells out the details of my educational background and experience which I believe would be an asset to your advertising firm. I would appreciate the opportunity to discuss how my qualifications might be applied to the Advertising Assistant position you have available. I may be reached weekdays between 9 A.M. and 5 P.M. at 555-1551. Thank you for your consideration.

The Closing

The closing should appear two lines below the body of your message. Keep it simple—"Sincerely" is usually enough. Space down a line or two and type your full name as it appears on your resume. If you are attaching your resume as a separate document, you may also wish to type your physical address, phone number, and e-mail address at the bottom of your e-mail message.

SAMPLE ELECTRONIC COVER LETTER

To: hstanhope@lisafleishmanassociates.com
From: rlbrandenburg@myemail.com
Subj: Advertising Assistant position

Dear Mr. Stanhope:

I am responding to your posting for an advertising assistant (Job #45678), which recently appeared at monster.com. I will be graduating in May from Colgate University with a Bachelor of Science in Marketing. In addition to developing excellent research, communication, editing, and interpersonal skills during my college career, I gained experience in various facets of marketing (e.g., advertising, direct marketing, and market research) by completing a student-team project for Bagel Bakery, Inc. I have also had exposure to international marketing through a summer study program in Moscow, as well as firsthand experience in retail sales.

The resume pasted below spells out the details of my educational background and experience which I believe would be an asset to your advertising firm. I would appreciate the opportunity to discuss how my qualifications might be applied to the Advertising Assistant position you have available. I may be reached weekdays between 9 a.m. and 5 p.m. at 555-1551. Thank you for your consideration.

Sincerely,

Rosemary L. Brandenburg

81 Sandypine Road
Joppa, MD 20707
(410) 555-1551
rbrandenburg@myemail.com

Chapter Fifteen

Sample Resumes and Cover Letters

This chapter includes more than 25 sample resumes with their corresponding cover letters. The resumes and cover letters are those of fictional college students and recent grads. They are intended to be used as a guide for writing your own job-winning resumes and cover letters.

The resumes included in this chapter cover a wide range of college majors, a combination of the currently most popular college majors and those which have been identified by several sources as the most employable. These majors are:

Accounting
Biochemistry
Business Administration
Civil Engineering
Communications
Computer Science/Programming
Culinary Arts
Earth Science/Forestry
Economics
Education
Electrical Engineering
English
Finance
Geography

Geology
Graphic Design
History
Interdisciplinary Studies
Journalism
Management Information
  Systems (MIS)
Marketing
Nutrition
Physics
Political Science/Government
Psychology
Sociology
Statistics

In addition to the sample cover letters and resumes in this chapter, you can also find resumes in Chapter 12, "Resume Makeovers," from students majoring in Biology, English Literature, Management, Mechanical Engineering, and Women's Studies.

19 Kellock Drive
Quincy, IL 60601

June 18, 2006

Ms. Amy Bauer
Accounting Manager
Deloit & Holt Associates
324 Main Street
Quincy, IL 60622

Dear Ms. Bauer:

Thank you for taking the time to speak with me on the phone today. As I mentioned, I would like to be considered for your opening for an Accounting Assistant.

I graduated last month from Wheaton College with a bachelor's degree in Accounting. Particularly valuable to me in my studies were the courses I took in Finance, Bookkeeping, Business Law, and Computer Science. I did extremely well in school, graduating summa cum laude with a GPA of 3.9.

In my junior year, I founded the Wheaton College Student Credit Union, a credit union run solely by and for college students, which has been very successful to date. During my senior year, I served as treasurer of the Senior Class Council and was responsible for administering an $18,000 budget.

In addition to having worked as a Research Assistant and as an Office Assistant at Wheaton College, I served as an Intern for a local accounting firm. In this position I handled accounts payable, resolving more than 32% of the company's past due accounts. I also made deposits performed data entry and handled other clerical duties as required.

I would like to meet with you to further discuss the position you have available. You may reach me between 9 a.m. and 6 p.m. weekdays at 312/555-2401. I look forward to hearing from you.

Sincerely,

Monica Duvalier

Monica Duvalier

Enc: Resume

MONICA DUVALIER

19 Kellock Drive

Quincy, IL 60601

312/ 555-2401

Education

WHEATON COLLEGE, Wheaton, Illinois

Bachelor of Science in Accounting awarded in May 2006. Coursework included Finance, Bookkeeping, Business Law, and Computer Science. 3.9 grade point average on a 4.0 scale. Graduated summa cum laude.

Founder of the Student Credit Union, a credit union run solely by and for college students. Treasurer of the Senior Class Council. Member of women's Rugby Team.

KNOX COLLEGE, Galesburg, Illinois

Studies included political science, sociology, and economics. Fall 2001 through spring 2003.

Internship

HOWE & HOWE ASSOCIATES, Wheaton, Illinois

Accounting Intern for the Vice President of the company. Handled accounts receivable, made deposits, performed data entry and some clerical duties. Cleared up more than 32% of the company's past due accounts. Summers 2004 and 2005.

Work Experience

WHEATON COLLEGE, Wheaton, Illinois

Office Assistant for the Career Development Office. Assisted students with career objectives, including writing resumes and cover letters, mapping out job search strategies, processing referral requests, phone calls, and general clerical duties. Part-time from 2003 to 2005.

WHEATON COLLEGE, Wheaton, Illinois

Research Assistant for political science professor. Performed research, prepared summary reports, compiled statistical and journalistic evidence of political dimensions of U.S. and Japanese economic relations for the professor's upcoming book. Summer 2003 and part-time through spring 2004.

Special Skills

Familiar with PC and Macintosh computers. Experience using Microsoft Word and Excel, Lotus 1-2-3, dBase, SAS, and SPSSX. Typing 90 wpm. Speak fluent French.

24 School Street
Norfolk, VA 23507
804/555-9855

March 2, 2007

Human Resources Manager
Brauman Industries
555 Industrial Park Drive
Fairfax, VA 22035

To the Human Resources Manager:

I am writing and enclosing my resume to apprise you of my interest in working for your Chemical Research Department.

I have just graduated from Radford University with a Bachelor of Science, in Chemistry, minoring in Biology with a concentration in Biochemistry. I am confident that my course-work in such areas as Anatomy & Physiology, Environmental Studies, Chemical Research, and Modern Laboratory Technology, as well as my independent study on marine pollutants, give me an excellent basis to begin a career in laboratory technology.

I have solid laboratory research experience as well, having worked as a Laboratory Assistant for the Chemical Research Department of a local fabrics manufacturer and as the assistant to the Head of the Chemistry Department at Radford, conducting research on noncombustible fuels. At Peller Laboratories, I developed a new fabric dye that is now being tested for use.

I have been recognized for academic excellence on several occasions. In 2004, I received the Curie Scholarship for Promising Students of Life Sciences. My independent study was recognized for excellence by the National Foundation for Scientific Research and was published in *Environment Today*.

It would be my pleasure to discuss with you any appropriate positions that are currently available or expected to be available at your company in the near future. I can be reached during business hours at (804) 555-8881, or you may leave a message for me at my home telephone listed above. I hope to hear from you soon.

Sincerely,

Martin H. Ericson

Martin H. Ericson

Enc.: Resume

BIOCHEMISTRY MAJOR

MARTIN H. ERICSON
24 School Street ❖ Norfolk, VA 23507 ❖ 804/555-9855

Objective: To obtain a challenging position in laboratory technology.

EDUCATION
Radford University, Radford, Virginia.
> Bachelor of Science in Chemistry awarded in December 2006. Minor in Biology with a concentration in Biochemistry. Courses include Anatomy & Physiology, Environmental Studies I-IV, Introductory Chemical Research, and Modern Laboratory Technology. 3.3 grade point average. Awarded the Curie Scholarship for Promising Students of Life Sciences.

Member of Students for Environmental Protection.
> Organized students into a clean-up crew and combed city for litter and trash. Established campus/city program for recycling paper, plastics, and aluminum cans. Recycled more than 50 tons of materials in the first year alone.

INDEPENDENT STUDY
Topic: The Effects of Petroleum-Based Pollutants on Crustacean Life and the Food Chain on the Mid-Atlantic Coast. Published in *Environment Today.* Recognized for excellence by the National Foundation for Scientific Research. Fall 2006.

RELATED WORK EXPERIENCE
Peller Laboratories, Norfolk, Virginia.
> Laboratory Assistant for Chemical Research Department of fabrics manufacturer. Assisted in research for development of new synthetic fabrics. Independently developed new red dye that won't fade or bleed, which is currently being tested for use. Summer 2006.

Chemistry Department, Radford University.
> Assistant to Department Head for government-commissioned research on non-combustible fuels. Conducted experiments, recorded and analyzed data, and redesigned flawed experiments. Spring-Summer 2005.

UNRELATED WORK EXPERIENCE
> Unrelated work experience includes Sales Clerk, Delivery Person, Warehouse Worker, and Waiter. 2002–2005.

References available upon request.

26 Mountain View Drive
Ladysmith, WI54891
715/555-6605

April 14, 2007

Mr. Frederick Gillette, Manager
Janston Athletic Gear Company
1022 Rodeo Drive
Salinas, CA 92004-1879

Dear Mr. Gillette:

The Campus Career Center at the University of Wisconsin suggested that I contact you regarding your management-training program.

I will be graduating next month with a Bachelor of Science in Business Administration. I have studied Marketing, Industrial Relations, Finance, Management, Accounting, Business Law, Economics, and Computer Applications, all of which I am confident will help me succeed in the world of business. I have worked very hard in school and have received a variety of academic honors and awards, including a Certificate of Merit for Outstanding Business Administration Graduates.

As my resume indicates, I have worked as a Data-Entry Clerk for the order department of a busy mailing list company. In this position, I gained experience processing orders on a computer, controlling inventory, handling customer inquires and problems, and packing and shipping. As the Office Assistant to a local shoe store owner, I learned all aspects of running a small retail store, including sales, accounting, inventory control, and advertising. When the store's owner went on vacation for two weeks, I successfully co-managed the store.

I am particularly interested in working for a sports-related company, as I have always been very athletic. I founded and directed the League of Women's Soccer in Madison and I teach and choreograph aerobics at a local fitness club. In 2003, I received the Wisconsin Times Scholar Athlete Award, which is given to the most outstanding female student athlete in Green County.

I feel that the combination of my business background and my athletic lifestyle makes me an excellent match for your company. If you agree, please give me a call. I look forward to meeting you.

Sincerely,

Alisia Petersham

Alisia Petersham

Enc.: Resume

ALISIA PETERSHAM

School Address: Permanent Address:
301 Temple Hall   26 Mountain View Drive
University of Wisconsin   Ladysmith, WI 54891
Madison, WI 53201   715/555-6605
414/555-5711

Education
2003–2007 UNIVERSITY OF WISCONSIN   MADISON, WISCONSIN
Candidate for the degree of Bachelor of Science in May 2007, majoring in Business Administration. Courses have included Marketing, Industrial Relations, Finance, Management, Accounting, Business Law, Economics, and Computer Applications. 3.4 grade point average.

Golden Key Society, Wisconsin University Fellowship, Certificate of Merit for Outstanding Business Administration Graduates. Varsity Soccer.

Experience
Summer 2006 GOODELL & HITE ASSOCIATES   MADISON, WISCONSIN
Data entry clerk for order department. Responsibilities included order processing, customer service, inventory control, and some packing and shipping.

Summer 2005 HIERLAND SHOES   LADYSMITH, WISCONSIN
Office Assistant for local shoe store. Assisted in all aspects of running the store, including sales, accounting, inventory control, advertising, and maintenance. Co-managed the store while owner was on vacation for two weeks.

Summer 2004
and Part-time
2004–present ISLAND FITNESS HEALTH CLUB   MADISON, WISCONSIN
Aerobics instructor and choreographer. Voted "Best Instructor" by members and staff.

Activities   Founderand director of League of Women's Soccer in Madison. Recipient of *Wisconsin Times* Scholar Athlete Award, awarded to the most outstanding female student athlete in Green County.

References   References available upon request.

567 Circle Drive
Columbus, OH
(614) 765-3210

February 2, 2007

Mr. James Baxter
Chief Engineer
City of Houston
6677 N.W. First Street
Houston, TX 77002

Dear Mr. Baxter:

I am writing to express my interest in securing a position as a civil engineer for the City of Houston. I received my Bachelor of Science in Civil Engineering from Northwestern University in January, with a major in Structural Engineering.

I have gained firsthand experience in the field through a summer internship with a consulting firm in Chicago, where I assisted in the design of municipal structures. In addition, I have worked with a contracting firm, overseeing the receipt and disbursement of construction materials on-site.

I will be in Houston the week of February 19; perhaps we can get together then? I will call you within the next week to discuss a mutually convenient time for an interview. In the meantime, I have enclosed my resume for your consideration. I look forward to meeting you.

Sincerely,

Patricia Cooke

Patricia Cooke

Enc: Resume

CIVIL ENGINEERING MAJOR

PATRICIA COOKE
567 Circle Drive
Columbus, OH 43211
(813) 555-5555

EDUCATION:
Northwestern University
Bachelor of Science in Civil Engineering, January 2007
Major course of study: Structural Engineering. 3.88 GPA. Member, Student Chapters, American Society of Civil Engineers and Society of Women Engineers.

EXPERIENCE:
Summer 2006
Tinker & Cooper Engineering Consultants, Chicago, IL
Engineering Intern. Assigned to the structural division; assisted with the design of municipal buildings and correctional facilities. Prepared blueprints, developed construction schedules, and calculated materials quantities.

2005–2006
School of Civil Engineering, Northwestern University, Evanston, IL
Tutor. Assisted students having difficulty in junior- and senior-level architectural engineering and structural steel design classes.

Summer 2004
Omega Contracting, Columbus, OH
On-Site Receiving Technician. Responsible for check-in and disbursement of building materials on various construction sites as needed.

ACTIVITIES AND INTERESTS
Architectural history, photography, fitness walking.

REFERENCES
Available upon request

1221 Oak Garden Road
Brookline, MA 02351
(617) 555-8850

April 1, 2007

Mr. Shawn Belleau, Director
WGUR TV-Channel 46
133 Business Park Drive
Brighton, MA 02215

Dear Mr. Belleau:

Sharon Lafferty, director of the "A.M. Boston" program, suggested I contact you regarding an opening you may have for a Production Assistant.

I am presently studying Communications at Emerson College and will be graduating next month. My coursework is concentrated in Broadcast Journalism and I have studied such topics as Ethics in Reporting, Broadcast Journalism I-IV, and Television Production. I was the top student in my Broadcast Journalism classes and was consistently recognized for academic excellence on the Dean's List.

I also have experience working in television, having worked as a Television Program Intern for "A.M. Boston." I was responsible for booking guests to debate controversial public interest topics with the host and fielding viewers' reaction calls provoked by on-air debates. Also, I gained valuable experience assembling and editing video clips of upcoming entertainment events and movies which were aired during the show.

My resume is enclosed. I would value the opportunity to meet with you to discuss a possible position with your station. I can be reached at the above address and telephone number.

I have included several writing samples and hope to have the chance to show you some of my other work soon. Thank you for your time.

Sincerely,

Jennifer Barnes

Jennifer Barnes

Enc: Resume
        Writing samples

JENNIFER BARNES

409 Walters Hall
Emerson College
Boston, MA 02116

1221 Oak Garden Road
Brookline, MA 02351
617/555-8850

Education
2003–present

EMERSON COLLEGE   **BOSTON, MA**
Candidate for the degree of Bachelor of Arts in May 2007, majoring in Communications with a concentration in Broadcast Journalism. Courses included Ethics in Reporting, Broadcast Journalism I-IV, and Television Production. Thesis topic: "The Future of Public Television in the United States." Dean's list.

Internship
Summer 2006

"A.M. BOSTON" – ABC Affiliate   **BOSTON, MA**
Television Program Intern. Responsible for booking guests to debate controversial public interest topics with host. Assembled and edited video clips of upcoming entertainment events and movies which were aired during show. Fielded viewers' reaction telephone calls provoked by on-air debates.

Experience
Summer 2005

JACOB & LAFFERTY CONSULTING   **BOSTON, MA**
Research Assistant. Used a variety of media including public forum, radio, telephone, and mailings to alert constituents about political issues. Supervised the phone bank and ran the national political hotline.

Summer 2004

BUFFORD & O'BRIAN ASSOCIATES   **CAMBRIDGE, MA**
Public Relations Assistant. Wrote press releases, designed and assembled product kits, handled typing, database management, and general clerical duties. Worked one-on-one with Vice-President on the LaJolie Cosmetics account.

Part-time
2002–present

Worked as an Office Assistant, Tutor, Waitperson, and Sales Clerk.

References

Available upon request.

2 Graham Street
Grove City, PA16126
412/555-5590

July 2, 2006

Sarah Cunningham
Opie Computer & Informational Systems
392 Richie Lane
Philadelphia, PA16002

Dear Ms. Cunningham:

I am enclosing my resume in response to your advertisement in the *Houston Times* for a computer programmer.

Briefly, I offer:

- B.S. in Computer Science and Programming from Gettysburg College
- Experience as an Applications Programmer with PC Systems, Inc.
- Experience as a Computer Lab Assistant and Tutor for introductory computer science courses
- Thorough knowledge of and experience with many programming languages, including COBOL, Java, C++, and PERL
- Experience using a variety of hardware, using Windows and Unix/Linux operating systems

I feel that I am well qualified for this position. If you would like to schedule an interview with me, I can be reached at the above listed number or at 412/555-8885 during daytime hours.

Thank you for considering me for this position.

Sincerely,

Leslie Pellham

Leslie Pellham

Enc.: Resume

LESLIE PELLHAM

2 Graham Street
Grove City, PA16126
412/555-5590

EDUCATION

Gettysburg College   **Gettysburg, Pennsylvania**

Awarded a Bachelor of science in Computer Science with a concentration in Programming. Key courses included: Computer Organization & Architecture, Logic Design and Switching Theory, Discrete Mathematical Structures I-II, Data Structures and Algorithms, Operating Systems & Computer Networks, and Software Engineering. 3.65 grade point average. Graduated Summa Cum Laude in May 2006.

Member of Gettysburg Society of Computer Programmers. Tutor for introductory computer science courses. Member and competitor in Cycling Club.

WORK EXPERIENCE

PC Systems, Inc.   **Philadelphia, Pennsylvania**
Applications Programmer   Summer 2005

Wrote business-related software, including programs used for inventory control and order processing using COBOL. Tested finished programs for bugs and made corrections as needed.

Gettysburg College Computer Center   **Gettysburg, Pennsylvania**
Computer Lab Assistant   Part-time 2003–2005

Assisted students with software, hardware, and printer questions and problems. Taught students and faculty how to use word processing, database, spreadsheet, and desk-top publishing programs. Maintained and repaired equipment.

LANGUAGES

Java	JavaScript	SQL
J2EEC++	PERL	ASP.NET

DATABASE SYSTEMS

SQL Server	MySQL	Oracle

APPLICATIONS

Outlook	Access	Excel	Microsoft Visual Studio
PhotoShop	FrontPage	Flash	

OPERATING SYSTEMS

Windows (XP, 2000, NT)	Unix/Linux

REFERENCES

Available upon request

178 Green Street
Cavendish, VT 05142
(802) 555-5555

July 5, 2007

Hugh Jenkins, Head Chef
The Lobster Hut
123 Any Street
Burlington, VT 05401

Dear Mr. Jenkins:

I read with interest your advertisement in the *Burlington Free Press* for an assistant chef. Enclosed is my resume for your review and consideration.

I graduated in May of this year from the Culinary Institute of America with a bachelor's degree in Culinary Arts. Here I took many fun and informative classes covering all major aspects of food preparation.

Over the past four years, I have gained much valuable experience from working in various restaurants. I have held positions ranging all the way from busperson to cook. I feel this experience gives me a good perspective on how a kitchen is run. I know this knowledge, along with my cooking skills, will prove valuable in the position of assistant chef at Lobster Hut.

I would appreciate the opportunity to discuss the assistant chef position with you. I will try to reach you by phone on Monday of next week. However, I know what a chef's schedule is like so I may be reached at the above number at your convenience. Thank you for your time, and I look forward to speaking with you.

Sincerely,

Chris Smith

Chris Smith

Enc.: Resume

Chris Smith
178 Green Street
Cavendish, VT 05142
(802) 555-5555

OBJECTIVE
To contribute acquired culinary skills to a restaurant position.

SUMMARY OF QUALIFICATIONS
- More than four years of progressively responsible food-related experience.
- Bachelor's degree in Culinary Arts.
- Dependable, detail-oriented team worker; capable of precisely following directions.

EDUCATION:
CULINARY INSTITUTE OF AMERICA, Hyde Park, NY
Bachelor's degree in Culinary Arts
Culinary Arts Diploma (2007)

UNIVERSITY OF WASHINGTON, Department of Correspondence Study
Nutrition Course – 3 semester hours credit (2006)

EXPERIENCE
AUTUMN OAKS INN, Cavendish, VT   2007–Present
Cook
Assist chefs in meal preparation. Responsibilities include cutting meat, making sauces, rotating food, cooking and serving special faculty functions and online service of more than 300 patrons.

SHADE HILL INN, Pleasant Valley, NY   2006–2007
Cook
Prepared breakfast for more than 200 patrons daily.

REDWING FOOD SUPPLY, Poughkeepsie, NY   2005–2007
Stock Person
Dated and rotated products. Supplied food to homeless shelter cafeterias.

THE WOLFSONG TAVERN, Butte, MT   Summer 2005
Prep Cook
General responsibilities as above.

Assistant Prep Cook   Summer 2004

Busperson   Summer 2003

32 North Shore Drive
Portland, OR 98651
503/555-4102

July 30, 2006

Mr. Jason R. Baxter, Director
Bureau of Land Management
U.S. Department of the Interior
Washington, DC 20240

Dear Mr. Baxter:

I am a recent college graduate with a degree in Earth Science and Forestry and am seeking a position in forestry in the Pacific states.

In June, I graduated from Oregon State University with a bachelor's degree in Earth Science and Forestry. I have studied many relevant courses including Forest Economics, Range Management, Ecology, Soil Science, Hydrology, Wildlife, and Agronomy. In 2005, I was recognized for outstanding achievement in the natural sciences when I was awarded the prestigious Tepper Badge.

I also offer on-site work experience, having interned last summer for the Oregon State Soil Conservation Service. In this position, I was exposed to all aspects of applied soil science. I provided technical assistance primarily to farmers and ranchers to promote the conservation of soil, water, and related natural resources. Equally important, I helped to develop programs to combat soil erosion and maximize land productivity without damaging the environment.

I gained valuable experience in forestry when I attended Oregon State University's Field Camp in Klamath Falls, where I planted and maintained trees and rare natural vegetation and recorded and charted their growth. In addition to testing soil and water samples, I tracked wildlife species and worked to preserve natural habitats for endangered species.

If you feel that I am suitable for a position with the Bureau of Land Management, I would greatly appreciate an interview. I may be reached at the above listed number during the morning hours. Thank you for your consideration.

Sincerely,

Douglas J. McNaughton

Douglas J. McNaughton

Enc.: Resume

DOUGLAS J. McNAUGHTON

School Address:
121 Main Street
Apartment 3A
Corvallis, OR 97335
Phone: 503/555-9546

Permanent Address:
32 North Shore Drive
Portland, OR98651
Phone: 503/555-4102

Education
2002–2006   *OREGON STATE UNIVERSITY*   CORVALLIS, OREGON
Awarded a Bachelor of Arts in June 2006, majoring in Earth Science and minoring in Forestry. Courses of study included Forest Economics, Range Management, Ecology, Soil Science, Hydrology, Wildlife, and Agronomy. Independent Research topic: The Effect of Hydrolechicin Treatment on Blue Alpine Firs Infected with Pulloma Disease. 3.7 grade point average.

Internship
Summer 2005   *OREGON STATE SOIL CONSERVATION SERVICE*   PORTLAND
Provided technical assistance to farmers, ranchers, and others concerned with the conservation of soil, water, and related natural resources. Aided in the development of programs designed to maximize land productivity without harm or damage. Developed programs to combat soil erosion.

Experience
Summer 2004   *OREGON STATE UNIVERSITY FIELD CAMP*   KLAMATH FALLS
Planted and maintained trees and rare natural vegetation, recorded and charted growth. Tracked wildlife species and worked to preserve natural habitats for endangered species. Tested soil and water samples.

Part-time
2002–2006   Unrelated work positions include Bus Person, Cashier, and Service Station Attendant.

References   Available upon request.

12 Island Road
Salinas, CA 21131

July 15, 2006

Mr. James R. Evans
Human Resources Department
B.G.R. Enterprises
192 East 47th Street, Ste. 708
New York, NY 10025

Dear Mr. Evans:

Having majored in Economics at Notre Dame College, where I also worked as a Telephone Salesperson for the Alumni contribution fund, I am confident that I would make a very successful International Sales Trainee in your International Sales Department.

In addition to my strong background in economics, I have studied International Relations, International Business Law, and Communications. I am sure that my fluency in German will also prove particularly useful in this position.

I am interested in pursuing a career in International Business because my extensive traveling has made me very much aware of and curious about the business world outside of the United States.

I am attracted to B.G.R. Enterprises because of its solid reputation and its numerous strong connections in Germany. I am convinced that I can make valuable contributions to your company.

Although my preference is to live in Germany, I am far more interested in working for a fine company with strong international ties. Enclosed is my resume that summarizes my qualifications. I will be glad to furnish any additional information that you may require. I am best reached weekdays between 8 a.m. and 1 p.m. at 619/555-9902.

Sincerely,

Nancy Allen

Nancy Allen

Enc.: Resume

ECONOMICS MAJOR

NANCY ALLEN

12 Island Road
Salinas, CA 21131
(619) 555-9902

EDUCATION
2002–2006   **NOTRE DAME COLLEGE**   **BAY CITY, OREGON**

Bachelor of Arts awarded in June 2006. Major in Economics, minor in German language. Courses included: International Relations, International Business Law, and Communications. Ranked 4 in a class of 53.

Dean's List. Resident Assistant for Freshman Dormitory for two consecutive years. Organized student activities and field trips and managed a budget of $500/semester.

1998–2002   **BAY CITY HIGH SCHOOL**   **BAY CITY, OREGON**

Received High School Diploma in June 2002. High honors list. Took advanced college-level courses in English, Mathematics, and Physics. Cheerleader for the Bay City Cougars Basketball team.

EXPERIENCE
Summers
2003–2005   **WATERSIDE BAR & GRILL**   **BAY CITY, OREGON**

Began work as busperson. Promoted to short-order cook.

Part-time
2004–2006   **NOTRE DAME COLLEGE**   **BAY CITY, OREGON**

Telephone salesperson for the Parents and Alumni Contribution Fund. Consistently solicited the highest donation levels for my sales group.

LANGUAGES   Able to speak fluently and write in German.

PERSONAL   Willing to travel and relocate, particularly in Europe.

INTERESTS   Enjoy photography, karate, and collecting antique books, particularly 19th-century German novels. Have traveled extensively in Europe, Asia, and South America.

REFERENCES   Available upon request.

14 Bradley Road
Boise, ID 49965
(451) 555-2222

April 8, 2006

Christine R. Davis
Human Resources Manager
Idaho School District 5
Boise, ID 49662

Dear Ms. Davis:

In response to last week's advertisement in the *Boise Chronicle* for an English teacher, I have enclosed my resume for your consideration.

I have recently graduated from the University of Idaho at Boise with a bachelor's degree in Secondary Education. I am certified to teach both English and Special Education. In addition to fulfilling my practice teaching requirement in your district, I participated in a volunteer literacy program to tutor both youths and adults with reading difficulties. I also organized and performed in a variety show at Boise Central High that benefited special needs students.

As I fulfilled my practice teaching requirement in District 5, I was continually impressed by its high educational standards and its long-standing record of producing students who achieve among the nation's highest SAT scores. I would consider it a great opportunity to teach in such an accomplished district.

I will be calling you on Monday, April 16 to confirm that you received my resume and answer any questions you may have. I look forward to speaking with you.

Sincerely,

Caleb J. Nash

Caleb J. Nash

Enc.: Resume

EDUCATION MAJOR

CALEB J. NASH
14 Bradley Road
Boise, ID 49965
(451) 555-2222

CAREER **OBJECTIVE:**	A classroom position teaching high school English and/or Special Education.
EDUCATION: 2002–2006	**UNIVERSITY OF IDAHO** **BOISE, IDAHO** Awarded a Bachelor of Arts in June 2006, majoring in Secondary Education. Concentration in English and Special Education. Thesis topic: "The Future of Special Education in Public Schools." 3.8 grade point average. Member of Volunteers in Action. Tutored illiterate adults and youths with reading difficulties. Organized and performed in variety show to benefit special needs students. Member of varsity wrestling team.
CERTIFICATION: May 2006	Idaho state certificate in English (Grades 9–12) and Special Education.
STUDENT **TEACHING:** 2005–2006	**CENTRAL HIGH** **BOISE, IDAHO** Assistant Teacher for a twelfth-grade college-level English Composition class. Took attendance, corrected papers, helped students with their writing skills, conducted workshop on preparing essays for college applications.
PROFESSIONAL **ASSOCIATIONS:**	National Council of Teachers of English. Council for the advancement and Support of Education.
INTERESTS:	Enjoy reading, basketball, and wrestling competitions.
REFERENCES:	References available upon request.

456 Duval Street
Fort Wayne, IN 60542

January 6, 2007

Recruiting Manager
Hewlett-Packard Company
4 Choke Cherry Road
Rockville, MD 20850

Dear Sir/Madam:

Having recently graduated form the University of Colorado at Boulder with a major in Electrical Engineering and a concentration in Computer Engineering, I am confident that I would make a very successful Computer Programmer at your prestigious company.

In addition to my strong educational background, I also offer significant hands-on experience, having worked as a Research Associates at the University of Colorado as well as having participated in the Scientific Supercomputing Workshop at UCB. In conjunction with my studies, I designed and built a short wave radio, developed a microprocessor-based system to measure heart rate and blood pressure, and successfully coordinated a method of producing a circuit board coplanar waveguide prototype.

I am sure that my coursework in microprocessor applications, digital systems, and computer organization, as well as my extensive computer skills and valuable experience, would prove particularly useful in the position of Computer Programmer.

Enclosed is my resume. I may be reached at 213/555-9857. I will be glad to make myself available for an interview at your convenience to discuss how my qualifications would be consistent with your needs. Thank you for your time and consideration.

Sincerely,

Sun Quan Lin

Sun Quan Lin

Enc.: Resume

ELECTRICAL ENGINEERING MAJOR

SUN QUAN LIN
456 Duval Street
Fort Wayne, IN 60542
213/555-9857

JOB OBJECTIVE:
To find a position as a computer programmer/engineer that will use my skills in microprocessor applications, digital systems, logic design, and computer programming.

EDUCATION:
University of Colorado at Boulder
B.S. in Electrical Engineering, Fall 2006. Area of concentration: Computer Engineering. GPA: 3.6/4.0.

Relevant Coursework:
- Microprocessor Applications and Organization
- Data Structures in C
- Digital Systems Engineering
- Computer Organization

Academic Honors:
- President's and Dean's List
- Trustees' Scholarship
- Member of Omega Honor Society

Extracurricular Activities:
- Student member of the American Society of Computer Engineers
- Volunteer for Disabled Student Services at UCB

EXPERIENCE:
University of Colorado at Boulder
Research Associate: **January 2003 to present**
Participated in Scientific Supercomputing Workshop at UCB and familiar with using the super-computers of Alliant FX-8 at Argonne National Laboratory, IBM 3090/600 series at University of California at Los Angeles, and Cray X-MP at Duke University.

Teaching Assistant: **January 2002 to present**
Taught college-level mathematics and basic computer skills.

COMPUTER SKILLS:
Languages:
- C++, Java, and ASP.NET

Operating Systems:
- UNIX/LINUX, MS DOS, and Windows

Projects:
- Developed microprocessor-based system to measure heart rate and blood pressure.
- Designed and built a short wave radio.
- Successfully coordinated a method of producing a circuit board coplanar waveguide prototype.

INTERESTS:
- Enjoy photography, basketball, and softball.

References available upon request.

102 Stonegate Lane
Auburn, AL 36849

June 14, 2007

William T. Harrison
FNW – Los Angeles
460 West End Avenue
Los Angeles, CA 92265

Dear Mr. Harrison:

I am writing in response to your advertisement in the *Los Angeles Sun* for an Assistant Buyer. I am interested in pursuing a career as a buyer and believe that I could make a significant contribution to your organization.

I will be graduating in December from Huntingdon College in Alabama. Although my degree is in English, I have taken many courses to prepare myself for a career in business, including Accounting, Finance, and Management. In addition, I offer solid work experience, having worked as an Assistant to the Financial Consultant and a Receptionist/Bookkeeper for busy, professional firms.

Enclosed is a copy of my resume. References will be forwarded upon request by the Student Resource Center at Huntingdon College.

I would greatly appreciate the opportunity to meet with you and discuss possible employment opportunities with your company. I may be reached at home at (205) 555-7771 or at school at (205) 555-3558.

Thank you for your time and consideration.

Sincerely,

Diane De Matto

Diane De Matto

Enc.: Resume

DIANE DE MATTO

School Address: Permanent Address:
36 Granite Street   102 Stonegate Lane
Montgomery, AL 36103   Auburn, AL 36849
(205) 555-3558   (205) 555-7771

Education

2003–present *HUNTINGDON COLLEGE*   MONTGOMERY, ALABAMA
Candidate for the degree of Bachelor of Arts in December 2007, major-
ing in English. Courses include Speech, Accounting, Finance, and
Management. 3.1 GPA overall, 3.5 in major. Dean's List honors.

Student Government representative. Volunteer tutor for underprivileged children.

Spring 2006 *UNIVERSITY COLLEGE OF IRELAND*   GALWAY, IRELAND
Studied courses in Irish literature, history, and culture. 3.2 GPA.

Experience

Summer 2006 *LILLITH & McGRATH ASSOCIATES* MONTGOMERY, ALABAMA
Assistant to the Financial Consultant. Worked closely with a vice president researching various stocks, keeping detailed records, supervising and conducting business in her absence, interacting with clients.
Learned how to fundamentally analyze a company and to construct a
balanced portfolio.

Summer 2005 *KENDALL & LAIRD, INC.*   AUBURN, ALABAMA
Receptionist/Bookkeeper. Greeted clients, answered phone inquiries
and performed assorted office tasks in an architectural firm. Processed
accounts payable and receivable, and prepared deposits.

Summer 2004 *SUNNYDAY CHILD CARE SERVICES*   AUBURN, ALABAMA
provided basic care, overnight, and weekly supervision for groups of
10–20 preschool children. Instituted and taught art classes; organized
art show for parents and relatives of children.

Interests   Travel, skiing, painting, and photography.

References Available upon request: Student Resource Center, Huntingdon College, Montgomery, AL 36106.

65 Cortland Avenue
Honolulu, HI 96804
(808) 555-3280

October 15, 2006

Stephanie Malone
Human Resources Director
Bank of Hawaii
32 Island Avenue
Honolulu, HI 96855

Dear Ms. Malone:

I would like to explore the possibility of joining your organization at the entry level, perhaps in your Financial Management Division. I believe that my Finance major and my recent work experience qualify me for such a position. I have enclosed my resume for your consideration.

I am seeking a position which will capitalize upon and further hone the skills I previously developed as a Sales Analyst for Tecchi Corporation, a Financial Accounting Assistant for Redden & Mitchell, an Investigator for First Hawaiian Bank, and a Statistical Analyst for Chaminade University. These jobs, particularly my position at the First Hawaiian Bank, confirmed my interest in the field of finance and in the banking industry. Also, I have extensive computer experience and knowledge of spreadsheet and statistical programs which I am confident will assist me throughout my banking career.

I am particularly interested in working for the Bank of Hawaii because of its long-standing reputation as a solid and trustworthy financial institution. I have been a customer of your bank all my life and have found your services to be excellent. I would consider it a great opportunity to contribute to the future success of such a fine institution.

I would like to interview with you at your convenience. I will be calling you the week of October 23 to make sure you received my resume. Perhaps we could schedule an interview at this time? In the meantime, thank you for your consideration of my qualifications.

Sincerely,

Arthur H. Goldman

Arthur H. Goldman

Enc.: Resume

FINANCE MAJOR

ARTHUR H. GOLDMAN
65 Cortland Avenue
Honolulu, HI 96804

(808) 555-3280

Education: **Chaminade University Of Honolulu** in Honolulu, Hawaii
Bachelor of Science in Finance.
Concentration: Investment Management
Date of graduation: May, 2006. GPA: 3.4
Dean's List, Who's Who Among College Students.

Relevant Courses:

Business Law	Entrepreneurship
Ethics in Business	Financial Accounting
International Economics	Macro & Microeconomics
Managerial Accounting	Statistics
Money & Credit	Calculus

Activities: Chairman of Finance Club. Freshman Orientation Counselor. Treasurer of Phi Gammu Nu Fraternity.

Experience: **Sales Analyst.** *Tecci Corporation,* Honolulu, HI. Summer 2005.
Prepared sales budgets and controlled inventory using Lotus 1-2-3. Interacted with Sales staff.

Financial Accounting Assistant. *Redden & Mitchell,* Honolulu, HI. Summers 2003–2004.
Worked closely with a vice-president researching various stocks, keeping detailed records, supervising and conducting business in his absence, interacting with clients. Learned how to fundamentally analyze a company and to construct a balanced portfolio.

Investigator. *First Hawaiian Bank,* Honolulu, HI. Summer 2002.
Evaluated branch operations, appraised the performance of bank tellers and customer service representatives.

Statistical Analyst. *Chaminade University,* Honolulu, HI. Part-time from January 2003 to April 2006.
Assisted Biochemistry professor in the analysis of data for a large-scale research project on the cell-regeneration capabilities of Brine shrimp using SPSSX.

Skills and Abilities: Proficient in the use of Lotus 1-2-3, Microsoft Excel, SASSE, and SPSSX. Excellent communication and interpersonal skills.

Personal: Single, in good health. Willing to travel and/or relocate.

References: References available upon request.

23 Lamar Street
Charlotte, NC 27601

February 21, 2007

Ms. Sandra Hall
Travel World, Inc.
23 Syracuse Street
Suite C
Charlotte, NC 27601

Dear Ms. Hall:

I was recently speaking with Dan Johnson of Tri-Travel Corporation about opportunities in the travel industry, and he recommended that I contact you. I am interested in pursuing a career in the tourism industry and would like to be considered for an entry-level position at your company.

Currently a senior at Duke University, I will be graduating this June with a bachelor's degree in Geography and International Studies. Although my area of study will no doubt assist me in the tourism field, I have taken additional courses which may also prove useful, including Business Management, Introductory Accounting, Computer Science, and Spanish. My participation in the Raths Debate Club helped me to enhance my verbal skills and communicate more effectively, which I'm sure will also increase my effectiveness in the travel industry.

In addition to my strong educational background, I offer solid work experience. As an Administrative Assistant in a wholesale glass and framing supplies company, I gained experience in all aspects of customer service, including taking large numbers of phone orders and assisting customers with questions and problems. My duties also included data entry, typing business letters, filing, and other clerical tasks.

I can type 50 WPM and have experience using a number of word processing, spreadsheet, and database programs. I am fluent in Spanish.

I would be very grateful if you would consider me for any entry-level positions for which you may have openings. I am especially interested in working as a travel agent or promotional assistant. I may be reached at 919/555-8881 after 3:00 P.M. or you may leave a message any time at 704/555-7891. Thank you.

Sincerely,

Margaret A. Reed

Margaret A. Reed

Enc.: Resume

GEOGRAPHY MAJOR

MARGARET A. REED

School Address:
203 Wing Hall
Duke University
Durham, NC 27706
919/555-8881

Home Address:
23 Lamar Street
Charlotte, NC 27601
704/555-7891

Education:
2003–present

DUKE UNIVERSITY   **DURHAM, NORTH CAROLINA**
Candidate for the degree of Bachelor of Arts in June 2007, majoring in Geography and minoring in International Studies. Courses include Business Management, Introductory Accounting, Computer Science, and Spanish.

Member of Raths Debate Club. Play second chair flute for the Duke University Band. Performed in annual Christmas concert to benefit the homeless.

2002–2003

ATLANTIC COLLEGE   **WILSON, NORTH CAROLINA**
Studied Physical Therapy and related health sciences fields for three semesters.

Experience:
summer 2006

MONARCH GLASS COMPANY CHARLOTTE, NORTH CAROLINA
Administrative Assistant to the President. Took phone orders, assisted customers with questions and problems, and handled data entry, some written correspondence, filing, and general clerical duties as assigned. Restructured and reorganized entire database system to increase efficiency.

Summers
2003–2005

THE CAJUN QUEEN   **CHARLOTTE, NORTH CAROLINA**
Hostess for popular local restaurant. Was promoted from busperson.

Part-time
2004–present

BI-LO CORPORATION   **DURHAM, NORTH CAROLINA**
Cashier and Inventory clerk for busy supermarket. Won employee of the month award on two separate occasions.

Skills:

Typing: 50 WPM. Working familiarity with Microsoft Word and Excel, MacWrite, Lotus, and rBase. Fluent in Spanish.

Interests:

Enjoy playing the flute, writing music, jogging, and speed walking for competition.

References:

Available upon request.

1222 College Blvd., #4
Boulder, CO 80305
(303) 444-4444

April 25, 2007

Mr. Robert Bowles
Director
Indiana State Geological Survey
2233 Every Street
Indianapolis, IN 46202

Dear Mr. Bowles:

I am writing and enclosing my resume to apprise you of my interest in working for the Indiana Geological Survey.

I will receive my B.A. in Geological Sciences with a double concentration in Geology and Geophysics from the University of Colorado in May. In addition to the courses required for my degree, I took classes in computer programming, environmental issues, geochemistry, and thermodynamics. Last summer, I served as a Geo-Corps America intern in California's Sierra National Forest, where I gained valuable hands-on experience in soil compaction assessment and water quality monitoring.

I would welcome the opportunity to speak with you personally about my qualifications. If you would like to schedule an interview with me, I can be reached at the telephone number cited above.

Thank you for your consideration and I look forward to your response.

Sincerely,

Jack Hollister

Jack Hollister

Enc: Resume

JACK HOLLISTER

1222 College Blvd., #4
Boulder, CO 80305
(303) 444-4444

EDUCATION:

University of Colorado, Boulder, CO
Candidate for a Bachelor of Arts in Geological Sciences, May 2007, with a double concentration in Geology and Geophysics.

Courses have included: Structural Geology, Mineralogy, Sedimentology, Geochemistry, Calculus, Critical Thinking in Environmental Sciences, Computer Programming, and Thermodynamics.

Member, Students for a Healthier Environment; Vice President, Student Association for Geological Sciences Students.

RELATED WORK EXPERIENCE:

Part-time, 2005–present
Department of Geological Sciences, University of Colorado
Laboratory technician. Assisted in the gathering and preparation of soil and mineral samples for use in undergraduate geology laboratory classes. Conducted independent experiments and participated in field trips as directed; maintained all laboratory equipment and tools in good working order.

Summer 2006
Sierra National Forest, California
Intern, GeoCorp America Program. Worked as a junior geologist on three primary projects: soil compaction assessment, cave inventory, and water quality monitoring.

UNRELATED WORK EXPERIENCE

Summer and part-time positions as: pizza delivery person, warehouse worker, and waiter/bartender, 2002–2005.

PERSONAL INTERESTS

Photography, hiking, camping, competitive cycling.

REFERENCES

Available upon request.

1621 Sycamore Street, Apt. 3
Raleigh, NC 27606
(919) 555-5555

June 12, 2007

Mr. Carl Ackermann
President
Ackermann Advertising
5678 Any Street
Raleigh, NC 27609

Dear Mr. Ackermann:

Carolyn Bentley, program director for Pines of Carolina Girl Scout Council suggested I contact you about a graphic design position with Ackermann Advertising. As a student member of the Raleigh Ad Council for the past two years, I have become a great admirer of your agency's excellent work and would welcome the opportunity to join a design team of such high caliber.

I graduated in May with a Bachelor of Graphic Design from North Carolina State University, where I distinguished myself as the winner of this year's "Best of Show" in the annual exhibition of student work sponsored by the College of Design. My work has also been honored by the Raleigh Ad Council.

My resume and several samples of my work are enclosed for your consideration. If you would like to schedule an interview with me, I can be reached at the above telephone number and address. I look forward to hearing from you.

Sincerely,

Andrea Macallister

Andrea Macallister

Enclosures: Resume, samples

ANDREA MACALLISTER

1621 Sycamore Street
Raleigh, NC 27606
(919) 555-5555

EDUCATION:
North Carolina State University, Raleigh, NC
Bachelor of Arts in Graphic Design, May 2007

Awarded "Best of Show," 2007 Exhibition of Student Work, North Carolina State, College of Design. Honorable Mention, 2006 Raleigh Ad Council competition, for Girl Scout summer camp brochure.

EXPERIENCE:
Part-time, 2005–present
Raleigh News and Observer, Raleigh, NC
Graphic artist. Designed ads and laid out pages for daily newspaper; assisted with design and production of special publications and promotional materials.

Summers, 2005, 2006
Macy's Department Store, Tampa, FL
Design Assistant, Merchandising Department. Prepared ads for placement in newspapers and magazines; assisted with design and installation of store displays.

September 2004–May 2005
Graphic Design Department, North Caroline State University
Assistant to a professor of Graphic Design; support staff in departmental office.

INTERNSHIP:
Tampa Bay Performing Arts Center–June 2006 to August 2006
Assisted in the design and production of print ads, brochures, playbills, posters, and other promotional materials related to summer and fall productions.

VOLUNTEER:
YMCA After School Program–September 2005 to May 2006
Coordinated and supervised arts and crafts activities as part of the after-school program offered to elementary and middle school students through the Raleigh YMCA.

Pines of Carolina Girl Scout Council–February 2006
Donated services to design brochure promoting summer camp opportunities Raleigh Girl Scouts. Received honorable mention in the not-for-profit category of the 2006 Raleigh Ad Council design competition.

SKILLS:
Demonstrated proficiency in use of Adobe Acrobat, Framemaker, QuarkXpress, and Microsoft Word. Accomplished photographer.

178 Green Street
Baltimore, MD 21218
(301) 555-5555

April 4, 2007

Arthur Holden, Museum Director
Natural History Museum
123 Any Street
Boston, MA 02118

Dear Mr. Holden:

Professor Plum of the history department here at the University of Maryland suggested that I contact you regarding any entry-level openings that you may have. I'm particularly interested in a position as an assistant to the director.

I will be graduating this May from the University of Maryland with a Bachelor of Arts in History. In addition to my core studies specializing in North American history, I have taken several courses in business administration, accounting, economics, and computers, all of which I'm confident will help me in position such as assistant to the director.

In addition to my coursework, I have gained real-life experience in the areas of sales, marketing, and administration. As owner and president of Blue Bayou Enterprises, I was responsible for the development, marketing, and sale of several innovative products and services, including course study guides and summaries for incoming freshmen, laundry services, and line-waiting services.

I look forward to discussing further any openings you may have. I can be reached at (301) 555-5555 until May and after that at (207) 444-4444. Thank you for your time.

Sincerely,

Carl Stevens

Carl Stevens

Enc: Resume

CARL STEVENS

Current Address
178 Green Street
Baltimore, MD 21218
(301) 555-5555

Permanent Address
23 Blue Street
Aurora, ME 04408
(207) 444-4444

OBJECTIVE

To contribute acquired skills and recent educational background to an entry-level administrative position within an organization offering opportunities for growth and advancement.

SUMMARY OF QUALIFICATIONS

- Adapt easily to new concepts and responsibilities.
- Diverse background in both business and outdoor skills.
- Self-motivated; detail-oriented; function well both independently and as part of a team.
- Proven oral and written communication skills.

EDUCATION

UNIVERSITY OF MARYLAND, College Park, MD
Bachelor of Arts, History, expected May 2007.

WORK HISTORY

THE SPORTS SPOT, Baltimore, MD   2006–Present
Sales Associate
Consistently meet/exceed monthly sales quotas in all market areas.

BLUE BAYOU ENTERPRISES, College Park, MD   2004–2005
Owner/President
Conceived, developed, marketed, and sold various products to a 30,000 student and faculty population.

BERMAN FOUNDATION, Aurora, ME   Summer 2004
Work Camp Supervisor
Responsible for twelve European University students through Volunteer for Peace Program.

Wilderness Trip Co-Leader   Summers 2001–2003
Co-led a seven-week canoeing and backpacking expedition for ten teenage participants in Northern Maine, 2001, 2002. Co-led a family canoeing trip on the Alaska Wilderness Waterway, ages 12 to 65, 2003.

UNIVERSITY OF MAINE, Orono, ME   Winter 2001–2005
Registrar's Office
Administrator
Processed transcripts; researched records on database, microfilm, and hard copy; responded to student inquiries/complaints. Required familiarity with PC and Mainframe data entry.

156 Newton Heights
Salisbury, MD 21804
301/555-9874

July 5, 2006

Ms. Marie Manette
Director
French-American Foreign Council
1127 Avenue of the Americas
New York, NY 10029

Dear Ms. Manette:

I am writing in hopes that you will consider me for the position of Translator as advertised in today's *New York Times*.

I graduated last month with a B.A. in International Relations and French Language from George Washington University. Consistently on the Dean's List and graduating one year early with honors and Advanced Standing, I was recognized throughout my academic career for excellent scholarship.

I was very active in college, having participated in many extracurricular events and organizations, including a residential honors program studying Ethics and Politics. By my junior year, I had become a Model United Nations Advisor, an Alumni Ambassador, and President of the International Affairs Society. Last summer, I participated in a valuable and exciting summer program at the College of International Relations in Paris called the International Studies Session.

I also have job experience in the field of international affairs, having worked as an interpreter and translator for a Parisian film corporation. In this position, I interpreted for negotiations over film co-productions and translated agreements, film scripts, scenarios, and foreign correspondence. I also worked as the Assistant to the Parisian Correspondent for Deshabilles Associates, a prestigious import/export company, where my duties included translation of documents, interpretation of telephone and live communications, and general office tasks.

I feel confident that an interview would demonstrate that my expertise in international affairs and French language and culture makes me well-qualified for this position. I am not limited by location and would enjoy the opportunity to live and work in New York City for the Foreign Council.

I look forward to meeting you, Ms. Manette, and will give you a call to follow up on this letter toward the end of next week.

Sincerely,

Lynne Ann Jordan

Lynne Ann Jordan

Enc.: Resume

INTERDISCIPLINARY STUDIES MAJOR: INTERNATIONAL RELATIONS/FRENCH LANGUAGE

LYNNE ANN JORDAN

156 Newton Heights
Salisbury, MD 21804
301/555-9874

Education
2003–2006

GEORGE WASHINGTON UNIVERSITY   WASHINGTON, D.C.
Awarded a Bachelor of Arts in June 2006, majoring in International Relations. Minor in French Language. Thesis concentration in International Law. Completed 4-year requirements in 3 years. Honors with Advanced Standing and Dean's List.

Participant in Ethics and Politics residential honors program. Model United National Adviser. President of International Affairs Society. Alumni Ambassador and Student Admissions Representative.

Summer 2005

COLLEGE OF INTERNATIONAL RELATIONS   PARIS, FRANCE
Participant in summer International Studies Session. Studied French, International Politics, Comparative Government, and History of the United Nations. Received Bilingual Proficiency Certification.

Experience
Summer 2004

FRENCH FILM PRODUCTION CORPORATION PARIS, FRANCE
Interpreted for negotiations over film co-productions, translated agreements, film scripts, scenarios, and foreign correspondence.

Part-time
2006

DESHABILLES ASSOCIATES   WASHINGTON, D.C.
Worked as an Assistant to Parisian Correspondent. Duties included translation of documents, interpretation for telephone and live communications, and general clerical tasks.

Part-time
2004–2005

Worked in unrelated jobs to pay for college tuition. Positions included: Sales Clerk, Bank Teller, Temporary Worker, Teaching Aide, and Research Assistant.

Personal Interests

Enjoy modern French literature and film, photography, and racquetball.

References   Available upon request.

JOURNALISM MAJOR

178 Green Street
Willamette, OR 97301
(503) 555-5555

June 4, 2007

Ms. Pauline Jacobs
President
Jacobs Public Relations
1234 Any Street
New York, NY 11012

Dear Ms. Jacobs:

Susan Larson, National Director of Kids Abroad, suggested that I contact you about the opening you have for a publicist. I am familiar with the excellent work your firm has done on the Ogilvy & Smith account and would like to contribute to a team of such high caliber.

I graduated this May with a Bachelor of Arts in Journalism from the University of Oregon. In addition to the usual communications courses, I took classes in computers and business administration which I feel will prove beneficial in my role as a publicist.

My resume is enclosed. I would value the opportunity to meet with you to discuss the publicist opening. I can be reached at the above telephone number and address.

I have enclosed several writing samples, including public relations materials I drafted while working with Kids Abroad. Thank you for your time.

Sincerely,

Anne Smith

Anne Smith

Enclosures: Resume
             Writing samples

ANNE SMITH
178 Green Street
Willamette, OR 97301
(503) 555-5555

EDUCATION:
University of Oregon, Eugene, OR
Bachelor of Arts in Journalism, May 2007

The Writer's Block, 2005–2007
Vice-President of a student-run journalism/writing group producing a biweekly newsletter and providing a forum for creative expression by students.

EXPERIENCE:
Kids Abroad 2006–2007
Administrative Director, Western Region USA; Supervised, from inception to completion, all incoming foreign exchange student programs. Assigned program location and coordinator. Annually monitored 800 high school exchange students. Acted as liaison between foreign clients and American personnel. Evaluated, edited, and chose texts used to teach English to the exchange students.

Kids Abroad April 2003–April 2007
Contributing columnist for public relations newspaper.

Kids Abroad Western Regional Office September 2003–April 2007
Managed 800 person field staff across United States. Placed, counseled, and monitored high school foreign exchange students and host families throughout United States. Tutored English As A Second Language. Annually directed French student orientation in Portland. Wrote public relations and promotional materials. Managed office.

Journalism Department University of Oregon September 2005–June 2006
Peer academic advisor; professor's assistant; office support staff.

INTERNSHIP:
Jade Ryder Enterprises July–September 2005
Researched and organized celebrity biographies for promotional flyers; writing and computer graphics; administrative duties.

VOLUNTEER:
Tutoring Program January 2004–June 2005
Participated in an independent tutoring program in which college students tutored junior and high school students in academic subjects and motivational skills.

SKILLS:
Microsoft Word, Lotus 1-2-3, Excel, Access, PowerPoint, hard copy and online editing.

12 Shady Lane
Brattleboro, VT 05211

July 17, 2007

Mr. Wayne Peterson
President
HBR Systems, Inc.
Science Park Road
Los Angeles, CA 90045

Dear Mr. Peterson:

Recently I completed the requirements for my B.S. in Management Information Systems at Adams State College. I am writing to you now because I am interested in a career at HBR Systems, Inc.

I believe that my intensive study of MIS during the past four years and my vast knowledge of computer hardware and software, along with my previous professional experience in MIS and other business areas, would make me a valuable Systems Analyst at HBR Systems.

I have enclosed my resume and would welcome the opportunity to speak with the appropriate person about current or anticipated openings at your company.

Thank you for your attention to this matter.

Sincerely,

Gigi D. Russell

Gigi D. Russell
802/555-8315

Enc.: Resume

GIGI D. RUSSELL
12 Shady Lane
Brattleboro, VT 05211
802/555-8315

Education

2003–2007   **ADAMS STATE COLLEGE**   **ALAMOSA, COLORADO**

Awarded a Bachelor of Science in May2007, majoring in Management Information Systems. Courses included Programming in Pascal, Programming in COBOL, Programming in FORTRAN, and Computer Engineering. 3.2 grade point average.

Member of the Beta Kappa Gamma Honor Society. Member of Delta Delta Delta sorority. Helped to organize the First Annual Adams State Computer Symposium.

Experience

Summer 2006   **D. MCGILL & ASSOCIATES**   **ALAMOSA, COLORADO**

Data Entry Clerk for busy accounting firm. Also maintained correspondence with key accounts. Found major accounting error that saved one account more than $50,000.

Summer 2005   **INCO SYSTEMS, INC.**   **DENVER, COLORADO**

Intern, Management Information Systems (MIS). Audited PC software with an emphasis on locating and eradicating viruses. Logged customer problems and performed extensive troubleshooting; dispatched appropriate technical support. Maintained disk arrays and tape storage devices and analyzed performance and security.

Summer 2004   **UNITED DELL CORPORATION**   **LAKEWOOD, COLORADO**

Assistant to the Finance Officer. Responsible for the monthly analyses of cash disbursements, accounts payable, petty cash, bank reconciliations, and expense reports. Aided in the preparation of the monthly budget report using Symphony software. Entered journal entries into the general ledger and produced financial statements using Platinum software package.

Skills

Working knowledge of BASIC, Microsoft Windows, dBase III Plus, dBase IV, HTML, Microsoft Word, Lotus 1-2-3, Microsoft Excel, MS-DOS, Nastec DesignAid Case 2000, RAMIS II MARVEL.

Experience with UNIX/C, Turbo Pascal, COBOL, C++, Intel 8086 Assembly Language, INTELESYS.

Exposure to VSE/SP, VSE/POWER, CICS/VS, JCL, CA-TOP SECRET.

References   Transcript and references available upon request.

81 Sandypine Road
Joppa, MD 20707
(410) 555-1551

March 22, 2007

Mr. Henry Stanhope
Personnel Manager
Lisa Fleischman Associates
2125 Wisconsin Avenue NW
Suite 202
Washington, DC 25507

Dear Mr. Stanhope:

I am writing in response to your advertisement in the *Washington Post* for the position of Advertising Assistant. Enclosed is my resume for your review and consideration.

I will be graduating in May from Colgate University with a Bachelor of Science in Marketing. Throughout my education, I have developed excellent research, communication, editing, and interpersonal skills. I have gained experience in various marketing capacities (e.g., advertising, direct marketing, and market research) by completing a student-team project for Bagel Bakery, Inc. I have also had exposure to international marketing through a summer program in Moscow which concentrated on the Russian culture and political and economic system.

Two summers of experience working in sales have given me the opportunity to employ my marketing knowledge while displaying initiative and responsibility. My ambitious attitude helped me win several employee incentive contests at The Limited. In both positions, I utilized my marketing background to make recommendations that improved employee efficiency and increased sales.

I believe that my skills and experience would be an asset to your advertising firm and I would appreciate the opportunity to discuss the Advertising Assistant position with you. I may be reached at the above listed phone number between 9 am and 5 pm for an interview at your convenience. Thank you for your consideration.

Sincerely,

Rosemary L. Brandenburg

Rosemary L. Brandenburg

Rosemary L. Brandenburg
81 Sandypine Road
Joppa, MD 20707
(410) 555-1551

OBJECTIVE An entry-level position in the advertising industry.

EDUCATION Colgate University, Hamilton, New York. Bachelor of Science in Marketing to be completed in May 2007. Courses include International Marketing, Marketing Research, Business Communications, and Statistics and Computer Programming. 3.4/4.0 grade point average.

Secretary of the Marketing Club. Member of Beta Gamma Sigma Honor Society for Business Administration Students. Member Women's Rugby Team.

RELATED EXPERIENCE *Direct Marketing Association's Collegiate CHO Competition*, Hamilton, NY – Fall Semester 2006.
Participated on student-team project to create direct marketing campaign for Bagel Bakery, Inc. Gained practical experience in developing marketing plans and reports.

Colgate in Moscow, Summer 2006.
Comprehensive study of Russian culture and thorough analysis of political and economic system.

WORK EXPERIENCE *The Limited*, Laurel, MD – Summer 2005.
Sales associates. Acquired retail sales experience and developed personal selling skills through excellent customer relations. Two-time winner of employee sales contests.

Janice's Boutique, Joppa, MD – Summer 2004.
Sales associate. Assisted in layout of store merchandise, stocking and quality control of inventory; operated cash register. Evaluated and presented recommendations for changes in store displays.

SPECIAL SKILLS *Typing:* 50 WPM.
Word Processing: 65 WPM.
Computer: Microsoft Word, dBase III, Lotus 1-2-3, Microsoft Excel, and Harvard Graphics.

PERSONAL BACKGROUND Enjoy rugby, horseback riding, reading fiction, and playing chess.

REFERENCES Available upon request.

178 Green Street
Bloomington, IN 47405
(812) 555-5555

March 3, 2007

Rex Winters, Laboratory Director
Brown Labs
12 Main Street
Bloomington, IN 47405

Dear Mr. Winters:

I am writing and enclosing my resume to apprise you of my interest in working for your laboratory as a research assistant.

I will be graduating this May from Indiana University with a Bachelor of Science in Nutrition. I am confident that my coursework in Organic Chemistry, Anatomy and Physiology, and Modern Laboratory Technology has given me a good base for joining your staff.

In addition to my schoolwork, I have gained valuable experience as an intern in the Nutrition Evaluation Laboratory at the Center on Aging at Indiana University. I assisted seven researchers in routine and complex biochemical analyses. This exposure has given me keen insights into laboratory procedures and practices.

I'm very impressed with what I have read about Brown Labs in *Nutrition Weekly*. I applaud your work on fat substitutes, and I would love to work for a team that is so obviously concerned about issues that affect people's everyday lives.

It would be my pleasure to discuss with you any possibility of working for you as a research assistant after my graduation in May. I can be reached after 4 p.m. at (812) 555-5555, or you may call earlier to leave a message. Thank you for your time, and I look forward to hearing from you.

Sincerely,

Jay Crawford

Jay Crawford

Enc.: Resume

JAY CRAWFORD

Current Address	**Permanent Address**
178 Green Street	23 Blue Street
Bloomington, IN 47405	Evansville, IN 47712
(812) 555-5555	(812) 444-4444

OBJECTIVE

To utilize acquired skills in biotechnology research toward project responsibility in nutrition/health industry.

EDUCATION

Bachelor of Science in Nutrition
INDIANA UNIVERSITY

- Degree Anticipated: 2007
- Courses include Organic Chemistry, Anatomy and Physiology, and Modern Laboratory Technology.
- Thesis topic: "Advances in Refrigeration Techniques and Their Application to the Fresh Meats Industry."

EXPERIENCE

2006 to Present: **Intern**
Nutrition Evaluation Laboratory, Human Nutrition Research
CENTER ON AGING AT INDIANA UNIVERSITY

- Assist seven researchers in routine and esoteric biochemical analysis. Implement 10 different nonclinical assays of vitamins, amino acids and other biomolecules in support of human and animal tissue culture studies. Develop and implement new types of assays and improve existing analytical techniques.
- Interact with investigators and assist in organization and implementation of analysis. Provide literature search and publication of developed methodologies in scientific journals.
- Provide maintenance for a wide variety of laboratory and analytical equipment.
- Train on microprocessor- and personal computer-driven analytical instruments and robots: Waters hardware and software, analytical, chromatography software.
- Initiated independent research project concerning detection of nonenzymatically glycated amino acid residues in proteins.

2005 to 2006: **Teaching Assistant**
Department of Biochemistry and Biophysics
INDIANA UNIVERSITY

- Led group of seven students in weekly laboratory experiments.
- Administered quizzes and evaluated lab results.

PERSONAL

Willing to travel.

332 Oakland Drive
Lake Charles, LA 70610
(318) 555-5557

March 16, 2007

Ms. Lisa Stanhope
Professional Recruiter
Eastman Kodak Company
121 Technology Drive
Rochester, NY 14650

Dear Ms. Stanhope:

Perhaps you are seeking an addition to your excellent team of physicists. A new person can provide innovative approaches and ideas to the challenges of research and development.

As you can see from my resume, I will be graduating in June from Loyola University with a bachelor's degree in Physics. I have also studied such related fields as chemical engineering, mathematics, and systems applications, all of which I am sure will help me in as a physicist with Eastman Kodak. I offer solid experience, having worked for two summers for the Physics Department at Loyola both as an intern and as a laboratory technician.

Additionally, I have a personal interest in photography, having been an avid amateur photographer for many years. I built my own darkroom and have won several awards for my photographs. Because of this, I feel that Eastman Kodak is an especially good match for my skills and interests.

Please advise me of any positions that may become available. Your consideration of my credentials is greatly appreciated.

Sincerely,

Bruce R. Sutherland

Bruce R. Sutherland

Enc.: Resume

BRUCE R. SUTHERLAND

Loyola University
Stone Hall
New Orleans, LA 70114
(504) 555-9951

332 Oakland Drive
Lake Charles, LA 70610
(318) 555-5557

EDUCATION

2003–Present **LOYOLA UNIVERSITY** New Orleans, Louisiana
Candidate for the degree of Bachelor of Science in June 2007, majoring in Physics. Additional areas of study include Chemical Engineering, Mathematics, and Systems Applications. 3.42 grade point average.

Golden Key Honor Society. Cycling Team. Varsity Wrestling. Helped establish Council on Racial Relations for New Orleans campus.

**WORK
EXPERIENCE**

Summer 2006 **LABORATORY TECHNICIAN** New Orleans, Louisiana
PHYSICS DEPARTMENT, LOYOLA UNIVERSITY
Designed and constructed signal filters and power amplifiers for research on bird behavioral patterns. Tested and modified equipment after preliminary use.

Summer 2005 **PHYSICS INTERN** New Orleans, Louisiana
PHYSICS DEPARTMENT, LOYOLA UNIVERSITY
Assistant to the department head. Helped to design and execute experiments testing electromagnetic waves and fields. Compiled and analyzed data.

Summer 2004 **ASSISTANT TO THE MANAGER** Ruston, Louisiana
FOLLEN'S VIDEO STORE
Maintained daily bookkeeping. Organized inventory and repair of video equipment. Rented videos and electronic equipment. Customer service and some sales.

Part-time 2006 **CIRCULATION ASSISTANT** New Orleans, Louisiana
KING MEMORIAL LIBRARY/LOYOLA UNIVERSITY
Processed borrowed books, assisted students and faculty with questions, managed and updated extensive library database.

SKILLS Familiar with Microsoft Word, WordPerfect, Lotus 1-2-3, dBase, and Fortran.

REFERENCES Available upon request.

107 Allston Way
Prairie View, TX 77644
409/555-4401

February 4, 2007

Mr. Robert J. Strauss
Program Director
Big Brother Program
42 Fulton Street
Houston, TX 76051

Dear Mr. Strauss:

Thank you for taking the time to speak with me on Wednesday. As I told you on the phone, I am interested in the position of Assistant Director which, you mentioned, should be opening up some time next month.

I graduated in December from Rice University with a bachelor's degree in Government and a dual concentration in Psychology and Sociology. I was consistently on the Dean's list and my final grade point average was 3.54.

I have had a good deal of experience in human services, having worked as a Management Intern for the United Way. Here, I learned the many aspects and responsibilities associated with management, including improving departmental efficiency, evaluating different charitable organizations, organizing fund-raisers, and budgeting funds.

At the Boy's Club of Prairie View, I worked as a Youth Counselor for two consecutive summers. I was responsible for orienting youngsters and new supervisors to the program, placing youths in various programs based on their abilities and interests, organizing fun and educational events for the boys, and assisting in the preparation of a weekly newsletter.

It was during my time at the Boy's Club that I decided that I would like to pursue human/social services as a career. I especially find working with children very rewarding and would love the opportunity to contribute to the Big Brother program.

Could we schedule an interview? I can be reached at 409/555-4401 during the late afternoon and evening hours. Thank you for your consideration.

Sincerely,

Michael Burke

Michael Burke

Enc.: Resume

MICHAEL BURKE

107 Allston Way
Prairie View, TX 77644
409/555-4401

Objective   An entry-level position in human/social services.

Education   Rice University, College of Arts and Sciences, Houston, Texas. Bachelor of
Arts awarded with honors in December 2006. Major: Government; Concen-
trations: Psychology/Sociology. Dean's List; 3.54 grade point average.

Relevant
Courses

U.S. Government	International Policy
Business Law	Sociology of Poverty
Ethics in Public Life	Comparative Politics
The Politics of Economics	Public Speaking

Experience

Management Intern *United Way of Texas*, Houston, Texas.
Analyzed efficiency of various departments, recommended areas for improve-
ment, visited and evaluated different charitable organizations, organized
fund-raisers, assisted in preparing budgets for the new fiscal year. Collected,
organized and evaluated data. Summer–Winter 2006.

Youth Counselor *Boy's Club of Prairie View*, Texas.
Responsible for orienting youngsters and supervisors in terms of the purpose
and rules of various programs, placing youths in various programs based on
their abilities and interests, organizing fun and educational events for the
youngsters, and assisting in the preparation of a weekly newsletter. Summers
2004–2005.

Paralegal Intern *Johnson & Wright*, Dallas, Texas.
Organized files, gathered information, met and received information from
clients, researched case and client histories in a general practice law firm.
Hired and trained other interns. Part-time 2004–2005.

Other
Positions   Worked as a Lifeguard, Summer Camp Counselor, Machine Operator,
Cashier, and Waiter. 2003–present.

Activities   Volunteer for VOTE AMERICA! Campaign. Chairman for the Committee
on Student Life, Intramural Athletic Chairman, and Member of Society for
Distinguished Collegiate Americans.

References   Available upon request.

233 Vetnor Avenue
Oklahoma City, OK 93304

November 13, 2006

Ms. Stephanie Long
Personnel Manager
Evans Corporation
1799 Business Park Drive
Sumter, SC 20034

Dear Ms. Long:

Can you utilize the talents of a competent, motivated, and well-organized Personnel Assistant who is interested in pursuing a career in the Human Resources field?

I am a college student at Furman University who is graduating this June with a bachelor's degree in Psychology and Sociology. I offer a strong talent for dealing with many different kinds of people, excellent communication skills, and a desire to learn and grow within your company.

I believe that Human Resources is the backbone of any company. After all, a company is only as good as the people working for it. If staffed poorly, a company will suffer and perhaps even fail. However, if Human Resources does a great job with staffing, then the company becomes strong and is likely to not only succeed but thrive.

I am particularly interested in Evans Corporation because it is such a dynamic firm. I was very impressed to discover that your company was among the fastest growing in the state. I would like to become a part of such a fine company, and the Human Resources Department that no doubt contributed to its success.

I would like to interview with you at your earliest convenience. I am best reached at (701) 555-9421 during business hours. Thank you for your consideration.

Sincerely,

Louis T. Barnes

Louis T. Barnes

Enc.: Resume

PSYCHOLOGY MAJOR

LOUIS T. BARNES
233 Vetnor Avenue
Oklahoma City, OK 93304
(701) 555-9421

Education
2003–2007   **FURMAN UNIVERSITY**   **GREENVILLE, SOUTH CAROLINA**
Candidate for the degree of Bachelor of Arts in June 2007, majoring in Psychology and minoring in Sociology. Courses include: Public Speaking, Mathematics, and Computer Science. Independent Study topic: The Psychological Impact of Commercial Advertising on Teenage Eating Disorders. Won the Alfred Pinder Award for Outstanding Students of Psychology in 2006.

Teaching Assistant for Introductory Psychology class. Member of Furman Cycling Club. Volunteer for local food shelter. Helped organize on-campus food donation drive for the needy; collected more than a half ton of food that was distributed to some 75 different families.

Summer 2006   **OXFORD UNIVERSITY**   **OXFORD, ENGLAND**
Participated in a summer abroad program, studying English popular culture. Thesis topic: The Role of Music in the English Punk Sub-Culture.

Experience
Summer 2005   **THE COCA-COLA COMPANY**   **PORTER, SOUTH CAROLINA**
Public Relations Assistant. Wrote promotional material, sent out mass mailings, and supervised company sponsorship of various charitable events.

Summer 2004   **ANNIE'S CANDIES**   **GREENVILLE, SOUTH CAROLINA**
Assistant candy-maker and counter person for local sweets shop.

Part-time
2003–2006   Part-time positions include Mail Clerk for college dormitory, Busperson at local restaurant, and Pizza Delivery Person.

Interests   Enjoy hiking, cycling, and building model cars. Compete in state-wide cycling races.

References   References available upon request.

76 Roanoak Avenue
Hartford, CT 06519
203/555-8877
April 4, 2007

Ms. Eileen Drexel, Director
State of Connecticut Agency of Aging
1222 Vermont Street
Hartford, CT 06522

Dear Ms. Drexel:

Thank you for taking the time so speak with me today. As I mentioned on the phone, I am interested in beginning a career in the field of gerontology.

I am currently a senior at Yale University, majoring in Sociology. I have studied a variety of subjects including Gerontology, which is how I first became interested in this field. Other related courses I've taken include Poverty and Crisis, The Political Economy of Health Care in the United States, Race Relations, and Women in Society. My current grade point average is 3.64 and I am a member of the Phi Beta Kappa honor society

In addition to my schoolwork, I am an active member of the student-run Volunteers for a Better World program. Some of the experiences I've gained through this organization include serving Thanksgiving dinner to homeless people at a local soup kitchen, tutoring underprivileged junior high school students in math and English, and co-directing a very successful annual campus food drive. As a contributing writer for *Vanguard Press*, I wrote many articles and editorials concerning various social issues, including the plight of the elderly.

As a result of my classroom studies and volunteer experience, I feel that I have an excellent grasp on the social and political issues that affect the elderly in the United States. Furthermore, I feel that at your agency, I could make a real difference in the lives of elderly people.

I've enclosed my resume and a sample article for your review. Thank you for your attention to this matter and I look forward to your response.

Sincerely,

Herbert Rosenwriter

Herbert Rosenwriter

Enc.: Resume
      Sample article

HERBERT ROSENWRITER
76 Roanoak Avenue
Hartford, CT 06519
203/555-8877

Objective:
A challenging position in the field of gerontology which would enable me to utilize my writing and analytical skills.

Education:
YALE UNIVERSITY
New Haven, Connecticut
Candidate for the degree of Bachelor of Arts in Sociology with a concentration in Economic Stratification and Social Hierarchies. Courses include Poverty and Crisis, The Political Economy of Health Care in the United States, Gerontology, Race Relations, and Women in Society. Independent Study topic: The Feminization of Poverty in the United States. 3.64 grade point average. Member of the Phi Beta Kappa honor society. Expected date of graduation: May 2007.

Member of student-run Volunteers for a Better World program. Served Thanksgiving dinner to homeless people at local soup kitchen, tutored four underprivileged junior high school students in math and English, co-directed campus food drive. Contributing writer for *Vanguard Press*.

Experience:
CUSTOMER SERVICE REPRESENTATIVE
ONTEGA SAVINGS BANK; Stamford, Connecticut
Duties included facilitating new account referrals, processing deposits, withdrawals, check cashing, balancing daily cash blotters and utilizing the CRT. Summers 2005, 2006.

ASSISTANT TO EXECUTIVE ASSISTANT U.S. ATTORNEY
U.S. ATTORNEY'S OFFICE, CRIMINAL DIVISION; Boston, Massachusetts.
Gathered and organized evidence for trial and filed complaints. Acted as a liaison between attorney and press. Summer 2004.

CREDIT CARD PAYMENTS CLERK
ONTEGA SAVINGS BANK; Stamford, Connecticut.
Responsibilities include data entry of new customer credit card accounts; sorting, balancing and posting credit card/home equity/cash advance payments to the CRT and general ledger; customer service. Part-time 2006–present.

References:
Available upon request.

460 Brook Road
Santa Fe, NM 87541
505/555-5561

August 5, 2007

Joseph C. Barber
Director of Human Resources
Kendall Pharmaceuticals
11241 Sundown Drive
Albuquerque, NM 87154

Dear Mr. Barber:

Please accept this letter as my application for the Statistician position currently available with your company, as advertised in Sunday's *Albuquerque Sun.* My resume is enclosed for your consideration, and I believe that you will find me well qualified.

I have a bachelor's degree in Statistics from New Mexico State University and I offer a solid background in computers, in addition to coursework in mathematics, economics, and business administration. To further my studies, I interned for a summer at the California Institute of Technology, where I took courses in Applied Mathematics and Advanced Macro Economics.

As an Assistant to a top Economist in the U.S. Department of Labor, I devised and interpreted the numerical results of surveys concerning the decline of manufacturing in the United States. In this position, I gained in-depth knowledge about the use of several statistical software programs, including SPSSX and SASS.

I am organized and detail oriented, work well under pressure, and have a great attitude. I'm looking for a challenging, growth-oriented position and would like the opportunity to learn more about your company and this position. I look forward to hearing from you to schedule a personal interview at your convenience.

Sincerely,

Alison Ann Granville

Alison Ann Granville

ALISON ANN GRANVILLE
460 Brook Road
Santa Fe, NM 87541
505/555-5561

Education		
2003–2007	**NEW MEXICO STATE UNIVERSITY**	**LAS CRUCES, NEW MEXICO**

Awarded a Bachelor of Science in May 2007, majoring in Statistics. Also concentrated studies in Mathematics, Economics, Business Administration, and Computer Applications. Thesis topic: New Applications of the Probability Theory Using Differential Equations. 3.1 grade point average.

Member of the Math Club. Recipient of the Connor Foundation Scholarship in2005. Varsity basketball.

1998–2003	**SANTA FE WEST HIGH SCHOOL**	**SANTA FE, NEW MEXICO**

Received High School Diploma in 2003. Achieved Advanced Placement Standing in Calculus. Scored highest math SAT score in history of high school. Junior varsity and varsity basketball. State Championships two years in a row.

Internship		
Summer 2006	**CALIFORNIA INSTITUTE OF TECHNOLOGY**	**PASADENA**

Studied Applied Mathematics and Advanced Macro Economics. Attended week-long seminar on "Future Applications of Mathematics and Statistics in Space-Age Technology."

Summers		
2004–2005	**UNITED STATES DEPARTMENT OF LABOR**	**WASHINGTON, DC**

Assistant to a top Economist. Devised and interpreted the numerical results of surveys concerning the decline of manufacturing in the United States. Used a variety of statistical programs, including SPSSX and SASS.

Summer–Winter		
2003	**BOHEM INDUSTRIES**	**SANTA FE, NEW MEXICO**

Data Entry Clerk. Promoted to Computer Operator within two months.

Personal Background	Enjoy chess, music, playing keyboard in a blues band, and basketball.

References	Available upon request.

Making the Right Impression

Chapter Sixteen

Before the Job Interview

Preparation is the key to successful interviewing.

Over the course of your job search, you will typically net relatively few interviews in relation to the number of companies you contact. But when you do get the call to come in for an interview, don't pass up the chance. Even if it appears to you at first that this is not exactly the right company or the perfect position, schedule the interview anyway. It could turn out to a better job than you thought and even if it doesn't, the interview will be good experience for when the right job opportunity does come along. Like anything else, your interviewing skills improve with practice. The more you interview, the better you become at interviewing, so why waste a single opportunity to improve your skills? Prepare yourself thoroughly, even for a "practice run," and you will eventually approach each interview with confidence and excitement.

Job Search Focus

Interview preparation should begin long before you actually start lining up interviews. If you've followed the advice in previous chapters, you have already taken the important first step of deciding which industry and job function to pursue. By limiting your job search in this way, you are showing a corporate recruiter that you are serious about a long-term professional career.

One favorite interview question employers use to eliminate candidates from consideration is, "What other firms are you interviewing with and for what positions?" In an effort to impress a prospective employer, candidates will often rattle off the names of several large firms in unrelated industries with completely different types of jobs. This is a mistake. What an employer wants to hear instead is that you are interviewing for *similar* jobs in the same industry at *similar* firms (even their competitors). It demonstrates your commitment to a specific industry and job function.

Company Research

Before you approach a particular company for the first time, do a little background research so that, when you make that initial phone call or networking contact, you can sound both knowledgeable about the firm and sincerely interested in securing a job there. While you may be tempted to try and find out as much as you can about every company you contact, it is best to concentrate your research efforts on the relatively small number of firms that might actually grant you an interview and, even then, don't delve too deeply just yet.

The time to get really serious about researching a particular company is when you have an interview scheduled there. Before the big day, you will want to find out everything you possibly can about the company, including its organizational structure and the names of the individuals holding key positions. In addition, you should try to learn as much as you can about the position for which you will be interviewing so that you can be prepared to demonstrate how your education and experience match the desired qualifications. The extra effort you take to learn about a prospective employer in advance could set you apart from the competition during that very first interview and well into the future.

At the very least, determine the following details about any firm at which you are interviewing:

- Principal products or services
- Types of customers
- Subsidiaries
- Parent company(ies)
- Type of ownership
- Approximate rank within the industry
- Sales and profit trends
- Announced future plans
- Organizational structure and key players
- Job description and qualifications desired for the specific position.

To find this information and more, you will need to explore every possible resource. A good place to start is the company's Web site. Click on every button and carefully read every page; you'll be amazed at what you can learn. And do use a search engine such as Google to unearth additional Web sources of information about the company. There is a wealth of information available on the Internet; take advantage of it.

When you have fully exhausted your Web resources, you might also check the business directories available at your local library for additional information. If the company is large and publicly owned, call the investor relations department to request an annual report. Check the local newspaper and business media for recent articles written about the company. Don't forget those all-important trade publications either. If you have been following the advice in previous chapters and have selected an industry in which to focus your job search, you are probably already reading those magazines or, at the very least, are familiar with them. Now is the time to comb through back issues in search of relevant articles.

Beware, however, that there could be a downside to this information gathering process. Your research could lead you to conclude that you don't want to work for the firm after all. If that happens, don't cancel your appointment; *interview anyway*. In a face-to-face meeting, you might come across something that changes your mind. And even if you don't, you will still benefit from the chance to practice and improve your interviewing skills.

Dressing for Success

How important is proper dress for a job interview? Well, let's just say that the final selection of a job candidate is rarely determined solely on the basis of what he or she wore. However, first impressions do count and inappropriate dress could narrow your chances early on. First-round candidates for an opening *are* often quickly eliminated by dressing inappropriately. This is not to suggest that you must rush out and buy a whole new wardrobe. But you should take some time now to look through your closet and determine if you have what you need to put together an adequate interview outfit.

For a man, a conservative two-piece suit, white dress shirt and simple tie is basic corporate wear. However, the trend is toward more casual attire and standards may vary depending on the industry, company, and region of the country. For some industries and/or companies, a quality sports jacket, pants, colored shirt and tie may be perfectly acceptable. If you're not sure what dress is appropriate at a particular firm, play it safe and opt for the traditional two-piece suit. Even at a company where fairly casual dress is encouraged, job seekers will not be out of place in somewhat more formal dress, and may, in fact, make a better impression. A man should always wear a jacket and tie to an interview—even if everyone else in the office is in shirtsleeves. Dressing more formally shows that you take your interview seriously and that you treat the company with respect. As for shoes, basic black is preferred, but if all you have is a pair of quality, conservative brown shoes, don't rush out and buy a new pair simply for the sake of an interview. Just make sure they are polished (or at least clean) and in good repair.

Because women have so many more fashion options, the rules are more difficult to discern. Generally speaking, however, women should either wear a relatively conservative dress or a skirted suit. In traditionally more conservative industries, such as investment banking, the suit is a safer bet. For most other industries, however, a professional-looking dress may be preferable; it makes a stronger statement of your individuality without being out of place. A tailored pant suit may also be acceptable in certain situations and industries.

In the long run, good grooming is more important than the perfect outfit. It indicates both thoroughness and self-confidence. Be sure that your clothes are immaculate and fit well—jackets and blouses should not be too tight, nor skirts too short. Your hair should be neat and freshly washed, your shoes clean and attractive. A basic pump or sling-back with a moderate heel is probably your best choice; leave the stilettos and flip-flops at home. Women should avoid excessive jewelry, makeup, or perfume. Men should be freshly shaven, even if the interview is late in the day.

You will also need to wear a watch, and carry a pen and pad of paper for taking notes. Finally, a briefcase or portfolio folder will help complete your professional look. Women should avoid carrying both a briefcase and a large, bulky purse. For a more professional appearance, transfer any essential items into a small bag you can store inside the briefcase. Since you may be asked to complete a job application at the time of your interview, be sure to bring along the necessary details you may need to supply, such as complete addresses and phone numbers of previous employers. And don't forget to bring along a few extra copies of your resume, too.

Have the Obvious Answers Ready

You can never be sure exactly what you will be asked during a job interview, but, since certain standard questions are on pretty much every interviewer's list, you should prepare yourself for them ahead of time. By developing solid answers in advance to questions that are likely to be asked, you will put yourself in a better position to answer the questions you hadn't anticipated.

Take a look at your resume, pretending for a moment that you are a corporate recruiter seeing it for the first time. What questions would you ask? Bear in mind that the questions you are asked in one interview are likely to be repeated in another. So, immediately after each interview, take a moment to write down each new question you were asked; consider how you answered it this time, then take a moment to prepare a solid response in case you are asked that same question again.

Some questions are relatively easy to anticipate and prepare for. For example, a recruiter is very likely to ask you for more information about your work history and academic achievements. Be prepared to talk about any one of them for approximately three minutes. You may also be asked about the personal interests you have listed on your resume; again, give some thought to what you might say. If your home address is significantly distant from your campus address, be prepared to discuss why you decided to attend college so far away from home. As you prepare for your interview, try to structure your responses in a way that suggests you are someone the recruiter would want to hire. In other words, project yourself as someone who is likely to stay with the company for a number of years, is achievement-oriented, will fit in well with other people, and is both mature and likeable. And by all means, try to project yourself as someone who is capable of doing the job in question extremely well.

For a list of commonly asked interview questions and their answers, see Chapter 18.

Be Prepared to Ask Questions

When it comes to asking and answering questions, job interviews are rarely one-sided. At some point, usually toward the end of the interview, the recruiter will likely ask if you have any questions. You should be prepared to ask about something; if you don't, you might be perceived as being uninterested in the company. *Do not* under any circumstances inquire about salary or benefits until after you have been offered the job. (During the first interview you are unlikely to receive a job offer—this usually happens only after one or more follow-up interviews.) During the first interview, you have three reasons to ask questions: to show your knowledge of the firm, to underscore your deep interest in the firm and the position, and to add to your chances of being invited back for a second interview. Save the questions about salary, benefits, and related issues for later, after you receive an offer; at this stage of the game, you don't want to seem too focused on money. You will still be free to negotiate—or to decline the position—later based on what you learn about the financial compensation package.

What questions should you ask? One possibility is: "What is the next position or positions that typically follow the entry-level job?" This question implies that you are seeking to work for a company where you can build a career and are less likely to change jobs in order to move up the career ladder.

Ask questions that will subtly show the recruiter your knowledge of the industry and of the firm. For example, "I noticed in the business press that your company is the market leader in industrial drill bits in North America. I am curious to know how much of the product line is sold overseas—and whether there are many career opportunities in marketing abroad."

Practice Interviewing

As in most things, practice makes perfect. Once you have developed solid responses to likely interview questions, write the questions on index cards. Shuffle the cards, then practice answering them into a tape recorder, moving quickly from one question to the next. Play the tape back. How did you do? Did you sound confident? Logical? Like a person who would be a good candidate for this job? What can you improve? Practice the same questions with some friends; ask them for feedback. Then, have your friends ask you as many questions as they can for which you *haven't* prepared answers. Are you able to formulate answers quickly? Do they make sense? If not, keep practicing until you feel comfortable with the concept of "thinking on your feet."

Overcoming Nervousness

As if formulating solid answers to interview questions isn't tough enough, you must also prepare how to overcome the nervousness you are almost certainly going to feel, at least during the first few interviews. You can take heart in the fact that you are not alone; virtually everyone is just as nervous as you are in an interview situation. In fact, next to speaking in public, job interviews are perhaps the most dreaded event in the average person's entire life.

You should expect to feel a little edgy—but not paralyzed with fright—as you go into a job interview. The best way to overcome your fears is to practice interviewing as much as you can—especially with real companies. Remember, the more often you do this, the more comfortable you will become.

If you happen to have a terrible interview—and just about everyone does at one time or another—don't let your confidence be shaken. And don't dwell on it, either. Simply chalk the terrible interview up to experience. Learn from your mistakes and work on your interview performance. Sooner or later you'll find another opportunity, and, this time, you'll shine.

Interview Strategy

Your first few interviews will be the toughest. So at least until you get a few under your belt and are feeling more confident, focus your efforts on remaining calm and collected. Listen carefully to what the recruiter is saying and concentrate on responding promptly and thoroughly to the questions. Don't try too hard. If you have been practicing your responses, you should be able to offer appropriate answers without too much difficulty and without sounding too rehearsed.

Once you begin to feel more confident about interviewing, you can start to think more strategically about each interview. One effective tactic is to adjust the speed of your speech to match that of the interviewer. People tend to talk at the speed at which they like to be spoken to. If you can adjust your speech rate to that of the interviewer without sounding unnatural, he or she is likely to feel more comfortable and to have a more favorable impression of you. After all, interviewing others isn't the easiest task, either. The interviewer may, in fact, be almost as nervous as you.

Another strategy is to adapt your answers to match the type of company at which you are interviewing. For example if you are interviewing for a job at a large product marketing company that emphasizes group decision-making and expends much of its energy on battles for market share with its competitors, you might want to talk about how much you enjoy team sports—especially being part of a team and competing, alongside and against others, to win.

Few companies seeking to fill professional career positions will make a job offer after only one interview. In most cases, the first interview is used to narrow the field of applicants to a small number of very promising candidates. During the first interview, then, your goal should be to stand out from a large field of competitors in the most positive way possible. To accomplish this goal, you should subtly emphasize one of your key, distinctive strengths as much as possible throughout the interview. (At the same time, however, be sure that you do not get so caught up in demonstrating that key strength that your responses seem awkward or become overbearing.)

During subsequent interviews, as the competition for the position drops off, recruiters will tend to look not for strengths, but for weaknesses. At this point, you should concentrate on presenting yourself as a well-balanced choice for the position. Listen carefully to the interviewer's questions so that you can determine his or her underlying concerns and dispel them.

Talk with Previous Interviewees

It never hurts to try and find out, in advance, what other job candidates have gone through. If you are interviewing with an on-campus recruiter, you may have an opportunity to talk with other students who have already been interviewed by that person. Check to see who else is on the interview schedule; perhaps someone you know is on the list. If so, and you are scheduled for a later interview, you may be able to find out what questions you are likely to be asked. Remember, however, that the names on the list are your competitors for the job, so be careful to make your inquiries only among people you can truly trust to provide you with accurate information.

Arrive on Time

Some college students have a tendency to arrive late for interviews. There are two major reasons for this: First, inexperienced candidates are likely to forget something or take a little unplanned extra time to prepare. Second, they often underestimate how long it will take them to arrive at the interview location.

The lesson in all of this is clear. You must allow yourself plenty of time to get ready and to travel to your job interview. It is bad form to arrive at the interviewer's office more than ten minutes in advance; by the same token, it is the kiss of death to arrive ten minutes late. To avoid either scenario, you should plan to arrive in the vicinity of the interview location at least thirty minutes early; you can then spend the next twenty minutes composing your thoughts in a nearby coffee shop or working off excess nervous energy with a walk around the block. Interviews are important enough to build in a little extra time. And here's another tip: If you have never been to the interview location before, make a trial run the day before so you know exactly where you are going and the best way to get there. There's nothing more frustrating than to get hung up by a one-way street you didn't know about or an unexpected detour when the clock is ticking.

Chapter Seventeen

At the Interview

So you've scheduled an interview.

Hopefully, by the time you head out for your first interview, you have spent a great deal of time preparing for job interviews in general and for this one in particular. But don't let your preparation become a disadvantage. Once the interview begins, your focus must be on interacting well with the interviewer who is in front of you—as opposed to trying to recall the exact responses you practiced at home. If you are well prepared for the interview, your conduct and responses will readily convey the image that you want to project. (If you did not prepare thoroughly, it's too late now to focus on making the ideal presentation. Instead, you should simply try to come across as a likeable, mature person who will fit in well with the company.)

The recruiter's decision about whether or not you will be invited back for a second interview will most likely be influenced more by your conduct during the first interview than by what you say. This is especially true if you are applying for your first professional position. Remember that recruiters' biggest concerns in hiring entry-level professionals are threefold: Is the candidate mature? Will the candidate fit in well in our organization? Will the candidate be enjoyable to work with? The answers to any one of these questions will not be determined so much by what you say in response to a specific interview question as by the overall impression you make. So, while preparing answers to interview questions in advance is certainly important and should not be left to chance, how you actually conduct yourself during the interview can make an even stronger impact.

Beware of appearing artificial; don't concentrate too much on trying to project the "perfect" image. Visualize yourself as confident, mature, and likeable, and you will project these very qualities.

The Crucial First Few Minutes

The first minutes of any interview are the most important. A recruiter begins sizing up your potential the instant you walk into the room. If you make a bad impression initially, the recruiter may rule you out immediately and not pay close attention to your performance during the rest of the interview. An excellent initial impression, on the other hand, will put a favorable glow on everything else you say and do during the rest of the interview—and could actually encourage the recruiter to ask less demanding questions.

How can you ensure that you make a terrific first impression? For starters, be sure you are dressed appropriately. When the recruiter meets you for the first time, he or she will notice your clothes and grooming first. And, as we noted in Chapter 16, nothing less than impeccable grooming will do. Your attire must be professional, well-fitted, and squeaky clean.

In virtually the same instant the recruiter takes notice of your clothes and grooming—even before either of you speaks—your body language will begin to affect the way you are perceived. Even an inexperienced recruiter who is not consciously seeking to make a "first read" will notice and react to your body language. Did you smile before greeting him? (Smiling sincerely is a universally attractive trait.) Did you walk straight up to her with a confident (but not overly aggressive) gait? Did you extend your right hand naturally to begin a firm (but not vise-like) handshake? Was your briefcase, note pad, and coat in your left hand or did you have to juggle them around in order to shake hands? Did you make just enough eye contact without staring at the recruiter? Did your eyes travel naturally to the recruiter's face as you began to talk? Did you remember the recruiter's name and pronounce it with confidence?

Did you wait for the recruiter to invite you to sit down, or did you just plop into the chair on your own? Alternatively, if the recruiter forgot to invite you to take a seat, did you awkwardly ask if you might be seated as though to point out the recruiter's lapse in etiquette? Or did you gracefully help yourself to a seat without comment? Did you make small talk easily, or did you act formal and reserved, as though under attack?

As you can see from this scenario, the first impression you make at an interview is dramatically affected by how relaxed and confident you feel. This is why it is so important to practice for each interview—so you can truly present your best first impression.

Greeting and Small Talk

The following is an example of proper greeting and initial small talk between a recruiter (Ms. Jane Smith) and a job candidate (Pauline Harris):

Assuming the door is wide open, Pauline pauses on the threshold of the doorway and waits to make eye contact with the recruiter. (If the door is fully or even partially closed, she should knock and wait for a response before entering the interview room.) As eye contact is made, Pauline smiles immediately at the recruiter and says, in an inquiring and pleasant tone:

> *Pauline:* Ms. Smith?
> *Ms. Smith:* *(Rising from her chair.)* Yes. Pauline Harris?
> *Pauline:* Yes, I am.
> *Ms. Smith:* Come in, please.

Pauline now walks to within about three feet of Ms. Smith. Presumably Ms. Smith has already extended her hand. If so, Pauline should grasp it in a firm but not vise-like grip. If not, and if Ms. Smith is not otherwise occupied, Pauline should extend her hand anyway. (In the unlikely event that Ms. Smith has neither extended her hand nor accepted Pauline's within a second or two, Pauline should withdraw her hand.)

> *Pauline:* It's a pleasure to meet you.
> *Ms. Smith:* It's nice to meet you too, Pauline. Please, have a seat.

Pauline sits down and respectfully waits a short time to give Ms. Smith a chance to initiate conversation. (If Ms. Smith does not initiate conversation after five seconds or so, Pauline may start the conversation herself with an innocuous comment such as "It's really a beautiful day today, isn't it?")

> *Ms. Smith:* How are you today, Pauline?
> *Pauline:* Fine, thank you. (Slight pause.) And yourself?
> *Ms. Smith:* Fine, thank you.

If Ms. Smith does not continue the conversation within a second or two, Pauline might now wish to add a short comment in hopes of further encouraging some small talk, which generally creates a more relaxed and amiable atmosphere for both parties at a job interview.

> *Pauline:* Tuesdays are always good days for me, because that's when I have two of my favorite classes.

Pauline has made use of an excellent conversational opener. She has given Ms. Smith the opportunity to ask what her favorite classes are. But she is not aggressively forcing the conversation by asking a direct question. She is also making a statement that she really enjoys at least two of her classes, thereby implying that she enjoys school in general. This allows the recruiter to infer that she would probably enjoy work and is a pleasant person to be around. Pauline is also discreetly guiding the interview toward one of the strengths—in this case, academics—that she wishes to highlight. If her strengths were elsewhere, Pauline might have made a different comment, such as: "Today's really been a great day for me—in fact, I just got back from a terrific track practice."

Structured or Unstructured?

Interviewing styles typically fall into one of two categories, structured and unstructured. In a structured interview, the recruiter will generally ask you a prescribed set of questions seeking relatively brief answers. In the unstructured interview, the recruiter asks more open-ended questions in an effort to prod you into giving longer responses and revealing as much as possible about yourself, your background, and your aspirations. Some recruiters will mix both styles, typically beginning with more objective questions and asking more open-ended, subjective questions as the interview progresses.

Listen carefully to each question so that you may answer them in the manner the recruiter desires. Try to determine as quickly as possible if the recruiter's interview style is structured or unstructured, then respond to the questions accordingly. As you answer the questions, watch for signals from the recruiter to determine whether your responses are too short or too long. For example, if there's a lot of dead air between questions, as if your interviewer might be waiting for more information, your answers are too short. If, on the other hand, the recruiter is nodding or looking away while you continue talking, that could be a signal that your answer is too long; wrap it up as quickly as possible.

It is vitally important that you follow the style the recruiter establishes during the interview. This will make the interview easier and more enjoyable for both of you and will leave the recruiter with a more favorable impression of you.

Staying Positive

Many inexperienced job candidates kill their chances for a job by making negative comments during an interview. A college student or recent grad should never make a negative statement about a former boss or teacher—even if it is completely true and fully justified. If the recruiter asks why you had an unsatisfactory grade in a particular course, *do not* say "the professor graded me unfairly" or "I didn't get along with the professor."

A recruiter would rather hire someone who gets and deserves an unsatisfactory grade in a course than someone who either doesn't get along with people or shifts blame to others. On the other hand, you can greatly increase your chances of getting any job by projecting a positive, upbeat attitude during your job interview. It's one of the very best ways you can stand out from the competition, in fact. How do you project a positive image? By smiling from time to time during the interview, by responding to interview questions with enthusiasm, by demonstrating excitement about your past accomplishments, and by showing optimism about the prospect of starting your career.

Handling Impossible Questions

One of the biggest fears that job candidates harbor about job interviews is the prospect of facing an unknown question for which they have no answer. And as if you aren't nervous enough about this issue, some recruiters may actually ask a question knowing full well that you can't possibly answer it.

They do this simply to see how you will respond. It's not that they enjoy watching you squirm in your seat, but rather they want to assess how you might respond to pressure or tension on the job. If you are asked a tough question that you simply can't answer, think about it for a few seconds. Then with a confident smile and without apology, simply say, "I don't know" or "I can't answer that question."

Answering Questions that Require Commitment

Even in some first interviews, you may be asked questions that seem to elicit a tremendous commitment on your behalf. For example, the recruiter might ask "Would you be willing to travel overseas for four-week stretches?" Or, "Would you be willing to move to our overseas technical training center for two years?" Or, "Would you be willing to work twelve-hour shifts on Saturdays and Sundays?" While it may be true that such questions are extremely unfair to ask during an initial job interview, you probably have nothing to gain and everything to lose by saying "No"—or even "I need to think about it." A negative answer could cost you the opportunity for a second interview. If you are asked such a question unexpectedly during an initial job interview, it's best that you simply answer in the affirmative. If you are actually offered a job at a later date, you can ask about specific work conditions and then decide if you wish to accept the position. Does this come under the category of lying to the interviewer, a practice we have warned against in previous chapters? No, because this is a hypothetical situation for which you have only sketchy details on which to base your answer; there should be no penalty for changing your mind once you learn the complete requirements of the job. Could this approach jeopardize your candidacy for any other, perhaps better jobs the recruiter might have? Probably not. Simply explain to the recruiter that now that you have had time to think about it, you cannot accept a position that involves (for instance) travel, but that you would like to be considered for other positions that become available.

Asking Your Own Questions

As the interview is coming to a close, the recruiter will probably say something like, "Are there any questions you would like to ask?" It is essential that you have a few questions to ask at this point, otherwise you are likely to be perceived as not serious about pursuing a career at this company. As part of your interview preparation, you should come up with a lengthy list of questions. Since some of your planned questions may already have been covered by the time you reach this stage of the interview, you will want to have plenty of extras in reserve.

Use the questions that you ask your interviewer to subtly demonstrate your knowledge of the firm and the industry, and to underscore your interest in seeking a long-term career position at the firm. But do not allow your questions to become an interrogation—pose only two or three in a thoughtful manner. Do not ask any questions that will be difficult or awkward for the recruiter to answer, or which might sound confrontational. This is not the time to ask, for example, "Does your company use recycled paper for all of its advertising brochures?"

It bears repeating that you should never ask about salary or fringe benefits until after you have received a firm job offer. If the recruiter brings up the subject by stating what the salary and benefits are, your best response is no response. If the recruiter specifically asks for your opinion, you should indicate that the terms seem acceptable, even if this is not necessarily true. Later, when you are offered the job, you can say that you have given the matter a good deal of thought and that you would like to negotiate the terms. (Please note, however, that this advice does not apply to a professional with years of solid work experience.)

The following are suggestions for some good questions to ask, assuming, of course, that these issues have not already been covered during the interview:

Assuming I was hired and performed well as a (the position you are applying for) for a number of years, what possible opportunities for promotion might be available to me?

This question implies you are looking to build a long-term career.

I have noticed in the trade press that your firm has a terrific reputation in marketing. What are the major insights into the marketing process that I might gain from this position?

This question implies that not only are you interested in a long-term career in this industry, but that you might lean toward taking a job with this firm because of its positive reputation, and that you have a real interest in building your job skills.

What skills are considered most useful for success in the job I'm applying for?

This question implies that you really care about being successful at your first job and also provides important information for further interviews—or your follow-up after this interview.

I would really like to work for your firm. I think it's a great company and I am confi-dent I could do this job well. What is the next step in the selection process?

More than a question, this is a powerful statement that will quickly set you apart from other job hunters. But beware—make this statement only if you really mean it. If you are offered the position on the spot (not very likely, but it's possible), then say you need two weeks to think it over, you will lose your credibility. However, even after making this statement, it is reasonable to ask for 24 or 48 hours to "digest the details."

Chapter Eighteen

Commonly Asked Interview Questions—and Their Answers

The following interview questions and suggested responses are provided as examples to show you how questions should be handled. They should not be used as the basis of "canned" or scripted answers. Adapt these responses to your own circumstances, but remember, too, that how you deliver the answer may be more important than what you say. Be positive, project confidence, smile and make eye contact with the interviewer, and listen carefully, then go with the flow!

Questions about School Grades

Question: Why didn't you get better grades in school?

Answer: I really enjoy school and learning. I study consistently, and I'm attentive in class. But I never cram before the night of an exam just to get a higher grade or stay up all night to finish a term paper. I believe I have learned just as much as many students who "went for the grades."

Question: Why are your grades so erratic?

Answer: I never hesitated to sign up for a course just because it had a reputation for being difficult. In fact, my American History professor, whose course I enjoyed tremendously, is notorious for giving out only one "A" grade per class. You may have noticed that, while my major is English, I did take four courses in physics. I did so because I thought these courses were important to round out my education, and I enjoyed the challenge they presented. Most of the other students in these courses were physics majors.

Questions about Academics

Question: What was your favorite class?

Answer: Outside of my major, one of the classes I particularly enjoyed was an introductory course in economics that I took last semester. It was a completely new subject area for me and I enjoy new challenges. I was particularly fascinated with macroeconomic theory in which complex mathematical equations are combined with psychology to explain past economic events and predict future trends.

Question: What course did you find most challenging?

Answer: Initially, I was completely overwhelmed by the introductory chemistry course I took last year. No matter how hard I studied, I seemed to be getting nowhere. I failed the first three quizzes. So I tried a new approach. Instead of just studying by myself, I asked a friend—a chemistry major—to help me with my studies. I also began to seek help periodically after class from the professor. And I found that more time spent in the lab was critical. I ended up with a B+ in the course and felt I achieved a solid understanding of the material. More than that, I learned that tackling a new field of study sometimes requires a new approach, not just hard work, and that the help of others can be crucial.

Question: How do you organize yourself for a large project such as writing a term paper?

Answer: Let me use the paper I wrote for my American History class last semester as an example. My first step was to read a book that presented a survey of the time period involved in order to narrow the topic and work up a tentative one-page outline. I also surfed the Web for possible resources and gathered all of the appropriate books for reference, then began compiling notes on index cards. I organized the index cards as logically as possible and developed a tentative thesis statement. After that, I composed a revised and much more detailed outline. Finally I put my thoughts on paper following both my outline and the index cards I had compiled.

Question: How do you prepare for a major examination?

Answer: Well, let's take a recent exam I had in 20th Century Art as an example. First I skimmed the material from two lessons that I felt particularly weak on. Then I went through all my class notes again, marking with a highlighting pen the most important points from each class. I went back through the chapter summaries in the basic textbook for every lesson except for those I had just read this last week. Then I reviewed the key points from each class that I had highlighted.

Question: Why did you decide to major in history?

Answer: It was a difficult choice because I was also attracted to government, international relations, and economics. But the study of history allowed me to combine all three, especially since I focused on economic history. What's more, I found several of the professors in the department to be exceptionally knowledgeable and stimulating; I enjoyed attending their classes.

Question: I see the title of your senior thesis is "A Comparative Study of Causal Analyses of the Great Depression." Tell me about your thesis and the conclusions of your study.

Answer: It's fascinating to me that even today, there is tremendous disagreement among scholars about the relative importance of various factors leading to the Great Depression. I examined the methodologies used in some of the most prominent works and critically compared their ability to explain this phenomenon. I concluded that the most meaningful analysis gave essentially equal weight to psychological and economic factors.

Questions about Extracurricular Activities

Question: Why did you participate so little in extracurricular activities?

Answer: I wanted to give as much effort as possible to my studies. I came from a high school in a very small town where I received mostly "As," but, sadly, this did not prepare me very well for college. So I have studied very hard to maintain the same level of academic achievement. Still, despite spending a lot of time with my books, I have found time to make many friends in the area, and I do enjoy informal socializing on the weekends.

Question: You seem to have participated a little bit in a lot of different extracurricular activities. Didn't any of them really hold your interest?

Answer: I've always felt it was important to have a well-rounded education, and I looked at extracurricular activities as an important part of that education. That's why I participated in many different activities—to broaden my experience and to meet new people. I did particularly enjoy the drama club and the cycling team, but I made a conscious effort not to spend too much time on any one particular activity, but to try new and different ones.

Question: You are certainly a talented athlete. You won a school-wide singles ping-pong championship, you have a low handicap at golf, and you participate in horse riding competitions. But I'm surprised that you don't list any team sports on your resume.

Answer: I'm the kind of person who enjoys staying with an activity for a long period of time and becoming extremely proficient at it. While I do play team sports on a "pickup" basis, I have chosen to focus on sports that I will be able to play for years to come, long after I have left college.

Question: I see you made the football team as a sophomore. Why didn't you play varsity football your junior or senior years?

Answer: While I enjoyed the comradeship and being "part of the team," I did find practices and drills to be tedious and unchallenging. I always was assigned to play guard, and how many different ways can you block a rusher? Instead I joined the Drama Club and was able to give some more time to my studies. While I didn't become a great actor, it was an enriching experience.

Question: I see that you were vice president of your class for three years. Did you run for president?

Answer: Yes, I ran for president every year and lost every year. If I wasn't graduating this year, I would run for president next year too—I never quit. I campaigned hard each year, but never to the detriment of my studies.

Question: Where would you like to be in five years?

Answer: I plan to remain in the banking industry for the foreseeable future following graduation. I hope that within five years I will have developed a successful track record as a loan officer, with consumer loans first perhaps, but then switching to business loans. Ideally, I would hope that within five years I will also have advanced to working with middle-market-sized companies.

Questions about Tough Academic Situations

Question: Your transcript reads "incomplete" for your second semester sophomore year courses. Why is that?

Answer: I was suspended from school for the second half of the semester for being at a party where there was excessive drinking and damage to school property. While I did not cause any damage to school property myself, I accept responsibility for the incident. I paid the penalty and learned my lesson. And I was grateful for the opportunity to return to school. I applied myself with vigor to my studies and have never been involved in any other incidents.

Question: I see that you failed two courses the last semester of your freshman year, then took a year off before returning to school. I assume there is a connection?

Answer: Four years ago, as a freshman, I didn't know what I wanted to study, what career I wanted to pursue, or what direction I was headed in. The year off from school was one of the most constructive experiences of my life. After working as a dishwasher in a restaurant for much of the year, I developed a greater respect for the value of a college education. I came back to school completely refreshed, embarked on a major in English and committed myself to pursuing a career in which I could use my mind a little more and my hands a little less.

Questions about Past Work Experience

Question: What were your responsibilities as a clerk during your summer job at Reliable Insurance Brokers?

Answer: The company was in the process of transferring its files to a new computer system. The primary task for which I was hired was to check the transferred files for accuracy vis-à-vis the previous files. I also recorded premium payments, prepared bank deposits, and sorted payables during the two weeks the bookkeeper was on vacation.

Question: Did you enjoy your summer job as a dishwasher at Washington Street Grill?

Answer: I wouldn't want to do it for the rest of my life, but it was fine for a summer job. The work was more interesting than you might think, I enjoyed my co-workers, and I had great rapport with my boss.

Question: I see you worked as a lifeguard one summer, mowed lawns another summer, and babysat during the two other summers. Which job did you find most interesting?

Answer: Actually, by far the most interesting job I held wasn't a summer job at all, but a part-time job I had at school performing research for my political science professor's just-published book entitled *The Disaffected Electorate*. The book is based on extensive surveys which show that most people feel that state and federal politicians are not responsive to their constituents. I personally conducted hundreds of door-to-door interviews to compile the information and helped tabulate the results. It was fascinating to be a part of this study almost from start to finish and at the same time it was dismaying to see, from the results, how disenfranchised people feel today.

Question: I see that you've been working as a waiter at Sam's Bar & Grill since graduation. How much notice would you have to give there if I offered you this position?

Answer: I would feel obliged to offer my current employer two weeks' notice. But if my boss does not object, I might be able to leave sooner.

Questions about Evaluating Your Former Employers

Question: Who was the toughest boss you ever had and why?

Answer: That would be Mr. Henson at Henson's Car Wash. He would push people to their limits when it got busy, and he was a stickler for detail. But he was always fair, and he went out of his way to be flexible with our work schedule and generous in advancing salaries when one of the kids was in a pinch. I would call him a tough boss, but a good boss.

Question: Tell me about a time last summer when your employer was not happy with your job performance

Answer: In the first week on the job there were two letters that had typos in them. Frankly, I had been a little sloppy with my proofreading. But that's all that comes to mind. Ms. Heilman did tell me on at least two occasions that she was very happy with my work.

Questions about Lack of Work Experience

Question: What did you do during the summer between your freshman and sophomore years at college? Your resume doesn't indicate anything about this period of time.

Answer: I tried to get a job, but the town I live in was hit very hard by the closings of a major automobile plant and several smaller industrial manufacturing facilities. I personally visited at least 100 businesses searching for work, but to no avail. That took most of June. I spent

July reviewing much of my calculus course, which was one of the toughest classes I ever took. Then in August, I moved in with a friend who had a small apartment near campus, sleeping on his living room couch. I did this so I could work temporary labor jobs in the city.

Question: I see that while you returned to your hometown each summer you worked at a different company. Why didn't you work the same job two summers in a row?

Answer: My career goal is to get a job in business after graduation. Because I attend a liberal arts college, I wasn't able to take any courses in business. So even though I was invited back to every summer job I held., I thought I could develop more experience by working in different positions at different companies. Although I didn't list high school jobs on my resume, I did work for almost three years at the same grocery store chain.

Question: I see that you traveled each of the last two summers rather than take a summer job. Do you expect to be traveling a lot after you graduate from college?

Answer: I figured that once I graduate from college I'll be spending the next forty years or so of my life working, so I might as well get in some extended travel while I have a chance. I hope to begin a career position immediately upon graduating, and I plan to stay with that company for some time to come.

Questions about Problems at Previous Jobs

Question: Were you ever fired from a summer or part-time job?

Answer: Yes. I had a part-time courier job during my freshman year. I became violently ill with a stomach bug after lunch one day and had to call in sick thirty minutes before my shift began. I was immediately fired. I knew it would be difficult for my boss to get a substitute courier on such short notice, but I really had no choice. I was very dizzy and thought there would be too much risk of an accident if I reported to work.

Questions about Future Plans

Question: Do you plan to attend graduate school?

Answer: Not on a full-time basis, but perhaps part-time. At some point, I might like to take courses at night that could contribute to my work performance.

Question: I see that you grew up in Hawaii. That's a long way away. Do you plan on going back there to live sometime in the future?

Answer: No. I would prefer to be based in a large mainland city, such as where your company is located, but I would be perfectly happy to go wherever my career might take me.

Questions about Your Work Preferences

Question: Why do you want to work in retailing?

Answer: I have been fascinated by the retail trade for as long as I can remember. To me, each store is a like a theater stage for its merchandise; there is an infinite variety of ways in which the exact same merchandise can be displayed and sold. I know retailing is a very challenging field.. Merchants need to think about many things: current fashion trends, the needs of local consumers, and building a niche in the market, as well as all the other aspects of running a business. Also, retail is a field that is changing very quickly today; I want to see firsthand what direction the industry takes in the future.

Question: What other types of positions are you interested in, and what other companies have you recently applied to for work?

Answer: Since I have definitely decided to pursue a career as a restaurant manager, I am only applying for restaurant management training programs. I have recently had interviews with several other large national fast-food chains, including Super Burger and Clackey's Chicken.

Question: Have you thought about why you might prefer to work with our firm as opposed to one of the other firms to which you've applied?

Answer: Yes. I like your policy of promotion from within. I think the company's growth record is impressive and I am sure it will continue. Your firm's reputation for superior marketing is particularly important to me because I want to pursue a career in marketing. Most important of all, it seems that your firm would offer me a lot of opportunities—not just for possible advancement but also to learn about many different product lines—all within one company.

Questions about You as a Person

Question: Tell me about yourself.

Answer: It takes me about thirty minutes in the morning to wake up, but after that I'm all revved up and ready to go. I have a tremendous amount of energy and love challenges at school, at work, and at home. This is true even when I'm performing mundane tasks, such as when I worked at the direct mail house last summer stuffing brochures into envelopes. I challenged myself to have the highest pace of anyone in the office; and I succeeded on every day but four during the entire summer. I also enjoy being around other people, working with them and doing anything I can to help them. For example, I really enjoyed tutoring freshmen in math. So while I push myself to high levels of performance and the achievement of constantly more challenging goals, I try to remain sensitive to the concerns of people around me.

Question: How would you like other people to think of you?

Answer: I like people to think that I am always there when they need me. But even more than that, I want to be thought of as always fair, considerate and even-handed with anyone I meet. I want everyone I come into contact with to be able to say, in retrospect, that meeting me was a positive experience.

Chapter Nineteen

After the Interview

Now that you've made it through the first round, what should you do? First, breathe a sigh of relief. Then, as soon as you've left the interview site, write down your thoughts about the interview while they're still fresh in your mind. Ask yourself key questions. What does the position entail? What do you like and dislike about the position and the company? Did you make any mistakes or have trouble answering any of the questions? Did you feel you were well prepared? If not, what could you do to improve your performance in the future? Carefully consider your answers to all of these questions; if you find that your performance was lacking, work to improve it.

Be sure to record the name and title of the person with whom you interviewed, as well as the names and titles of anyone else you may have met during your visit to the company. Don't forget to write down the next agreed-upon step. Will they contact you? How soon?

Writing Your Follow-Up Letter

Next, write a brief follow-up letter thanking the interviewer. Do this immediately—within one or two days of the interview—in order to make sure that you stay in the forefront of the recruiter's mind. Your letter should be typewritten and no longer than one page. Express your appreciation for the opportunity to interview with the recruiter and your continued enthusiasm about the position and the company. Above all, make sure that the letter is personalized—do not send out a form letter!

An example of a letter you might send to a prospective employer after a job interview can be found at the end of this chapter.

Calling to Follow Up

After sending your follow-up letter, allow the employer approximately a week to ten days to contact you. If, after ten days or so, you still have not heard anything from the employer, you should follow up with a phone call of your own. Express your continued interest in the firm and in the position; inquire as to whether or not any decisions have been made or when you might be notified.

What's Next?

Don't be discouraged if you do not get an immediate response from an employer—most companies interview many applicants before making a final decision. The key is to remain fresh in the recruiter's mind. Once you have sent your thank you letter and made a follow-up call, it's pretty much a waiting game.

But don't just sit by the phone! Take advantage of this time: contact other firms and schedule more interviews so that if rejection does come, you have other options open. This is a good idea even if you do end up receiving a job offer because you'll have a number of options to choose from and you'll be in a better position to make an informed decision. If you place too much importance on a single interview, you will not only waste time and energy, you will also increase the chances of a drop in your morale if the initial offer doesn't come through. So keep plugging away at your job search. Who knows what wonderful things might result?

Handling Rejection

Rejection is inevitable, and it will happen to you as it happens to all other job-hunters. The key is to not take it personally.

One way to turn rejection around is to contact each person who sends you a rejection letter. Thank the recruiter for considering you for the position and, if you feel comfortable doing so, ask for feedback so that you can improve your resume or subsequent interview performances. Ask for suggestions that might help you improve your chances for getting a job in the industry. Ask for the names of people who might require your skills—or just be willing to talk with you about the industry. Ask, "What would you do in my situation? Who would you call?"

Two cautions are in order here. First, do not ask an employer to tell you specifically why you weren't hired. Not only does this put the employer in an awkward position, it will probably generate an extremely negative reaction. And second, realize that even if you contact employers solely for impartial feedback, not everyone will be willing to provide it. As our society grows ever more litigious, the employer who didn't hire you, for whatever reason, may not want to talk for fear of legal repercussions.

Regardless of whether or not you choose to contact recruiters who have rejected you, don't use rejection as an excuse to give up on your job search. Stay positive and motivated, and learn from the process. Okay, so you didn't get this job, but you might get the next one. Success could be just around the corner.

SAMPLE FOLLOW-UP LETTER

460 Brook Road
Santa Fe, NM 87541
505/555-5561

September 22, 2007

Joseph C. Barber
Director of Human Resources
Kendall Pharmaceuticals
11241 Sundown Drive
Albuquerque, NM 87154

Dear Mr. Barber:

Thank you for the opportunity to discuss your opening for a statistician. I enjoyed meeting with you and Ms. Tate and learning more about Kendall Pharmaceuticals.

I believe that my experience at the Department of Labor and my educational background in statistics, economics, and business administration qualify me for the position. My extensive knowledge of computers and statistical software would also be especially valuable to me as a statistician with your firm.

I was particularly impressed with Kendall's strong commitment to innovation and growth, as well as its plans to expand into the overseas market. I feel that this type of environment would challenge me to do my best work.

I look forward to hearing from you within the next two weeks. In the meantime, please call me if I can provide more information or answer any additional questions to assist in your decision.

Sincerely,

Alison Ann Granville

Alison Ann Granville

IV

Landing the Job

Chapter Twenty

The Job Offer

Congratulations! You've received a job offer—or maybe several. What do you do now?

Let's begin with some basic details you should take into consideration as you evaluate the offer. What is the minimum salary you can live on? What is the going rate in the current market for this particular position? You shouldn't have to scramble to come up with these figures. If you've been following the guidelines in previous chapters, this is information you should have already accumulated as part of your research into possible jobs and preferred industries. You will need to pull it now before you enter into negotiations with a potential employer.

To consider an offer seriously, you should feel confident that this is a job you really want, that the field is one in which you'd like to pursue a career, and that you are willing to live and work in the area in question. Ask yourself this: Is the lifestyle and work schedule associated with this potential new occupation one I could enjoy? Presumably, during the interview process, you've had time to think about these issues and about whether or not this particular position satisfies your basic financial requirements.

Important Factors to Consider

Once you're received a firm offer, you should have all the information about the position necessary to make a sound decision. This includes:

- Start date
- Job title and associated responsibilities
- Potential for career progression
- Salary, overtime pay, and other compensation
- Bonus structure
- Tuition reimbursement or possible graduate studies

- Vacation and parental leave policy
- Life, disability, medical, and dental insurance coverage
- Pension or 401(k) plan
- Job location
- Travel expectations

If you are unsure about any of these details, do not simply assume that everything will be to your satisfaction. Contact the company's human resources representative or the recruiter to confirm all important details.

Money

Money may seem like the most important criterion for accepting a job, but beware; the prospect of a substantial salary can often color the decision-making process. Don't accept a job you are less than enthusiastic about simply because the starting salary is a few thousand dollars higher than another offer you have received. (After taxes, that few thousand dollars may be virtually meaningless anyway.) Concern yourself, instead, with finding a job that lets you do something you enjoy; all the money in the world will not make up for working, day after tedious day, at a job you hate. Ask yourself whether the job presents a career path with upward mobility and the opportunity to acquire valuable experience, whether it will enable you to establish yourself in a particular field and have greater career opportunities in your future. Don't make the mistake of convincing yourself that you "want" a job solely because the salary looks good.

Benefits

Benefits can make a huge difference in your compensation package—don't overlook them! Given the cost of hospitalization and pharmaceuticals these days, health insurance is perhaps the most important benefit to consider. Evaluate the company's health insurance plan carefully. It is unusual today to find an employer that pays for the full cost of their employees' health coverage. Typically, companies pay a portion of the cost of health insurance with the remainder coming from the employee's salary. (One positive here: the money you pay for health coverage is frequently not subject to federal taxes.) Find out what percentage and dollar amount of health insurance payments you will be responsible for. Health care plans also differ on the amount you pay out of your own pocket before your insurance kicks in to cover the rest. Consider how much you might need to pay, even with insurance, for ordinary or unexpected medical situations.

What about life, disability, and dental insurance? Does the company have a bonus structure? (This can contribute significantly to your salary.) Is there a retirement plan? If it's a 401(k), what is the company's policy on matching the contributions you make?

What about vacation days, sick time, and personal leave? These are all factors that you should consider carefully in making your decision to accept or reject an offer.

If graduate school is in your future plans, find out if the company will pay for your education and if you'll be given time off to attend classes. Some organizations offer tuition incentives but require so much overtime it is almost impossible to take advantage of the education benefit.

Career Progression

Career progression is another important factor in evaluating any offer. Some organizations may bring you on board at a relatively high level, then curtail your ability to move up the career ladder. Be clear about future opportunities for advancement. Find out how often performance reviews are conducted, a factor which could have a considerable impact on your salary in the long run. Don't let a low starting salary discourage you too much. Understand the long-range income potential as well.

Work Environment

Another important factor to consider is the kind of environment in which you will be working. Is the atmosphere comfortable, challenging, exciting? Consider specifics, too, such as whether you will have a private office or work in a cubicle. If possible, ask to see your actual work station. How much privacy will you have in relation to other staff? How much desk space will you have? What kind of computer system and software will you be using? What is the ambiance in terms of noise level and lighting?

Then, too, there's the matter of interaction among co-workers. Some organizations strongly encourage teamwork and dialogue among staff, while others prefer to emphasize individual accomplishment and discourage a great deal of interaction among employees. Which approach do you prefer? It's important to consider all of these factors carefully; if you don't like the work environment before you accept the job, there's a pretty good chance you won't grow to like it as an employee.

Do Your Homework

Supplement the information provided by the organization by searching journals and newspapers for articles about the company. If possible, talk to current or past employees. Try to get objective comments. Information from someone who was recently fired by the company is likely to be unreliable. Alumni of your college or university who hold similar positions or are employed by the same organization may be excellent sources of information.

The Art of Negotiation

If you are disappointed or dissatisfied with any of the conditions of the offer you receive, don't just turn it down; find out first what may be negotiable. Some organizations offer flexible benefits packages or "menu" benefit plans that allow an employee to choose from a variety of options. Now is the best time to inquire about such plans.

If you are unable to negotiate an arrangement with which you feel comfortable, it may be an indication that you should consider other offers or continue looking for a position that better meets your needs. Don't make the mistake of accepting a position that you are unhappy with. Listen to that little voice in your head and trust your instincts. If you are dissatisfied with an employer even before your start date, it is unlikely that your attitude will change once you accept the job. The uncertainties you are feeling now will almost surely have a negative impact on your work and your success.

At the same time, however, you must keep in mind that competition for jobs is fierce in today's tough economy. Employers don't have to look very far to find someone else to fill the position you turned down. Keep your expectations realistic and don't ask for the stars right now. After all, you are just fresh out of college and have a lot of working to do before you can begin making demands. Once you've been working for a particular employer for a while and have proven yourself to be a valuable commodity, you can attempt further negotiations.

Making Your Final Decision

The most important thing to consider in evaluating an offer is whether you will be happy with the job and be able to accomplish what is important to you. Don't accept a job because your friend works at the company or because a relative thinks you'd be crazy to turn it down. By all means, talk the offer over with other people, but trust your own reasoning abilities. If you are confused, discuss your concerns with a career counselor and then make an informed decision based on what is right for you. Remember, this is your job, and your choice.

Chapter Twenty-One

Any Questions?

On the following pages, we've provided answers to some of the most common questions college students and recent grads have about job searching.

How many companies should I expect to contact before I actually find a job?
This varies from person to person, but you can be sure that you will have to contact a lot of companies—possibly as many as 100 or 200—before you find an acceptable job. Occasionally, a student gets lucky and lands a job soon after beginning the search, but such cases are few and far between.

Remember, the more effort you put into your job search and the more companies you contact each week, the more likely it is that you'll get a job sooner than someone who is only searching casually and sending out just one or two resumes a week. It bears repeating: making only a half-hearted stab at your job search effort is a major error. Students who make this mistake typically find themselves discouraged after making little or no progress over the course of several months, and often settle for the first offer that comes along—even if it isn't for a job they really want.

How do I decide which job to seek?
Consider the good part-time jobs you've had, the classes you enjoyed most, or your extracurricular interests. Identify the activities or skills you'd like to develop further. Do you prefer to work alone or with a team? Your answer will help you determine whether you would enjoy a work environment where there is a lot of teamwork and socializing, or one in which individual problem solving is the norm. What kinds of people do you like to work with? You may shine among imagina-

tive people who like to brainstorm solutions, or you may prefer to associate with highly-organized co-workers who make data-driven decisions quickly.

Do you prefer to work on many projects at once, or to concentrate on one assignment at a time? What about your social and lifestyle preferences? Some jobs require certain behaviors and dress. Can you see yourself talking on the phone for several hours a day, sitting in meetings or in front of a computer terminal for long stretches of time, making presentations to clients or co-workers, or being outdoors a good share of every week? You may decide that the values and goals of the organization you work for are more important to you than the tasks you perform or the physical environment in which you work.

Companies vary greatly in work environments—and in what they expect from their employees. It is up to you to determine what you like most and the skills or qualities you want to develop in yourself. Using what you discover about yourself, you can decide whether a given job represents a good match.

Another way to gain insight is to meet with people already employed in the field. Contact your career services office and/or your alumni association office to see if they have mentor programs or if they can refer you to alumni or other contacts who can help you meet with established professionals in a particular field. This is one of the best ways to get inside information about a job. And when you meet with these contacts, don't be afraid to ask questions: What do you like (and dislike) about your job? How did you get started in the field? If you decide to pursue a job in this area, you'll not only have gathered valuable information, you'll have gained a potential contact as well.

Above all, keep in mind that first jobs do not necessarily reflect what you will do for the rest of your life. A career can take many years to develop. So rather than ask yourself, "What career is right for me?" ask instead, "What would I like to try first?"

Will it hurt my chances of getting a good job if I take time off the summer after graduation?

Unfortunately, it probably will. Companies like to hire students who want to go to work right away. You have a much stronger chance of getting a great job while you are still a student preparing for graduation than you do after the fact. Of course, you can still get a good job after graduation, especially if you are aggressive about it. But, if at all possible, you shouldn't wait until after you leave school to start looking for a job. Your best bet is to begin your job search early in your senior year so that you have an advantage over other those students who do procrastinate. Remember, you're just one of a whole host of other graduates who are also looking for jobs; the sooner you get started, the more successful you will be.

I'm having a hard time getting informational interviews. What should I do?
Many people who are contacted by job seekers automatically assume that the person on the other end of the phone is calling to ask for a job. In order to counter this misperception, tell your contact up front that all you are asking for is an opportunity to learn more about the industry or company in question. Also, unless specifically requested, do not send your resume to someone with whom you'd like to meet for an informational interview. Cluttering your request with a resume is almost certain to give the wrong impression.

What benefits should I expect?
That depends on the size of the company. A small company with fewer than a dozen or so employees may not offer any benefits at all. A large company with hundreds or thousands of employees, on the other hand, will probably offer a very attractive benefits package. The most commonly offered benefit (besides paid vacation and sick days) is health care. Typically, companies offer either a health insurance plan that allows you to choose your own doctor, or a Health Maintenance Organization (HMO) plan that requires you to choose a health care provider from a specified list. In either case, however, very few companies today pay for 100% of an employee's health insurance or HMO costs. At some companies you may be expected to pay as much as 50% or more of these costs. The amount that you will be expected to pay out of your own pocket for health care is certainly an important factor to consider when weighing job offers.

Other benefits that might be offered include life insurance, disability insurance, tuition reimbursement, pension or 401(k) plans, and profit-sharing plans. When evaluating job offers, be sure that you fully understand the fringe benefits; they can make a significant difference in your decision to accept one offer over another. And remember, it is bad form to even ask about benefits until after you have been offered the position.

Can I expect to find a job if there is a high unemployment rate in my city or town?
No matter how high the unemployment rate is in a particular area, jobs will still be available. However, they may be more difficult to find and the competition may be more intense. In such cases, you might be better off trying to find a job in another city where the unemployment rate isn't quite so high. On the other hand, no matter where you are, there is always movement within the workforce itself—the regular transition of people entering and leaving the workforce, changing jobs, new jobs being created, etc. As a result, many opportunities may be available even when the unemployment rate is high.

So don't let statistics scare you. Remember, you are looking for just one job, and you have a considerable amount of control over the kind of job you get and how long it takes you to land it because you control how much effort you put into your job search campaign.

I'm a full scholarship student. Won't employers understand if I don't buy a professional outfit for interviews?

No. Employers fully expect that every applicant, regardless of his or her financial situation, will come to the interview dressed professionally. You don't need to be on the leading edge of fashion, but the clothes you wear to your interview must be clean, somewhat on the conservative side, and fit well.

I'm sending out lots of letters—but I'm not getting interviews. What should I do?

Perhaps you are sending out enough letters—but are you making enough follow-up phone calls? Many students try to avoid making phone calls, assuming that employers will contact them. Following up your resume and cover letter with a phone call will dramatically increase your chances of getting an interview.

But what if you are sending out lots of letters *and* making lots of phone calls, and you still aren't getting interviews? If this is the case, then you really need to reconsider all aspects of your job search campaign. Ask yourself:

- Given my education and experience, is this position a realistic one for me?
- Does my resume look sharp?
- Is my cover letter personalized, or does it resemble a form letter?
- Am I sending out a large number of letters each month or just a few dozen?
- Am I contacting companies that are smaller and less known? Am I using *all* the job-search methods outlined in Chapter 4?
- Am I networking as much as I should be?

If you are getting lots of interviews but no job offers, chances are you need to work on your interviewing skills. Remember, you should consider not only what you say during job interviews but how you say it. Do you present yourself as mature and confident or are you nervous and unsure of your answers? If you need to polish your interview performance, you might want to pick up a copy of *Knock 'Em Dead: The Ultimate Job Search Guide* by Martin Yate. The most popular job-hunting book ever written, *Knock 'Em Dead* offers tips that can help you improve your interview skills dramatically and increase your chances of winning job offers.

Whatever you do, *practice, practice, practice!* There is simply no substitute for it. Practice interviewing with different relatives and friends—even on your own in front of the mirror. The more you practice, the more confident you'll become and the better you'll be able to present yourself during actual interviews.

Is the phone book a good place to find companies to contact?

The phone book can certainly be a useful source of company listings for job hunters. However, there are many other resources (such as the *JobBank* series discussed in Chapter 7) which, in addition to addresses and telephone numbers, provide information about the company, typical positions that might be available, and the names of contact persons. And, of course, don't overlook the company Web site. You'll find a wealth of valuable information there.

I really want to work for a certain large company. How can I get a job there?

As a general rule, it's a bad idea to target a single large company. One of the keys to successful job searching is to apply at many different companies—and not just five or six or even twenty, but hundreds. While it's fine to set your sights on your "dream job," don't make the mistake of waiting for one company to call you. If you do, your chances of getting a good job will be extremely slim, and you will cut yourself off from other great opportunities that might be available.

If, despite these warnings, you still insist on working for a certain large company, there are a few things you] can do to improve your chances. First, find out everything there is to know about the company in question. Comb trade publications for information, find articles written about the company, read books about the company (if you can find them), as well as books about the industry in general. Apply for every job you see advertised by the company in newspapers or online; send your resume and cover letter to the human resources office as well as to the head of the department in which you want to work.

And don't forget to network. It's the number one way to land a job. If the firm is very large, there's a good chance that someone you know from high school or college may work there. If this doesn't yield any leads, request an informational interview with someone at the company to find out more about the industry and the company itself. If you can't find contacts through your alumni association or friends and family, ferret out networking leads on your own. Check the business section of your local newspaper, trade publications and the company Web site to find names of people you might contact.

Many large companies have an internal newsletter that is distributed within the organization; job openings are often listed in these publications. Try to get a copy of one from the human resources department—it could be a valuable resource for job leads.

Don't most companies hire almost exclusively through college recruiting, and mostly in the spring?

No! Most companies, even those that recruit on campus, will tell you that about half of their hires are the result of unsolicited resumes and walk-in candidates. And they hire throughout the year, not just in spring. In fact, fall is actually a good time to look for a job, because that's when production cycles begin in many industries.

If I have to travel a long distance for an interview, can I expect the company to pay for my expense?

Not necessarily. While this used to be the norm, companies are increasingly cutting back on recruitment expenses. This means that some companies are relying more heavily on telephone screening, online applications and career fairs, which allow them to review hundreds of applicants per day. If you are looking for a job in a distant city, there's a good chance that the costs of transportation and hotel stays may have to come out of your own pocket. Some companies that are still willing to pay for travel often cut costs by accomplishing more in fewer visits. You may be asked to complete all of your interviews, competency tests, physical exams, and the like during your first—and only—visit.

I'm very shy and the thought of going on job interviews petrifies me. What should I do?

Shyness is not a major problem for most employers unless it interferes with your work. In fact, shy employees may actually be highly valued because they tend to get along well with other workers and don't participate in office politics. Shyness can, however, hurt your chances of landing a job if you resist contacting new people and communicating what you have to offer to a particular company and position.

There are several steps you can take to overcome shyness. First, when networking, contact only people you feel comfortable with and ask them to introduce you to others. This way, you don't have to call any strangers and you know that all of your inquiries will be welcomed. Beginning with friends, relatives, and neighbors, you will soon be well on your way to making important contacts.

Another way to counteract shyness is to seek out volunteer work or an internship in the field you would like to enter. Nonpaying positions allow you the opportunity to demonstrate your skills and abilities rather than having to describe them verbally in a pressure-filled interview. Many employers prefer to hire applicants that have volunteer and internship experience because they are known quantities.

Unfortunately, you probably won't be able to avoid job interviews altogether, so your best bet is to manage your shyness as best you can. For the first few minutes of your interview, just listen to the interviewer talk, interject a few questions or comments here and there as you feel comfortable doing, and allow yourself time to relax. When you are asked about your accomplishments, simply tell what you did rather than try to impress the recruiter with your "brilliance" or suitability for the job he has available. Let recruiters come to their own conclusions; they'll not only see the positive qualities that led to your accomplishments, they'll appreciate your modesty as well.

If it makes you feel more comfortable, tell the recruiter right away that you tend to be shy and that you're feeling a little nervous. This often breaks the ice and will keep the employer from assuming your apparent discomfort is a sign that you are trying to hide something.

Who are the best people to use as references?

The best references are the people for whom you've worked. Recruiters are always more interested in what previous employers have to say about your on-the-job performance than what a professor or friend thinks about you. Your current employer is probably your best reference, but don't be shy about asking previous employers, too.

If you ask someone to provide a letter of recommendation, have the letter sent directly to you rather than to a prospective employer; that way, you know the letter was actually written and sent and you can see its content. When you receive a letter of recommendation, promptly send a thank-you note to the person who wrote it, even if the letter isn't an enthusiastic one. You never know when that person might be called by a prospective employer for a verbal reference. (However, if the letter of recommendation isn't glowing, do not forward it on to a prospective employer.)

How many letters of recommendation do I need?

You don't really need any letters of recommendation to get hired. It's more important that you are able to provide solid references if the employer asks (and he or she probably will). It doesn't hurt, however, to have two or three letters available to present at the interview. (Also, letters of recommendation can substitute for references if the employer has a hard time reaching the people on your list.)

Should I apply to ads in the newspapers that don't identify the employer?

Yes. As you've already learned, you're less likely to get a job through newspaper ads than through other methods such as networking or direct contact. Still, many legitimate job opportunities are advertised through "blind" ads. Companies may choose to run blind advertisements for many good reasons, not the least of which is to avoid being deluged with phone calls. It's possible, too, that a company may be looking to replace someone who has not yet been terminated.

In most cases, blind ads are legitimate, but you should be aware that on rare occasions, they have been used for deceitful purposes. For example, there have been instances in which blind ads were used as a means of selling employment marketing services or for obtaining sexual favors from the applicant.

When newspaper ads ask for salary requirements, should I give them?

State your salary requirements—but as a range. For example, your cover letter may read, "I seek a starting salary between $25,000 and $30,000." If you prefer not to be specific, you may also write "salary is negotiable."

Should I join a professional organization?

For networking purposes, you want to make as many contacts as you possibly can in situations that you feel comfortable in. If you feel comfortable attending meetings of professional associations and don't mind asking people for jobs or advice when you get there, then by all means, join a professional association. If you're not sure how you would feel in such a situation, attend a meeting and find out. Professional association membership can be helpful, but it is certainly not mandatory.

What should I do if I'm asked an illegal interview question?

Some of the people who conduct job interviews simply may not know which interview questions are legal and which are not. Questions about age, race, religion, and marital status are among those that may not, by law, be asked. For more information on this issue, see *Knock 'Em Dead: The Ultimate Job Search Guide* by Martin Yate.

If you are asked an illegal interview question, you may either answer the question or gracefully point out that it is illegal and decline to answer it. Avoid reacting in a hostile manner. There's no point in antagonizing your interviewer (he may just be ignorant of the law) and you can always decide later if this is a company you really want to work for.

Shouldn't I find a job that justifies the investment in my education?

Your salary is important to the extent that it enables you to meet your financial obligations after college. If you choose a job primarily because of the financial rewards, you need to be aware that you are on dangerous ground. Putting money ahead of personal satisfaction is rarely a good idea in the long run.

Conclusion

"No person who is enthusiastic about his work has anything to fear from life."
—*Samuel Goldwyn*

"Nothing happens until you make it happen."
—*Anonymous*

By the time you reach this point in the book, you should be pretty well along in your planning or actual job search. Hopefully, you're turning up more contacts and job leads every day—and if not, you're reevaluating and revising your plan accordingly. Perhaps you're even interviewing and receiving job offers!

Whatever stage you happen to be at right now in your job search, recognize that this can be a long process and that you will likely experience some setbacks along the way. At times you may feel anxious and frustrated, and some days you simply won't want to send out any resumes or make any networking calls. This is perfectly normal. When you come up against such obstacles, however, the key is to make sure you don't let your job search come to a standstill. If you feel that you need to take a break, by all means do so. Just don't stop searching altogether. Simply slow down the pace for a day or two, then get back to full force. In the meantime, even if you're sending out only one letter or making one phone call a day, give yourself a pat on the back; at least you're making some progress.

Job searching is tough for everyone—but if you work hard and focus on your goals, the possibilities for success are practically endless. Your first job can be a source of great personal satisfaction and when you find the right one, you will know that your efforts were worth the price you had to pay in terms of time and energy.

Keep trying, keep learning. You'll land the job that's right for you and the rest will fall into place.

Great Jobs for College Grads

This appendix includes descriptions of some great jobs for college graduates, with an emphasis on those occupations that have especially strong growth outlooks for the next decade or so. For each position, there is a brief description of what the job entails, the background or qualifications you would need for entering and advancing in that occupation, and an indication of working conditions. The outlook for employment in the industry is also provided. The occupations listed are as follows:

Accountant/Auditor
Advertising Worker
Biochemist
Claims Representative
Computer Software Engineer
Computer Systems Analyst
Dietitian/Nutritionist
Economist
Engineer
Financial Analyst/Personal
  Financial Advisor
Forester/Conservation Scientist
Geographer
Geologist/Geophysicist
Graphic Designer
Human Resources and Labor
  Relations Specialist
Industrial Designer
Insurance Agent/Broker

Lodging Manager
Medical Services Manager
Physician Assistant
Physicist
Psychologist
Public Relations Specialist
Purchasing Agent
Quality Control Supervisor
Reporter/Editor
Sales Representative for
  Manufacturers/Wholesalers
Securities, Commodities, and
  Financial Services Sales
  Representative
Social Worker
Statistician
Teacher
Technical Writer/Editor
Underwriter

Accountant/Auditor

Accountants prepare and analyze the reports that furnish important financial information. Four major fields are: public, management, and government accounting; and internal auditing. Public accountants typically have their own businesses or work for public accounting firms. Management accountants, also called industrial, cost, or private accountants, handle the financial records of the company for which they work. Government accountants examine the records of government agencies and audit private businesses and individuals whose activities are subject to government regulation or taxation.

Accountants often concentrate on one phase of accounting. For example, many public accountants specialize in auditing, taxes, or estate planning. Others specialize in management consulting and give advice on a variety of topics. Still others focus on forensic accounting, which involves investigating and interpreting white-collar crimes, such as securities fraud and embezzlement, bankruptcies, and contract disputes. Management accountants provide the financial information corporate executives need to make sound business decisions. They may work in areas such as taxation, budgeting, cost management, performance evaluation, or investments. Internal auditors verify the accuracy of their organization's internal records to ensure adherence to generally accepted accounting practices and efficient, economical operations. Government accountants work in the public sector to maintain and examine the records of local, state, and federal agencies. Accountants and auditors employed in the federal government are often Internal Revenue Service agents or are involved in financial management and budget administration.

About 60 percent of all accountants do management accounting. An additional 25 percent are engaged in public accounting through independent firms. Other accountants work for government, and some teach in colleges and universities. Accountants and auditors are found in all business, industrial, and governmental organizations.

Although the best way to enter the accounting field is with a four-year accounting degree, liberal arts grads should not overlook this field—especially when jobs are scarce. One disadvantage for the non–accounting major is that he or she would probably have to start in a clerical position and learn on the job in order to make career advances.

A typical entry-level position might be general accounting clerk, payroll clerk, accounts receivable clerk, or accounts payable clerk. In applying for any of these positions, a background in computers or data-entry experience is a must. Previous experience in accounting can help an applicant get a job; many colleges offer students the opportunity to gain experience through summer or part-time internship programs at public accounting firms. Such training is invaluable in gaining permanent employment in the field. Professional recognition through certification (CPA designation, for example) or licensure provides a distinct advantage in terms of career advancement.

Employment for accountants and auditors is expected to increase by 18 to 26 percent through 2014. Changing financial laws and regulations and increased scrutiny of company finances as a result of accounting scandals at several large corporations in recent years are helping to drive job growth in this field.

Advertising Worker

Several different occupations are commonly associated with the field of advertising. Advertising managers direct the advertising program of the business for which they work. They determine the size of the advertising budget, the types of ads and media to use, and which outside advertising agency, if any, to employ. Managers who decide to seek outside assistance work closely with the advertising agencies to develop the advertising program for their company's products and services. On the advertising agency side, account executives serve as the liaison between the agency and the client, overseeing the campaign and working with the creative, media, and research directors to ensure that client needs are heard and addressed. Copywriters develop the text and headlines to be used in the ads. Media directors negotiate contracts for advertising space or air time. Production managers and their assistants arrange to have the ad printed for publication, filmed for television, or recorded for radio. Market research analysts compile data, develop research tools, and interpret statistical data to assess past performance and predict future direction of advertising campaigns.

Entry-level positions in most advertising agencies and departments require a bachelor's degree. Some employers seek persons who have degrees in advertising with heavy emphasis on marketing, business, and journalism; others prefer graduates with a liberal arts background. Entry-level creative positions may not require a bachelor's degree. It is possible, for example, to land a job as an assistant art director with a two-year degree from an art or design school or as a junior copywriter with no college credits at all.

Opportunities for advancement in this field are generally excellent for creative, talented, and hard-working people. For example, copywriters and account executives may advance within their specialties or to managerial jobs if they demonstrate the ability to work well with clients. Some especially capable employees may become partners in an existing agency, or they may establish their own agency.

The glamour of the advertising business attracts many more job seekers than there are positions available, which means that competition for jobs is keen. However, employment is projected to grow by 22 percent over the next ten years as the economy expands and generates more products and services to advertise.

Biochemist

Biochemists study the chemical composition and behavior of living things. They often study the effects of food, hormones, or drugs on various organisms in order to analyze the complex chemical reactions involved in metabolism, reproduction, growth, and heredity. The methods and techniques of biochemists are applied in such broad areas as medicine and agriculture. Three out of four biochemists work in basic and applied research activities; some combine research with teaching at the college and university level. A few biochemists work in industrial production and testing activities. Approximately one-half of all biochemists in the workforce are employed by colleges or universities, and about one-fourth work in private industry, primarily in companies manufacturing pharmaceuticals, insecticides, and cosmetics. Some biochemists work for nonprofit research institutes and foundations; others for federal, state, and local government agencies. A few self-employed biochemists act as consultants to industry and government.

In most cases, the minimum educational requirement for many entry-level jobs as a biochemist, especially in research and teaching, is an advanced degree. A Ph.D. is a virtual necessity for persons who hope to contribute significantly to biochemical research and advance to many management or administrative jobs. However, a bachelor's degree in biochemistry, biology, or chemistry may qualify some individuals for entry-level jobs as research assistants or technicians. Graduates with advanced degrees may begin their careers as teachers or researchers in colleges or universities. In private industry, advanced degrees are often a ticket to research jobs; with experience, those who hold graduate degrees may advance to positions in which they plan and supervise research.

While advanced degrees remain important in this field, the outlook for those with bachelor's degrees in the biological sciences is expected to improve as the number of science-related jobs in sales, marketing, and research management grows.

Claims Representative

The people who investigate insurance claims, negotiate settlements with policy holders, and authorize payments are known as claim representatives—a group that includes claims adjusters, appraisers, and examiners. When a casualty insurance company receives a claim, the claims adjuster determines whether the policy covers it and the amount of the loss. Adjusters use reports, physical evidence, and the testimony of witnesses, if applicable, in investigating a claim. When their company is liable, they negotiate with the claimant and settle the case. Some adjusters work with all lines of insurance. Others specialize in claims from fire, marine loss, automobile damage, workers' compensation loss, or product liability.

A growing number of casualty companies employ special adjusters to settle small claims. These workers, generally called "inside adjusters" or "telephone adjusters," contact claimants by telephone or mail to request copies of repair costs, medical bills, and other statements from the policy holder. In life insurance companies, the counterpart of the claims adjuster is the claims examiner, who investigates questionable claims or those exceeding a specified amount. They may check claim applications for completeness and accuracy, interview medical specialists, consult policy files to verify information on a claim, or calculate benefit payments. Generally, examiners are authorized to investigate and approve payment on all claims up to a certain limit. Larger claims are referred to a senior examiner. Another occupation within this field is that of the appraiser, whose role is to assess the cost or value of an insured item. The majority of appraisers employed by insurance companies and independent adjusting firms are auto damage appraisers; they inspect damaged vehicles following an accident and estimate the cost of repairs.

Training and entry requirements vary for claims adjusters, appraisers, and examiners. Although many who work in this field do not have college degrees, more and more companies now prefer to hire college graduates. No specific field of study is recommended, although courses in insurance, economics, or other business subjects are certainly helpful. Most large insurance companies provide beginning claims adjusters and examiners with on-the-job training and home study courses. Claims representatives are encouraged to take continuing education courses designed to enhance their professional skills and to keep them abreast of changes in the law as well as court decisions that may affect how claims are handled and who is covered by insurance policies. Beginning adjusters, appraisers, and examiners work on small claims under the supervision of an experienced employee. As they learn more about claims investigation and settlement, they are assigned claims that are either higher in loss value or more complex. Trainers are promoted as they demonstrate competence in handling assignments and progress in their course work. Employees who show superior abilities in claims work or outstanding administrative skills may be promoted to more responsible managerial or administrative positions. Qualified adjusters and examiners sometimes transfer to other departments, such as underwriting or sales.

As many insurance carriers downsize their claims staffs in an effort to contain costs, the availability of jobs shrinks. However, as long as more insurance policies are being sold to accommodate a growing population, there will be a need for adjusters, appraisers, and examiners.

Computer Software Engineers

Computer software engineers working in applications or systems development analyze users' needs, and design, construct, test, and maintain computer applications software or systems. Software engineers may be involved in the design and development of many types of software, including software for operating systems and network distribution, and for compilers, which convert programs for execution on a computer.

Computer software engineers typically fall into two broad categories: applications and systems. Computer applications software engineers design, construct, and maintain general computer applications software or specialized utility programs; some develop both packaged systems and systems software, or create customized applications. Computer systems software engineers coordinate the construction and maintenance of a company's computer systems with an eye to future growth. Among their responsibilities is the coordination of each department's computer needs—ordering, inventory, billing, and payroll recordkeeping, for example—in order to make suggestions about possible technical direction.

For the position of computer software engineer, most employers prefer to hire persons who have at least a bachelor's degree in computer science or computer information systems, plus broad knowledge of and experience with a variety of computer systems and technologies. More complex jobs may require graduate-level degrees. Entry-level computer software engineers are likely to test and verify ongoing designs. As they become more experienced, they may become involved in designing and developing software. Later, they may advance to a position as project manager or manager of information systems.

Computer software engineers are expected to be among the fastest-growing occupations over the next ten years. Rapid employment growth in the computer systems design and related services industry, which employs the greatest number of computer software engineers, should result in plenty of good job opportunities for students coming out of college with at least a bachelor's degree in computer engineering or computer science and practical experience working with computers.

Computer Systems Analyst

Computer systems analysts solve computer problems and apply computer technology to meet the individual needs of an organization. In addition to helping an organization realize the maximum benefit from its investment in equipment, personnel, and business processes, systems analysts may plan and develop new computer systems or devise ways to apply the existing systems' resources to additional operations. Systems analysts typically begin an assignment by discussing the systems problem with managers and users. After defining the goals of the system and dividing the solutions into individual steps and procedures, systems analysts use such techniques as structured analysis, data modeling, information engineering, mathematical model building, sampling, and cost accounting to plan the system. Once it is accepted, the systems analyst determines, acquires, and tests the necessary computer hardware and software to ensure smooth operation and implementation of program requirements.

The type of education and training necessary for entry-level positions in this field depends largely on the specific needs of the employer. Typically, however, companies seek applicants who have at least a bachelor's degree in computer science, information science, or management information systems (MIS), coupled with strong problem-solving and analytical skills. Since this job requires a good deal of interaction with other employees to determine their requirements for a well functioning computer system, good interpersonal skills are also necessary. Those who show leadership ability may move up to become project managers or advance into such positions as manager of information systems or chief information officer.

Employment of computer systems analysts is expected to grow at a rate of 27 percent or more within the coming decade. Job increases will be driven by very rapid growth in computer system design and related services, which is expected to be among the fastest growing industries in the U.S.

Dietitian/Nutritionist

Dietitians, sometimes called nutritionists, are professionals trained in applying the principles of nutrition to food selection and meal preparation. They counsel individuals and groups; set up and supervise food service systems for institutions such as hospitals, correctional facilities, nursing homes, and schools; and promote sound eating habits through education and administration. Dietitians also conduct research. Clinical dietitians, sometimes called therapeutic dietitians, provide nutritional services for patients in hospitals, nursing homes, clinics, or doctors' offices. They assess patients' nutritional needs, develop and implement nutrition programs, and evaluate and report the results. Clinical dietitians confer with doctors and other health care professionals to coordinate the medical and nutritional needs of individual patients based on their health history, diagnosis, and treatment protocols.

Community dietitians counsel individuals and groups on sound nutrition practices to prevent disease and to promote good health. Employed in such places as public health clinics, home health agencies, health maintenance organizations, and human services agencies that provide group and home-delivered meals, their job is to evaluate individual needs, establish nutritional care plans, and communicate the principles of good nutrition in a way that individuals and their families can understand and apply. Research dietitians are usually employed at academic medical centers or educational institutions, although some may work in other settings such as community hospitals or not-for-profit agencies. Using established research methods and analytical techniques, they conduct studies in areas ranging from basic science to practical applications. Research dietitians may examine changes in the way the body uses food over the course of a lifetime, for example, or study the interaction of drugs and diet. They may investigate such topics as the nutritional needs of persons with particular diseases, behavior modification as it relates to diet and nutrition, or dietary applications to food service systems and equipment.

The basic educational requirement for this field is a bachelor's degree in dietetics, food and nutrition, food service management, or a related field.

Of the 46 states and jurisdictions with laws governing dietetics, 31 require licensure, 14 require certification, and one requires registration; requirements vary by state. Although not required in many jurisdictions, the Registered Dietitian designation is recommended. The Commission on Dietetic Registration of the American Dietetic Association awards the Registered Dietitian (RD) credential to those who pass an exam after completing their academic coursework and supervised experience.

Employment in this field is expected to grow faster than the average for all occupations as the result of increasing emphasis on disease prevention through improved dietary habits.

Economist

Economists study the way a society uses scarce resources such as land, labor, raw materials, and machinery, to produce goods and services. They conduct research, collect and analyze data, monitor economic trends, and develop forecasts. Their research might focus on such wide-ranging topics as energy costs, inflation, interest and exchange rates, business cycles, unemployment, tax policy, and farm prices. Having the ability to present economic and statistical concepts in a meaningful way is particularly important for economists whose research is policy directed. Economists who work for business firms may be asked by management to provide information on which decisions about the marketing or pricing of company products are made; to look at the advisability of adding new lines of merchandise, opening new branches, or diversifying the company's operations; to analyze the effects of changes in the tax laws; or to prepare economic or business forecasts. Business economists working for firms with operations abroad may be asked to prepare forecasts of foreign economic conditions.

The majority of economists—approximately 58 percent—are employed in the public sector. The remaining economists work in private industry, particularly in scientific research and development services and management, scientific, and technical consulting services.. A number of economists combine a full-time job in government, business, or academia with part-time or consulting work in another setting.

A bachelor's degree in economics is sufficient for many beginning research, administrative, management trainee, and business sales jobs. However, graduate training is rapidly becoming mandatory for advancement to more responsible positions as economists. In government research organizations and consulting firms, economists who possess master's degrees can usually qualify for more responsible research and administrative positions. A Ph.D. may be necessary for top positions in some organizations; it is required for appointment as an instructor at most colleges and universities. Experienced business economists may advance to managerial or executive positions in banks, industrial concerns, trade associations, and other organizations where they formulate practical business and administrative policy.

Rising demand for economic analysis in virtually every industry should bode well for future employment opportunities in this field.

Engineer

Engineers apply the theories and principles of science and mathematics to develop economical solutions to tactical technical problems. Often, their work is the link between a scientific discovery and its useful application. Engineers design machinery, products, systems, and processes for efficient and economical performance. Engineering is a highly specialized field; the work of an engineer varies greatly by industry.

Aerospace engineers design, develop, test, and help produce commercial and military aircraft, missiles, spacecraft, and related systems. They play an important role in advancing the state of technology in commercial aviation, defense, and space exploration. Aerospace engineers often specialize in an area of work such as structural design, navigational guidance and control, instrumentation and communication, or production methods. They also may specialize in one type of aerospace product, such as passenger planes, helicopters, satellites, or rockets.

Biomedical engineers develop devices and procedures that solve medial and health-related problems by combining their knowledge of biology and medicine with engineering principles and practices. They may assist in the development and evaluation of artificial organs, prostheses, instrumentation, medical information systems, and health management and care delivery systems. Biomedical engineers may also design the devices used in various medical procedures, such as imaging systems or instruments for automated insulin injection. Most engineers in this specialty need a strong background in another engineering specialty, such as mechanical or electronics engineering, in addition to biomedical training.

Chemical engineers are involved in many phases of the production of chemicals and chemical products. They design equipment and chemical plants as well as determine methods of manufacturing these products. Often, they design and develop chemical processes such as those used to remove chemical contaminants from waste materials. Because the duties of the chemical engineer cut across many fields, these professionals must have knowledge of chemistry, physics, and mechanical and electrical engineering. This branch of engineering is so diversified and complex that chemical engineers frequently specialize in a particular operation such as oxidation or polymerization. Others specialize in a particular field, such as materials science, or in the development of specific products.

Civil engineers, who work in the oldest branch of the engineering profession, design and supervise the construction of roads, harbors, airports, tunnels, bridges, water supply and sewage systems, and buildings. Major specialties within civil engineering are structural, water resources, construction, environmental, transportation, and geotechnical engineering. Many civil engineers are in supervisory or administrative positions ranging from construction site supervisor, to city engineer, to top-level executive. Others teach in colleges or universities, or work as consultants in design, construction, and research.

Electrical engineers design, develop, test, and supervise the manufacture of electrical. equipment. Electrical equipment includes power-generating, -controlling, and transmission equipment used by electrical utilities; electric motors; machinery controls, lighting and wiring in buildings; automobiles; aircraft; and radar and navigation systems. Although the terms "electrical" and "electronics" engineering are sometimes used interchangeably, they are not the same. Electrical engineers focus on the generation and supply of power, while electronics engineers work on the applications of electricity to control systems or signal processing. Electrical engineers generally specialize in such areas as power systems engineering or electrical equipment manufacturing.

Electronics engineers (except computer engineers) are responsible for a wide range of the technologies we take for granted, from portable music players to the global positioning system (GPS) in our cars. Electronics engineers design, develop, test, and supervise the manufacture of electronic equipment such as broadcast and communications systems. They may specialize in such areas as communications, signal processing, and control systems, or have a specialty within one of those areas, such as industrial robot control systems or aviation electronics.

Environmental engineers develop solutions to environmental problems using principles drawn from biology and chemistry. Their work encompasses water and air pollution control, recycling, waste disposal, and public health issues. Environmental engineers conduct hazardous-waste management studies, design municipal water supply and wastewater treatment systems, conduct research on the environmental impact of proposed construction projects, and perform quality-control checks. They may also be involved in the protection of wildlife. Many environmental engineers work as consultants, helping businesses comply with regulations and clean up hazardous sites.

Industrial engineers determine the most effective ways for an organization to use the basic factors of production—people, machines, materials, information, and energy—to make a product or provide a service. They are more concerned with people and methods of business organization than are engineers in other specialties, who generally are concerned more with particular products or processes, such as metals, power, or mechanics. To solve organizational, production, and related problems most efficiently, industrial engineers design data processing systems and apply mathematical concepts. They also develop management control systems to aid in financial planning and cost analysis, design production planning and control systems to coordinate activities and control product quality, and design or improve systems for the physical distribution of goods and services. Many industrial engineers move into managerial positions because the work they do is so closely related to the work of managers.

Mechanical engineers research, develop, design, manufacture, and test mechanical devices, including tools, engines, and machines. They work on a variety of power-producing machines, such as electric generators, internal combustion engines, and steam and gas turbines, as well as power-using machines, such as refrigeration and air-conditioning equipment, machine tools, material handling systems, elevators and escalators, and robots used in manufacturing. Mechanical engineers typically work in production operations in manufacturing or agriculture, maintenance, or technical sales; many are administrators and managers.

Mining and **geological** engineers find, extract, and prepare minerals for manufacturing industries to use. They design open pit and underground mines, supervise the construction of mine shafts and tunnels in underground operations, and devise methods for transporting minerals to processing plants. Mining engineers are responsible for the economical and efficient operation of mines and mine safety, including ventilation, water supply, power, communications, and equipment maintenance. Some mining engineers work with geologists and metallurgical engineers to locate and appraise new ore deposits. Others develop new mining equipment or direct mineral processing operations, which involve separating minerals from the dirt, rock, and other materials they are mixed with. Mining engineers frequently specialize in the mining of one specific mineral such as coal or copper. With today's increased emphasis on protecting the environment, many mining engineers have been working to solve problems related to mined land reclamation and water and air pollution.

Petroleum engineers are primarily involved in exploring and drilling for oil and natural gas. They work to achieve the maximum profitable recovery of oil and gas from a petroleum reservoir by determining and developing the best and most efficient methods for extraction. Since only a small proportion of the oil and gas in a reservoir will flow out under natural forces, petroleum engineers develop and use various enhanced recovery methods, including injecting water, chemicals, gases, or steam into an oil reservoir to force out more of the oil, and doing computer-controlled drilling or fracturing to connect a larger area of a reservoir to a single well. Recognizing that even the best techniques recover only a portion of oil and gas in a reservoir, petroleum engineers research and develop technology and methods to increase recovery and lower the cost of drilling and production operations.

A bachelor's degree in engineering from an accredited engineering program is required for almost all entry-level engineering jobs. Most engineering degrees are awarded in branches such as electrical, electronics, mechanical, or civil engineering; engineers trained in one branch may work in related branches. College graduates with a degree in science or mathematics and experienced engineering technicians may also qualify for some engineering jobs, especially in engineering specialties that are in high demand. Graduate training is essential for engineering faculty positions but is not required for the majority of entry-level engineering jobs. All 50 states require licensing for engineers whose work may affect life, health, or property, or who offer their services to the public.

Beginning engineering graduates usually work under the supervision of experienced engineers, and, in larger companies, may receive seminar or classroom training. As engineers advance in knowledge, they may become technical specialists, supervisors, or (as noted earlier) managers or administrators within the field of engineering. Some engineers obtain advanced degrees in business administration to improve their growth opportunities, while others obtain law degrees and become patent attorneys.

Overall job opportunities in engineering are expected to be favorable in the immediate future, with the number of engineering students roughly in balance with the number of job openings available. The biomedical and environmental specialties are expected to show significantly higher growth than some other, more traditional engineering specialties.

Financial Analyst/Personal Financial Advisor

Financial analysts and personal financial advisors provide analysis and guidance to businesses and individuals in order to help them with their investment decisions. Both types of specialists gather financial information, analyze it, and make recommendations to their clients. The difference between the two comes in the type of investment information they provide and the clients for whom they work. Financial analysts assess the economic performance of companies and industries for firms and institutions with money to invest. Personal financial advisors, on the other hand, assess the financial needs of individuals and offer them options for investing their money. Financial analysts typically work for banks, insurance companies, mutual and pension funds, securities firms, and other businesses. They read company financial statements and analyze commodity prices, sales, costs, expenses, and tax rates to determine a company's value and projected future earnings. Using spreadsheet and statistical software packages, they analyze financial data, spot trends, and develop forecasts in order to make recommendations to buy or sell a particular investment or security. Personal financial advisors use their knowledge of investments, tax laws, and insurance to recommend financial options for individual investors based on that person's short- and long-term goals. Some of the issues they may address include retirement and estate planning and funding for college, as well as general investment opportunities.

A college degree is required for financial analysts and strongly preferred for personal financial advisors. Most companies require financial analysts to have at least a bachelor's degree in business administration, accounting, statistics or finance. An M.B.A. degree is desirable, along with advanced courses in options pricing or bond valuation and knowledge of risk management. For personal financial advisors, a bachelor's degree in accounting, finance, economics, business, mathematics, or law provides good preparation. Courses in investments, taxes, estate planning, and risk management are also helpful. Although not required, certification can enhance professional standing and is strongly recommended for both financial analysts and personal financial advisors. Following successful completion of three exams, financial analysts with a bachelor's degree and at least three years of experience, may receive the Chartered Financial Analyst (CFA) designation from the CFA Institute. Personal financial advisors may obtain the Certified Financial Planner (CFP) credential after passing a comprehensive examination on such topics as insurance and risk management, employee benefits planning, taxes and retirement planning, and investment and estate planning. The Chartered Financial Consultant (ChFC) designation is also available to personal financial advisors from the American College.

Job opportunities in both fields are expected to increase; however, personal financial advisors may benefit more than financial analysts as baby boomers save for retirement and as a generally better educated and wealthier population requires investment advice.

Forester/Conservation Scientist

Foresters plan and supervise the growing, protection, and harvesting of trees. They plot forest areas, approximate the amount of standing timber and future growth, and manage timber sales. Some foresters also protect the trees from fire, harmful insects, and disease. Some foresters may also protect wildlife and manage watersheds; develop and supervise campgrounds, parks, and grazing lands; and conduct research. Foresters in extension work provide information to forest owners and to the general public. Related occupations include conservation scientist (they devise ways to use and improve the land without damaging the environment) and soil and water conservationists (they provide technical assistance to farmers, ranchers, forest managers, government agencies, and others concerned with soil, water, and related natural resources).

A bachelor's degree in forestry, biology, ecology, natural resource management, environmental sciences, or a related discipline is the minimum educational requirement for professional careers in forestry or conservation science. Most land-grant colleges and universities offer bachelor's or higher degree in forestry; the Society of American Foresters accredits 48 such programs throughout the country. A Ph.D. is usually required for teaching or research positions.

Approximately one in three workers in this field is employed by the federal government, primarily in the U.S. Departments of Agriculture and Interior. Another 21 percent of conservation scientists and foresters work for state governments and about 11 percent for local governments. Continuing emphasis on environmental protection, responsible land management, and water-related issues is expected to drive job growth in this industry, most of which will come in private sector consulting firms.

Geographer

Geographers study the interrelationship of humans and the environment. Economic geographers deal with the geographic distribution of resources and economic activities. Political geographers are concerned with the relationship of geography to political phenomena. Physical geographers study variations in climate, vegetation, soil, and landforms, and their implications for human activity. Urban and transportation geographers study cities and metropolitan areas, while regional geographers specialize in the physical, economic, political, and cultural characteristics of regions ranging in size from a single congressional district to entire continents. Medical geographers investigate health care delivery systems, epidemiology (the study of the causes and control of epidemics), and the effect of the environment on health.

The minimum educational requirement for an entry-level position is a bachelor's degree in geography. However, a master's degree is increasingly required for many entry-level positions. Applicants for entry-level jobs will find it helpful to have training in a specialty such as cartography, remote sensing data interpretation, and statistical analysis or environmental analysis. Since most geographers use geographic information systems (GIS) technology to assist with their work, computer skills are a must. To advance to a senior research position in private industry and perhaps gain a spot in management, a geographer would need to have an advanced degree.

The outlook for jobs in this field is positive as geographers have increasing opportunities to use their skills to advise government, real estate developers, utilities, and telecommunications firms on where to build new roads, buildings, power plants, and cable lines. The prospects for employment are especially bright for geographers with a solid background in GIS technology for application to nontraditional areas such as emergency assistance and homeland security.

Geologist/Geophysicist

Geologists study the structure, composition and history of the earth's crust. By examining surface rocks and drilling to recover rock cores, they determine the types and distribution of rocks beneath the earth's surface. They also identify rocks and minerals, conduct geological surveys, draw maps, take measurements, and record data. Geological research helps to determine what is going on beneath the earth's surface, and may result in significant advances, such as in the ability to predict earthquakes. An important application of the geologist's work is locating oil and other natural and mineral resources. Geologists usually specialize in one or a combination of general areas: earth materials, earth processes, and earth history.

Geophysicists study the composition and physical aspects of the earth and its electric, magnetic, and gravitational fields. Geophysicists usually specialize in one of three general phases of the science—solid earth, fluid earth, and upper atmosphere. Some may also study other planets.

A bachelor's degree in geology or geophysics is adequate for entry- to some lower-level geology jobs, but better jobs with good advancement potential in private industry, federal agencies, and state geological surveys usually require at least a master's degree in geology, geophysics, or earth science. People with strong backgrounds in physics, mathematics, or computer science also may qualify for some geophysics jobs. A Ph.D. is essential for most high-level research positions. Graduates with bachelor's degrees in geoscience may find excellent opportunities as high school science teachers.

Graphic Designer

Graphic designers—graphic artists as they are sometimes called—plan, analyze, and create visual solutions to communications problems. Using a variety of methods, such as color, type, illustration, photography, animation, and various print and layout techniques, they decide the most effective way to get a message across in print, electronic, and film media. Graphic designers develop the overall layout and production design of magazines, newspapers, journals, corporate reports, brochures, catalogs, and other publications. They also produce displays and packaging for products and services, design distinctive logos for products and businesses, and develop signs and signage systems for business and government. An increasing number of designers are also involved in developing material for Web pages, interactive media, and multimedia projects.

To assist in their designs, graphic designers typically use a variety of graphics and layout computer software. Those who create Web pages and other interactive media designs may also use computer animation and programming packages. Graphic designers are typically employed by large advertising, publishing, or design firms; they may also work for a private business, such as a manufacturing or financial services firm, or a health care provider. Designers in smaller design consulting firms, or those who freelance, generally work on a contract, or per job, basis.

A bachelor's degree, with an emphasis in graphic design is required for most entry-level and advanced graphic design positions. In addition to creativity and above-average communications and problem-solving skills, graphic designers must be familiar with computer graphics and design software. Entry-level graphic designers usually receive a good deal of on-the-job training and normally need from one to three years of professional experience before they can advance to higher level positions. Experienced graphic designers in large firms may advance to chief designer, art or creative director, or other supervisory positions.

The demand for graphic design continues to increase from advertisers, publishers, and computer design firms. Graphic designers should have no trouble finding employment in the future, thanks in large part to the rapidly expanding markets for Web-based information and video entertainment.

Human Resources and Labor Relations Specialist

Human resources and labor relations specialists provide a necessary link between management and employees by helping management make effective use of employees' skills, and by helping employees find satisfaction in their jobs and working conditions. Human resources specialists interview, select, and recommend applicants to fill job openings. They handle wage and salary administration, training and career development, and employee benefits. Labor relations specialists usually deal in union-management relations; the people who specialize in this field typically find work in unionized public and private sector agencies. They help management officials prepare for collective bargaining sessions, participate in contract negotiations with the union, and handle day-to-day matters of labor relations agreements.

In a small company, human resources work consists mostly of interviewing and hiring, and one person typically handles all phases. By contrast, a large organization needs an entire staff, which might include recruiters, interviewers, counselors, job analysts, wage and salary analysts, education and training specialists, and benefits supervisors, as well as technical and clerical staff. For a taste of what human resources work entails, you need look no further than the recruiters or employment interviewers who visit college campuses in search of promising job applicants. These specialists talk to a wide range of applicants, then select and recommend those who appear qualified to fill vacancies at the companies they represent. They often administer tests to applicants and interpret the results. Job analysts and salary and wage administrators, on the other hand, examine detailed information about specific jobs, including job qualifications and worker characteristics, in order to prepare employee manuals and other materials for training courses; they also determine the types of training that may be needed for specific positions and explore new methods for delivery. These human resources professionals may counsel employees on the various training opportunities available to them, which may include on-the-job, apprentice, supervisory, or management training.

Employee benefits supervisors oversee the employer's benefits programs, which may include health insurance, life insurance, disability insurance, and pension or 401(k) plans. Human resources specialists also often coordinate a wide range of employee services, including cafeterias and snack bars, recreational facilities, newsletters and employee communication, and counseling for worker-related personal problems. Counseling employees who are reaching retirement age is a particularly important part of the job.

Labor relations specialists provide advice on labor management relations. Nearly three out of four work in private industry——for manufacturers, banks, insurance companies, airlines, department stores, etc. The rest work for government agencies.

The educational backgrounds of human resources and labor relations specialists vary considerably due to the diversity of duties and level of responsibility. While some employers look for graduates with degrees in human resources, human resources administration, or industrial and labor relations, others prefer graduates with a technical or general business background, or a well-rounded liberal arts education. Graduate study in industrial or labor relations is often required for jobs in labor relations. For those involved in contract negotiations, mediation, and arbitration, a law degree, or at the very least, extensive knowledge of the law is highly desirable.

Entry-level human relations specialists usually come into the field through formal or on-the-job training programs in which they learn how to classify jobs, interview applicants, and administer employee benefits for a particular company. New workers are typically assigned to specific areas in the human resources department to gain experience. Later, they may advance within their own company, transfer to another employer, or move from human resources to labor relations work. Human resources workers in the middle ranks of a large organization often transfer to a top job in a smaller company. Employees with exceptional ability may be promoted to executive positions, such as director of human resources or director of labor relations.

Thanks to increasing legislation regarding occupational safety and health, equal employment opportunity, wages, health care, pensions, and family leave, there's a growing need for knowledgeable human resources specialists. Job opportunities in this field are expected to remain strong well into the next decade.

Industrial Designer

Industrial designers combine artistic talent with a knowledge of marketing, materials, and methods of production to improve the appearance and functional design of products so that they compete favorably with similar goods on the market. Although most industrial designers are engaged in product design, others focus on the creation of favorable public images for companies and government agencies; some develop the trademarks or symbols that appear on a firm's products and advertising. Industrial designers also develop the containers and packages that both protect and promote their contents. They may also prepare individual display exhibits or the entire layout for industrial fairs. Some design the interior layout of special purpose commercial buildings such as restaurants and supermarkets.

Industrial designers may either work for a specific company or as independent consultants. Corporate designers usually work only on products made by their employer. They may be involved in filling the day-to-day design needs of the company, or they may assist in the long-range planning and design of new products. Independent consultants who serve more than one industrial firm may plan and design a great variety of products. In either case, most designers work for large manufacturing companies designing either consumer or industrial products, or for design consulting firms. Others work as freelancers, or are on the staffs of architectural and interior design firms.

A bachelor's degree in industrial design, architecture, or engineering from a university, art school, or technical college is required for most entry-level positions in the field. Beginning industrial designers are frequently assigned to simple projects as part of a design team. As they gain experience, they may begin to work on their own, and many become supervisors with major responsibility for the design of a product or group of products. Those who have an established reputation and the necessary funds may start their own consulting firms. Because many talented individuals are attracted to this field, the competition for jobs is keen. Designers with strong backgrounds in engineering and computer-aided design, as well as business expertise, have the best prospects for success in the field.

Insurance Agent/Broker

Agents usually sell one or more of the three basic types of insurance: life, property and casualty, and health. Some insurance agents, called captive agents, work exclusively for one insurance company. Independent insurance agents, or brokers, represent several companies and place insurance policies for their clients with the company that offers the best rate and coverage. Life insurance agents specialize in selling policies that pay beneficiaries in the event of the policyholder's death. Life insurance agents may also sell annuities that provide retirement income. Property and casualty insurance agents sell policies that protect individual policyholders from financial losses resulting from automobile accidents, fire, theft, storms, and other events that might damage property. They also sell industrial or commercial lines, such as workers' compensation, product liability, or medical malpractice insurance. Health insurance agents sell policies that cover the costs of hospital and medical care and/or loss of income due to illness or injury. They may also sell dental insurance and short- and long-term disability policies. Many agents also offer securities, such as mutual fund shares or variable annuities.

Insurance agents spend most of their time discussing insurance needs with prospective and existing clients. Some time must be spent in office work to prepare reports, maintain records, plan insurance programs that are tailored to prospects' needs, and draw up lists of prospective customers. Specialists in group policies may help an employer's accountant set up a system of payroll deductions for employees covered by the policy.

All insurance agents must obtain a license in the state where they plan to sell insurance. In most states, licenses are issued only to applicants who complete specified pre-licensing courses and pass written examinations covering insurance fundamentals and state insurance laws. Agents who plan to sell mutual fund shares and other securities also must be licensed for the sale of those products by the state.

While a bachelor's degree is not required to sell insurance, most companies and independent agencies prefer to hire college graduates. Courses in finance, mathematics, accounting, economics, business law, and marketing help insurance agents understand business and economic conditions as they relate to the insurance industry; courses in psychology, sociology, and public speaking may prove useful in improving sales techniques. New agents usually receive training at the agencies where they will work, and frequently at the insurance company's home office. Beginners sometimes attend company-sponsored classes to prepare for the examination. Others study on their own and accompany experienced sales workers when they call on prospective clients.

Future demand for insurance sales agents and brokers depends largely on the volume of sales of insurance and other financial products. Sales of health and long-term-care insurances are expected to rise as the population ages. Multilingual agents should be in particular demand.

Lodging Manager

Lodging managers work in traditional hotels and motels, inns, camps, guesthouses, and recreational resorts. They are responsible for operating their establishments profitably and efficiently and for satisfying the needs of their guests. In a small establishment with limited staff, the manager may oversee all aspects of operation. In large hotels, on the other hand, where the staff may number into the hundreds, the manager oversees several assistant managers who are assigned to various departments, such as reservations, food and beverage, front office operations, housekeeping, maintenance, security, and guest relations. When management is combined with ownership, these activities may expand to include all aspects of the business. Regardless of the size, however, handling problems and coping with the unexpected are important aspects of the job.

Although general managers of large hotels usually have several assistants or department heads who manage various parts of the operation, they are ultimately responsible for overall operations. Because hotel restaurant and cocktail lounges are important to the success of the entire establishment, they are almost always operated by managers with experience in the restaurant field.

Other areas that may be handled separately include advertising, rental of banquet and meeting facilities, marketing and sales, human resources, and accounting. Large hotel and motel chains often centralize some activities, such as purchasing and advertising, so that individual hotels in the chain may not need managers for these departments. Managers who work for chains may be assigned to organize a newly built or purchased hotel, or to reorganize an existing hotel or motel that is not operating successfully.

Experience is the most important consideration in selecting hotel managers and promotion from within is quite common in this industry. However, employers are increasingly looking for management candidates with college degrees. A bachelor's degree in hotel/restaurant administration provides particularly strong preparation for a career in hotel management. Most hotels promote employees with proven ability; a typical career track might be from front office clerk, to front desk manager, to assistant manager in charge of reservations, and eventually general manager. Hotel and motel chains may offer better employment opportunities because employees are able to transfer to another hotel or motel in the chain, or to the central office if an opening occurs. Salaries vary according to the level of responsibility as well as to the size and location of the lodging establishment. Employment is expected to grow in this field and job openings are readily available as experienced managers move up the career ladder, transfer to other properties or leave the field altogether due to long hours and stressful working conditions.

Medical and Health Services Manager

Like any other business, health care needs good management to keep things running smoothly. Medical and health care services managers plan, direct, coordinate, and supervise the delivery of health care. Medical and health services managers may be either specialists or generalists. Specialists are in charge of specific clinical departments or services; generalists, on the other hand, manage or help mange an entire facility or system.

As the structure and financing of health care changes, medical and health services managers must be prepared to deal with evolving integrated health care delivery systems, technological innovations, an increasingly complex regulatory environment, restructuring of work, and increased focus on preventive care. Increasingly, medical and health services managers will be called upon to improve efficiency in health care facilities and the quality of the care they provide. Large facilities usually have assistant administrators to aid the top administrator and to handle many of the day-to-day decisions. In small facilities, however, top administrators handle more of the details of daily operation. Clinical managers have training or experience in specific clinical areas; typically, they establish and implement policies, objectives, and procedures for their departments; evaluate personnel; develop reports and budgets; and coordinate activities with other managers. In group practices and managed care settings, medical and health services managers work closely with physicians and may have some responsibility for community outreach.

Medical and health services managers must be familiar with management principles and practices. A master's degree in health services administration, long-term care administration, health sciences, public health, public administration, or business administration is the standard requirement for most generalist positions. However, for some entry-level positions in smaller facilities and at the departmental level within health care organizations, a bachelor's degree may be adequate. For those who want to become heads of clinical departments, a bachelor's degree in the appropriate field and work experience may be sufficient for an entry-level position, but a master's degree in health services administration or a related field might be necessary for advancement.

Employment of medical and health services managers is expected to grow quite quickly over the next few years as the health care industry continues to expand and diversify. Job opportunities will be especially available in the offices of health practitioners, general medical and surgical hospitals, home health care services, and outpatient care centers. Applicants with work experience in the health care field and strong management skills will enjoy the best opportunities.

Physician Assistant

Physician assistants (PAs) practice medicine under the direct supervision of physicians and surgeons. Not to be confused with medical assistants, who perform routine clinical and clerical tasks, PAs are formally trained to provide diagnostic, therapeutic, and preventive health care services, as delegated by a physician. Working as members of the total health care team, they take medical histories, examine and treat patients, order and interpret laboratory tests and X-rays, and make diagnoses. They also treat minor injuries by suturing, splinting, and casting. In 48 states and the District of Columbia, physician assistants may prescribe medications.

PAs work under the supervision of a physician. However, in some settings, such as rural or inner city clinics where a physician is present only one or two days a week, the physician assistant may be the principal care provider. PAs may make house calls or go to hospitals and nursing care facilities to check on patients, after which they report back to the physician.

The specific duties of a physician assistant are determined by the supervising physician and by state law. Many PAs work in primary care specialties, such as family medicine and pediatrics; other specialty areas include general and thoracic surgery, emergency medicine, orthopedics, and geriatrics.

All states require that PAs complete an accredited, formal education program and pass a national exam to obtain a license. PA programs typically last at least two years and are full-time. Admission requirements vary, but many programs require two years of college and some work experience in the health care field prior for admission. Students considering a PA program should take courses in biology, English, chemistry, mathematics, psychology, and the social sciences.

The occupation of physician assistant ranks among the fastest growing in the United States, due to anticipated expansion of the health care industry and the increasing emphasis on cost containment, which has resulted in greater utilization of PAs by physicians and health care institutions. PAs relieve physicians of many routine duties and procedures and are thus considered a cost-effective and productive member of the health care team.

Physicist

Through systematic observation and experimentation, physicists describe the structure of the universe and the interaction of matter and energy in fundamental terms. Working with lasers, particle accelerators, telescopes, mass spectrometers, and other equipment, physicists develop theories that describe the fundamental forces and laws of nature. The majority of physicists work in research and development. Some perform basic research to increase scientific knowledge; others, who are more engineering-oriented, conduct applied research and help develop new products. Many physicists teach and do research in colleges and universities. A small number work in inspection, quality control, and other production-related jobs in industry, while others do consulting work.

Most physicists specialize in one or more branches of the science; a growing number of physicists are specializing in fields that combine physics and a related science. Furthermore, the practical applications of a physicist's work have become increasingly merged with engineering. A growing number of physicists work in interdisciplinary fields, such as biophysics, chemical physics, and geophysics. Private industry employs more than half of all physicists, primarily in companies manufacturing chemicals, electrical equipment, and aircraft and missiles. Many others work in hospitals, commercial laboratories, and independent research organizations.

Because the practitioners in this field are so heavily involved in research and development, graduate training in physics or a closely related field is essential even for most entry-level jobs in physics, and, certainly, for advancement into all types of work. A Ph.D. is normally required for faculty status at colleges and universities, and for industrial or government jobs administering research and development programs. Those with a master's degree qualify for many research jobs in private industry and in the federal government. In colleges and universities, some teach and assist in research while studying for their Ph.D. degrees. Those with bachelor's degrees rarely qualify for positions in research or teaching at the college level; however, they may qualify for some applied research and development positions in private industry and in government. In addition, some holding bachelor's degrees may be employed as technicians or research assistants in colleges and universities while studying for advanced degrees. Many also work in engineering and other scientific fields.

Physicists, even those with advanced degrees, often begin their careers performing routine laboratory tasks. After gaining experience, they are assigned more complex tasks and may advance to work as project leaders or research directors. Some work in top management jobs. Physicists who develop new products sometimes form their own companies or join new firms to exploit their own ideas.

Employment opportunities for physicists are expected to increase in the coming decade, but only by about 8 percent. Federal research expenditures are the primary source of physics-related research funds; limitations on science funds over the next ten years may impact the growth in employment and career opportunities.

Psychologist

Psychologists study human behavior and mental processes in order to understand, explain, and modify people's behavior. Research psychologists investigate the physical, cognitive, emotional, and social aspects of human behavior. Psychologists in applied fields counsel and conduct training programs; engage in market research; or provide mental health services in hospitals, clinics, or private settings.

Since psychology deals with human behavior, psychologists apply their knowledge and techniques to a wide range of endeavors including human services, management, education, law, and sports. In addition to the variety of work settings, psychologists specialize in many different areas. **Clinical** psychologists—who constitute the largest specialty within the field—generally work in hospitals or clinics, or maintain private practices. Many clinical psychologists help mentally or emotionally disturbed clients adjust to life. Others counsel people who are dealing with life stresses such as divorce or aging. Clinical psychologists interview patients; give diagnostic tests; provide individual, family, and group psychotherapy; and design and implement behavior modification programs. They may collaborate with physicians and other specialists in developing treatment programs. Some clinical psychologists work in universities, where they conduct research and train graduate students in the delivery of mental health services. Others administer community mental health programs.

Counseling psychologists use several techniques, including interviewing and testing, to advise people on how to deal with problems of everyday living from a personal, social, educational, or vocational perspective. **Developmental** psychologists study the patterns and causes of behavioral change as people progress through life from infancy to adulthood. Some concern themselves with behavior during infancy, childhood, and adolescence, while others study changes that take place during maturity and old age. **Educational** psychologists design, develop, and evaluate educational programs. **Experimental** psychologists study behavior processes in human beings and in animals such as rats, monkeys, and pigeons. Prominent areas of experimental research include motivation, thought, attention, learning and retention, sensory and perceptual processes, effects of substance abuse, and genetic and neurological factors affecting behavior.

Industrial and **organizational** psychologists apply psychological techniques to the workplace with regard to personnel administration, management, and marketing problems. They are involved in policy planning, applicant screening, training and development, psychological test research, counseling, and organizational development and analysis, among other activities. For example, an industrial psychologist may work with management to develop better training programs and to reorganize the work setting to improve worker productivity. **School** psychologists work with students in elementary and secondary schools. They collaborate with teachers, parents, and school administrators and other personnel to resolve students' learning and behavior problems; create safe, healthy, and supportive learning environments; counter substance abuse; assess students with learning disabilities; and improve teaching, learning, and socialization strategies. **Social** psychologists examine people's interactions with others and with the social environment. Prominent areas of study include group behavior, leadership, attitudes, and interpersonal perception.

Other areas of specialization within the field include cognitive psychology, community psychology, comparative psychology, consumer psychology, engineering psychology, environmental psychology, family psychology, forensic psychology, health psychology, neuropsychology, psychometrics, population psychology, psychopharmacology, and military and rehabilitation psychology.

Although a doctorate or a master's degree is generally required for employment as a psychologist, a college grad with a bachelor's degree in psychology is qualified to assist psychologists and other professionals in community mental health centers, vocational rehabilitation offices, and correctional programs; to work as a research or administrative assistant; and to take a job as a trainer in government or private industry. However, without additional academic training, advancement possibilities are limited. In the federal government, candidates having at least 24 semester hours in psychology and one course in statistics qualify for entry-level positions. Competition for these jobs is keen, however, because this is one of the few areas in which it is possible to work as a psychologist without an advanced degree.

Given the increased demand for psychological services in schools, hospitals, social service agencies, mental health centers, substance abuse treatment clinics, consulting firms, and private companies, employment of psychologists is expected to rise at pace of approximately 18 to 26 percent over the next 10 years.

Public Relations Specialist

Public relations specialists help businesses, government, universities, and other organizations build and maintain a positive public image. They apply their talents and skills in a variety of different areas, including media, community, or consumer relations; political campaigning; interest-group representation; fund-raising; and employee recruitment. Public relations is more than simply telling the employer's story, however. Understanding the attitudes and concerns of customers, employees, and various other segments of the general public, and effectively communicating this information to management to help formulate policy is an important part of the job.

Public relations staffs in very large firms may number in the hundreds, but in most firms the staff is much smaller, sometimes only one or two. The director of public relations, who is often a vice-president of the company, typically develops the overall public relations plans and policies in partnership with a top management executive. In addition, large public relations departments employ writers, researchers, and other specialists who prepare material for the various media, stockholders, customers, and other groups the company wishes to reach.

Manufacturing firms, public utilities, transportation companies, insurance companies, and trade and professional associations are among the entities that employ many public relations workers. A sizeable number also work for government agencies, schools, colleges, museums, and religious, human service and other not-for-profit organizations. The rapidly expanding health care field also offers many opportunities for public relations work. Job opportunities are also available at public relations agencies/consulting firms, which furnish services to clients for a fee. In addition, public relations specialists may work for advertising agencies, overseeing the public relations activities that coincide with advertising campaigns created on behalf of clients.

A college degree along with public relations experience, usually gained through an unpaid internship, is excellent preparation for work in this field. Although most beginners in the field have a college degree in communications, public relations, or journalism, some employers seek applicants with communication skills and training or experience in a field related to the firm's business—information technology, health, science, engineering, or finance, for example. Other firms want college graduates who have worked for the news media. In fact, many editors, reporters, and workers in closely related fields enter public relations work, in large part because it tends to pay better than jobs in the media. Some companies, particularly those with large public relations staffs, have formal training programs for new workers. In other firms, new employers work under the guidance of experienced staff members.

Promotion to supervisory jobs may come as workers demonstrate their ability to handle more demanding and creative assignments. Some experienced public relations workers start their own consulting firms. The Public Relations Society accredits public relations specialists who have at least five years of full-time work or teaching experience in public relations and have passed comprehensive written and oral examinations. Successful candidates earn the Accredited in Public Relations (APR) designation.

As in advertising, the number of qualified applicants for jobs in public relations exceeds the number of openings. The good news, however, is that job opportunities are expected to grow as the increasingly competitive business environment spurs demand for public relations specialists in organizations of all types and sizes.

Purchasing Agent

Purchasing agents, also sometimes called industrial buyers, obtain the goods and services that a company or institution needs to either resell to customers or use in-house. When choosing suppliers and merchandise, purchasing agents consider price, quality, availability, reliability, and technical support, and they try to get the best deal for their company—the highest quality goods at the lowest possible cost. Agents who work for manufacturing companies may purchase maintenance and repair supplies. Those working for government agencies may purchase such items as office supplies, furniture, business machines, or vehicles.

Purchasing agents usually specialize in one or more specific groups of commodities, such as steel, lumber, cotton, or petroleum products. In large organizations, agents are typically assigned to sections, headed by assistant purchasing managers, who are responsible for a group of related commodities. In smaller companies, purchasing agents generally are assigned certain categories of goods. About half of all purchasing agents work for manufacturing firms.

At one time, most purchasing agents worked their way up through the ranks, learning the job as they went. Today, however, most large organizations require their purchasing agents to have a bachelor's degree, and many prefer applicants with an M.B.A. degree. Familiarity with the computer and its use is essential to understanding and implementing the systems aspect of the purchasing profession. Following an initial training period, junior purchasing agents usually are given the responsibility of purchasing standard and catalog items. As they gain experience and develop expertise in their assigned areas, they may be promoted to positions as senior purchasing agents. For those who want to advance their careers, continuing education is a must. In addition, purchasing agents are encouraged to participate in frequent seminars offered by professional societies, and to take courses in the field at local colleges and universities.

In private industry, the recognized marks of experience and professional competence are the Accredited Purchasing Practitioner (APP) and Certified Purchasing Manager (CPM) designations, conferred by the Institute for Supply Management, and the Certified Purchasing Professional (CPP) and Certified Professional Purchasing Manager (CPPM) designations, conferred by the American Purchasing Society. The National Institute of Governmental Purchasing has similar designations for purchasers in the public sector. In all cases, certifications are awarded only after a specified number of years in the field and completion of oral and written exams.

Quality Control Supervisor

A quality control supervisor may either be involved in the spot checking of items being manufactured or processed or in assuring that the proper processes are being followed. As a general rule, the quality control supervisor oversees a quality control system, which involves selection and training of personnel, product design, the establishment of specifications, procedures and tests, the design and maintenance of facilities and equipment, the selection of materials, and recordkeeping. In an effective quality control system, all these aspects are evaluated on a regular basis, and modified and improved when appropriate.

While some quality control positions, such as those involved with supervising the production of simple items may require little background other than on-the-job training; quality control for the production of highly technical or scientific equipment may require a specialized degree in engineering, chemistry, or biology. While all manufacturing firms require some degree of quality control, many are increasingly coming to rely on automated systems to provide it. As a result, there is less need for quality control supervisors. One exception to this rule, however, is the pharmaceutical industry. Some drug manufacturers for example, may assign one out of every six production workers to oversee quality assurance functions alone.

Reporter/Editor

Reporters investigate leads and news tips, gather information on current events, and interview sources in order to write stories for daily or weekly newspapers. They may either return to the newsroom to write their stories on stationary computer terminals or compose their stories on laptop computers at remote locations; in either case, the material is electronically submitted to editors who review the work for grammar and style, attach a headline, and "send" it the composing room for placement on the page. Radio and television reporters often compose stories and report "live" from the scene.

At times, they may tape an introduction or commentary at the studio later for attachment to their live reports.

Large newspapers and radio/television stations frequently assign reporters to gather news about specific topics, such ass crime or education. General assignment reporters write local news stories on a wide range of topics, from public meetings to human interest features.

Reporters with a specialized background or interest in a particular area may write, interpret, and analyze the news in fields such as medicine, politics, foreign affairs, sports, fashion, art, theater, consumer affairs, travel, finance, social events, science, education, business, labor, religion, and other topics. Critics review literary, artistic, and musical works and performances while editorial writers present viewpoints on topics of interest. Reporters on small newspapers cover all aspects of local news, and may also take photographs, write headlines, lay out pages, and write editorials. On some small weeklies, they may also solicit advertisements, sell subscriptions, and perform general office work. The work of a reporter is deadline-oriented and often quite hectic. Reporters must be highly motivated, and are expected to work long hours. Broadcast journalists must often air their reports with little or no time for preparation.

Most media outlets will only consider applicants with a bachelor's degree in journalism or mass communications, which includes training in the liberal arts in addition to professional training in journalism. Large-city newspapers and broadcasting stations may prefer applicants with a bachelor's degree in a subject-matter specialty such as economics, political science, or business. Experience at school newspapers or broadcasting stations or as a part-time "stringer" is very helpful in finding full-time employment as a reporter; internships with recognized news organizations are a real plus. Most beginning reporters start on weekly or small daily newspapers; a small number of outstanding journalism graduates at the top schools may find entry-level work with large daily newspapers, although this is a rare exception. Large dailies generally look for at least three years of reporting experience, acquired on smaller newspapers. In all cases, familiarity with the use of computers, scanners, and other electronic communications equipment is essential.

Beginning print and broadcast reporters are assigned duties such as reporting on civic and community meetings, summarizing speeches, writing obituaries, interviewing important community leaders or visitors, and covering police, government, or courthouse proceedings. As they gain experience, they may report on more important events, cover an assigned beat, or specialize in a particular field. Newspaper reporters may advance to large daily newspapers or state and national newswire services; broadcast reporters may move on to local stations in larger markets or network news positions. However, competition for such positions is fierce, and news executives are flooded with applications from highly qualified reporters every year. Some experienced reporters become columnists, correspondents, editorial writers, editors, or top executives; these people represent the top of the field, and competition for these positions is extremely keen. Other reporters transfer to related fields, such as public relations, writing for magazines, writing copy behind-the-scenes for radio or television news programs, or writing text for Web sites.

Sales Representative for Manufacturers/Wholesalers

Sales representatives market their company's products to manufacturers, wholesale and retail establishments, government agencies, and other institutions. Regardless of the type of product sold, the primary job of a sales representative is to interest wholesale and retail buyers and purchasing agents in their merchandise (as opposed to retail salespersons who sell directly to consumers).

Manufacturers' and wholesale sales representatives spend much of their time traveling to and visiting with prospective buyers. During a sales call, they may show catalogs that describe their company's products or actual product samples. Because the prospective customers is most likely considering products from many competing vendors, the sales rep must use product knowledge and interpersonal skills to persuade the customer that the product he/she represents is best. Sales representatives also take orders and help resolve problems or complaints with merchandise. Sales representatives may also promote their company's products at trade shows and conferences. Other duties of a sales rep might include analyzing sales statistics, preparing reports, and handling administrative duties. Obtaining new accounts is an especially important part of the job. To do so, sales representatives follow leads from other clients, track advertisements in trade journals, participate in trade shows and conferences, and sometimes, drop in on prospective clients unannounced.

A career as a sales representative for a manufacturer or wholesaler has many benefits including high pay, travel, and the opportunity to meet many new people. However, this field is not for the meek or soft-spoken. The most difficult part of the job, referred to as "cold calling," requires the salesperson to call prospective customers who have yet to express any interest in the company's products or services and may have little or no interest in even talking to the sales person, let alone making a purchase.

A sales position is the best way to get into a top management position at many companies. This is because sales work provides a strong overall view of the company's products, an understanding of the nature of the competition, and an appreciation for the needs of the customer base. An entry-level position in sales is the closest thing to a fast-track management training program that many companies offer.

The background needed for sales jobs varies by product line and market; however, because job requirements have become more technical and analytical, a college degree is increasingly desirable. Any summer or part-time experience in sales will also be greatly beneficial to the college student seeking a career in this field. Continued growth in the variety and number of goods sold is expected to fuel the number of job opportunities available for sales representatives in the years ahead.

Securities, Commodities, and Financial Services Sales Representative

Most investors, whether they are individuals with a few hundred dollars or large institutions with millions to invest, use securities, commodities, and financial sales representatives when buying or selling stocks, bonds, shares in mutual funds, insurance annuities, or other financial products. Securities and commodities sales representatives also provide many related services for their customers. Depending on a customer's knowledge of the market, the representative may explain the meaning of stock market terms and trading practices, offer financial counseling, devise an individual financial portfolio, including securities, corporate and municipal bonds, life insurance, annuities, and other investments, and offer advice on the purchase or sale of particular securities.

Sometimes called private bankers or relationship managers, financial services sales representatives sell a variety of banking and related services. They call on various businesses to solicit applications for loans and new deposit accounts for banks or savings and loan associations, and for participation in consumer credit card programs. They also locate and contact prospective customers to present their bank's financial services and to ascertain the customer's banking needs. At most small and medium-sized banks, branch managers and commercial loan officers are responsible for marketing the bank's financial services. As banks offer more and increasingly complex financial services, for example, securities brokerage and financial planning—the job of financial services sales representatives— assumes greater importance.

A college education is becoming increasingly important, as securities and commodities sales representatives must be well informed about economic conditions and trends. Although employers seldom require specialized academic training, courses in business administration, economics, and finance are helpful. Securities and commodities sales representatives must meet state licensing requirements, which generally include passing an examination and, in some cases, furnishing a personal bond. In addition, sales representatives must register as representatives of their firm with the National Association of Securities Dealers, Inc. (NASD). Before beginners can qualify as registered representatives, they must pass the General Securities Registered Representative Examination (Series 7 exam), administered by NASD, and be an employee of a registered firm for at least four months.

Banks and other credit institutions prefer to hire college graduates for financial services sales jobs. A business administration degree with a specialization in finance or a liberal arts degree that includes courses in accounting, economics, and marketing serves as excellent preparation for this job. Financial services sales representatives often learn their jobs through one-the-job training under the supervision of bank officers. Outstanding performance can lead to promotion into managerial positions.

The demand for securities, commodities, and financial services sales representatives is expected to grow right along with individual disposable income. While growth in the volume of stocks traded over the Internet may limit job growth, the overall increase in investment among baby boomers will likely spur additional job opportunities.

Social Worker

Social workers help people function the best they can in their environment, deal with their relationships, and solve personal and family problems. Social workers often see clients at their worst—when they are facing a life-threatening illness or a social problem, such as inadequate housing, unemployment, disability, or substance abuse. Social workers also assist families that have serious domestic conflicts, sometimes involving child or spousal abuse. Most social workers elect to specialize; although some conduct research or are involved in planning or policy development, the vast majority of social worker prefer to work in an area of practice where they interact with clients.

Child, family, and school social workers provide social services and assistance to improve the social and psychological functioning of children and their families in order to maximize family well-being and improve academic performance. Social workers in this specialty may assist single parents, arrange for adoptions, or help find foster homes for neglected, abandoned, or abused children. Child, family, and school social workers typically work for individual and family services agencies, schools, or state and local government. Medical and public health social workers provide individuals, families, and vulnerable populations with the social support they need to cope with chronic, acute, or terminal illnesses, such as Alzheimer's disease, cancer, or AIDS. These social workers may work for hospitals, nursing and personal care facilities, individual and family services agencies, or local governments. Mental health and substance abuse social workers assess and treat individuals with mental illness or substance abuse problems, including abuse of alcohol, tobacco, or other drugs. Sometimes known as clinical social workers, they are likely to be employed in hospitals, substance abuse centers, individual and family services agencies, or local governments.

A bachelor's degree in social work is the most common minimum requirement for an entry-level position in this field; however, majors in psychology, sociology, and related fields may also qualify. For positions in health care settings and clinical work, a master's degree in social work is typically required. Some jobs in public and private agencies may also require an advanced degree; college and university teaching positions and most research appointments require a doctorate. In addition, all states and the District of Columbia have licensing, certification, or registration requirements regarding social work practice and the use of professional titles; for details, it is best to check with the individual states as regulations may vary from one place to another.

The demand for social workers is, not surprisingly, highest in cities; however, opportunities are also available in rural areas, where it is often difficult to attract and retain qualified staff. As the rapidly growing elderly population generates greater demand for health and social services, employment of social workers will continue to increase in the coming years.

Statistician

Statisticians devise, carry out, and interpret the numerical results of surveys and experiments. In doing so, they apply their knowledge of statistical methods to a particular subject area, such as economics, human behavior, the natural sciences, or engineering. They may use statistical techniques to predict population growth or economic conditions, develop quality control tests for manufactured products, or help business managers and government officials make decisions and evaluate the results of new programs. Although nearly every government agency employs some statisticians, more than half of all those working in the field are in private industry, primarily in manufacturing, finance, and insurance firms.

Although employment opportunities exist for individuals with a bachelor's degree, a master's degree in statistics or mathematics is the minimum educational requirement for most statistician jobs. Research and academic positions typically require at least a master's degree and, more often, a Ph.D. in statistics. Beginning positions in industrial research often require a master's degree with several years of experience. For entry-level jobs in the federal government, however, a bachelor's degree, including at least 15 hours of statistics or a combination of statistics and mathematics, may be sufficient In either case, beginning statisticians with lower-level degrees typically spend their time performing routine work under the supervision of an experienced statistician. Through experience, they may advance to positions of greater technical and supervisory responsibility. As the use of statistics by business and government continues to grow, the demand for qualified statisticians will remain strong. However, opportunities for promotion are best for those with advanced degrees.

Teacher

Gone are the days when a teacher stood up in front of the class and lectured at a classroom of students. Today's teachers act as facilitators or coaches, using interactive discussions and "hands-on" approaches to help students learn and apply concepts in such subjects as science, mathematics, social studies, and English. Utilizing "props" or "manipulatives," teachers help children understand abstract concepts, solve problems, and develop critical thought processes. To encourage collaboration, students increasingly work in groups in order to discuss and solve problems together, and teachers provide the environment that enables them to practice the kinds of interaction and logical thinking they will need to use later in life. Preschool and kindergarten teachers capitalize on children's play to further language and vocabulary development, improve social skills, and introduce key scientific and mathematics concepts. Elementary school teachers typically instruct one class of children in several subjects; in some schools teachers work in teams of two and are jointly responsible for a group of students in at least one subject. Middle and secondary school teachers help students delve more deeply into subjects introduced in elementary school and expose them to more information about the world. Additional responsibilities at this level may include career guidance and job placement.

Teachers often work with students from varied ethnic, racial, and religious backgrounds. In so doing, they must design classroom presentations that meet individual and collective students' needs and abilities. They must also work with parents and school administrators to ensure that academic requirements are met and that problems are readily addressed and corrected.

All 50 states and the District of Columbia require public school teachers to be licensed. Although specific requirements for licensure may vary from one state to the next, all agree on one point: general education teachers must have a bachelor's degree and have completed an approved teacher training program with a prescribed number of subject and education credits, as well as supervised practice teaching. In addition, almost all states require applicants for a teacher's license to be tested for competency in basic skills and to exhibit proficiency in his or her subject. In an effort to relieve shortages in certain subjects, such as math and science, some states offer alternative licensure programs for teachers who have a bachelor's degree in the subject they will teach, but lack the necessary education courses required for a regular license. In some cases, provisional licenses may be available which allow recent college graduates who did not complete education programs to teach in the classroom while they work toward the necessary credit hours in education theory and practice.

Whereas twenty years ago, there was a glut of teachers in the marketplace, today there are too few in many areas. As school enrollments rise and mandates for smaller class sizes take effect in many states, the demand for teachers at all levels continues to rise. Shortages of qualified teachers in some regions and subject areas will likely continue, which bodes well for employment opportunities.

Technical Writer/Editor

Technical writers and technical editors put technical information into easily understandable language. They research, write, and edit operating and maintenance manuals, catalogs, parts lists, assembly instructions, sales promotion materials, and project proposals; they may also produce audiovisual materials. To ensure that their work is accurate, technical writers must either be expert in the subject area in which they are writing or work closely with others who are. Editors are also responsible for the accuracy of material on which they work. Some organizations use job titles other than technical writer/editor, such as staff writer, publications engineer, communications specialist, industrial writer, industrial materials developer, and others. Technical writers set out either to instruct or inform, and in many instances they do both. Some of the materials they create will be used by end-users; others will be used by sales representatives who sell machinery or scientific equipment or by the technicians who install, maintain, and service it.

Technical writers often serve as part of a team, working closely with scientists, engineers, accountants, and other technical types. Technical editors take the material technical writers produce and further polish it for final publication and use. Many technical writers and editors work for large firms in the electronics, aviation, aerospace, ordinance, chemical, pharmaceutical, and computer manufacturing industries. Firms in the energy, communications, and computer software fields also employ many technical writers, and research laboratories make use of their skills in significant numbers.

Employers seek applicants for technical writing and editing positions whose educational background, work experience, and personal pursuits indicate they posses both writing skills and appropriate scientific knowledge. Knowledge of graphics and other aspects of publication production may also be helpful in landing a job in the field. An understanding of current trends in communication technology is an asset, and familiarity with computer operations and terminology is essential.

Many employers prefer to hire candidates with degrees in communications, English, or journalism. Increasingly, however, technical writing requires a degree in, or at least some knowledge about, a specialized field, such as engineering, business, or one of the sciences. Persons with training and/or experience in technical writing are often preferred over candidates with little or no technical background.

Beginning technical writers may assist experienced writers by doing library research work and preparing drafts of reports. Experienced technical writers in companies with large writing staffs may eventually move to the job of technical editor, or to an administrative position in the publications or technical information departments. The top job is usually that of publications manager (or some similar title), who supervises the people directly involved in producing the company's technical documents. The manager oversees not only the technical writers and editors, but also staff members responsible for illustrations, photography, reproduction, and distribution.

While the outlook for jobs in technical writing is favorable, expect there to be a lot of competition, as many people with general writing or journalism training are attracted to this occupation. As online publications and services grow in number and sophistication, so too will the demand for writers and editors with Web experience.

Underwriter

Underwriters are employed by the insurance companies to appraise and select the risks they will insure. With the aid of computers, underwriters analyze information in insurance applications, reports from loss-control consultants, medical reports, and actuarial studies to determine whether a risk is acceptable and will not result in a loss. They then decide whether to issue a policy and, if so, the appropriate premium to charge. Most underwriters specialize in one of the three major categories of insurance: life, property and casualty, and health. They may further specialize in group or individual policies.

For entry-level underwriting jobs, most large insurance companies seek college graduates who have degrees in business administration or finance with courses or experience in accounting. However, a bachelor's degree in liberal arts—plus courses in business law and accounting—may be sufficient to qualify for a beginning position. In either case, computer skills are essential. Underwriter trainees typically begin by evaluating routine applications under the close supervision of an experienced risk analyst. Continuing education is necessary for advancement to senior-level positions. Insurance companies generally place great emphasis on completion of one or more of the many recognized independent study programs. Many companies pay tuition for underwriting courses; some offer salary incentives. The Insurance Institute of America offers both a program titled "Introduction to Underwriting" for beginning underwriters, and the specialty designation of Associate in Commercial Underwriting (ACU). Those interested in developing a career underwriting personal insurance policies may earn the Associate in Personal Insurance (API) designation. The American Institute for Chartered Property Casualty Underwriters awards the Chartered Property and Casualty Underwriter (CPCU) designation after successful completion of 10 exams and at least three years of insurance experience. Other professional designations are Chartered Life Underwriter (CLU) and Registered Health Underwriter (RHU) from the American College.

Demand for underwriters is expected to increase in the years ahead as economic and population growth result in increased insurance needs by businesses and individuals. Job opportunities should be best for those with a background in finance and strong computer skills.

Online Job-Hunting Resources

Searching for a job today is vastly different than it was ten, or even just five, years ago. Electronic resumes, Internet service providers, and the World Wide Web are continuing to change the definition of what it means to be a job seeker. If you want to stay ahead of the game, you will need to change your definition, too.

These days it is practically impossible to search for a job unless you have access to a computer and the Internet. More and more employers are requesting that applicants send their resumes to e-mail addresses rather than by fax or traditional "snail mail." If you are unable to comply, you could be missing out on many opportunities. Then, too, there's the proliferation of career Web sites where job seekers can not only reply to online classifieds for the available positions listed but also post their resumes so that employers from around the world may see what they have to offer and, hopefully, contact them. In recent years, the World Wide Web has become *the* place to look for jobs. And with good reason. There are dozens of career resources on the Web devoted to job listings, and more are springing up every day. While many are general—offering job hunting advice and services for job seekers in broad categories, such as banking and finance, health care, sales and marketing, etc.—there are specialized sites, too. Some are devoted to job listings in a single, narrow industry category, such as higher education, aerospace, advertising, or entertainment; some professional associations have online listings of availabilities by specific job functions. Still others focus solely on geographic locale. There are sites that list job opportunities only in Chicago or California, or the United Kingdom, for example. Which Web-based resources will be most valuable for you is largely a matter of personal choice. If you have done your research, as suggested in earlier chapters, and have decided on an industry or job focus, you will have an easier time of determining which sites to use.

Where to Find Job Listings on the Web

The popularity of the World Wide Web as a source of career information and job listings is due in large part to its user-friendly, graphical interface. Gone are the days when job seekers were required to scroll through long lists of job openings on the cumbersome, text-based Internet. Today, a job hunter can simply access a search engine like Google, enter his or her desired job category, and *voila*! A list of career Web sites pops up in a flash. A click to one of them and you have instant access to a wealth of resources for improving your job hunt, plus a list of jobs available in specific industry categories and geographic locales. While interesting graphics were what first drew job hunters to the Web, it is the veritable mountain of job-related information to be found that has kept them there. The Web has dozens of career sites offering listings of specific jobs currently available, plus hundreds more with general job-hunting resources, such as resume banks and employer databases.

As a whole, the Web contains hundreds of thousands of job listings. Here, you can find jobs in government or private industry, jobs that require either technical skills or creative abilities, entry-level jobs for new graduates or jobs for people with years of experience. What's more, they may be permanent, temporary, full- or part-time positions. Surfing the Web, you might find a position in your own hometown, but you could just as easily look for jobs in Australia, Japan, or in a state two time zones away, which is what makes the Web an especially attractive destination for anyone considering relocation. Then, too, there's the added advantage of 24/7 accessibility. You can hunt for jobs any time of the day or night from the comfort of your own home.

Web-based job sites vary greatly in both the quality and quantity of their job listings. Due to an aggressive marketing campaign, Monster.com is perhaps the best known. But there are many others, including CareerBuilder.com, TrueCareers.com, Jobs.com, Jobs.net, BestJobsUSA.com, and HotJobsYahoo.com, to name just a few.

Each Web-based job site has its individual specialties and quirks, and some are more user-friendly than others. The most comprehensive are perhaps Monster.com and CareerBuilder.com. At either one, in addition to thousands of job listings, you can get expert advice on specific job-hunting skills, such as putting together a resume and preparing for interviews; access helpful books, articles, and software; and find information on thousands of employers and links to many company Web sites.

Since Web-based job sites vary so much in terms of what they offer to job seekers, rather than recommend one over another, we believe your best bet is to consult the list on the following pages, then try these Web sites out for yourself. You will probably find a couple of favorites that contain more job listings in your chosen field than others, or that provide the tools you particularly need. Be sure to bookmark those sites where you find good information, so you can return to them easily and often.

As you peruse the job listings, you will soon come to recognize one advantage of scanning the Web for employment: the quantity of information the job listings provide. Some job postings on the Web run as many as 500 words, a far cry from the minuscule classifieds in your Sunday newspaper. These larger ads contain detailed information about the position, such as a lengthy job description and a specific list of required skills.

You may also find, however, that a number of the listings in the major job databases overlap. The same search performed on Monster.com and CareerBuilder.com, for example, will likely retrieve many of the same listings, simply because, for the broadest reach, companies often advertise on several sites at once. Be sure to keep careful records so you don't mistakenly send your resume to the same company twice for the same job listing; it looks sloppy if you do.

In addition to the listings that follow, you may want to check out some job-related online Metalists, which provide additional links to other online career resources. The Career Resource Center *(www.careers.org)* contains thousands of links to job resources on the Web, which are broken down into categories, such as financial services, computers, engineering, and marketing. Another Metalist to consult is Stanford University's JobHunt *(www.job-hunt.org)*. In addition, The Riley Guide *(www.rileyguide.com)* is a superb source of job-related resources on the Web, too. A quick way to find job listings on the Web when you don't know the specific Web address is to perform a keyword search in a search engine such as Google or Yahoo! Try using keywords like "employment opportunities," "job listings," or "positions available." You'll be amazed at how many links pop up. Finally, an individual company's Web page is often an excellent source for job listings and company background information.

To get you started, here's a list of some of the major job-hunting sites currently available on the World Wide Web:

America's Job Bank   *www.ajb.dni.us*
This is an immense database of jobs culled from the combined job databases of some 1,800 state employment offices covering professional, technical, blue collar, management, clerical, and sales positions.

Best Jobs USA   *www.bestjobsusa.com*
Features an extensive general jobs database and a secondary database focusing exclusively on health care positions.

CareerBuilder   *www.careerbuilder.com*
One of the most comprehensive career sites on the World Wide Web today, CareerBuilder offers job listings in more than 50 different categories, including an entry-level category, plus resume, cover letter and general job-hunting advice. A weekly newsletter and Spanish-language articles are also available. Note: the former CareerCity, CareerMosaic, and CareerPath sites have been absorbed into the CareerBuilder network of job-related Web sites.

Career Exposure *www.careerexposure.com*
Covers all areas, but seems to focus primarily on skilled technical job postings. This 100% women-owned site is essentially a compilation of job listings from large corporate Web sites.

CareerMagazine *www.careermag.com*
Includes a resume database, employer profiles, and a job database covering most major career areas. Look here for industry-specific "career channels" where you can find job listings, plus employment trends, job descriptions, keyword lists, and educational opportunities related to specific fields.

CareerMosaic. See CareerBuilder.

CareerPath. See CareerBuilder.

Career Shop *www.careershop.com*
Contains links to job fairs and employer home pages in addition to job and resume databases. One interesting feature for job hunters is the "personal job shopper service," which regularly browses the jobs database and automatically generates e-mail messages regarding new job postings that match your career interests based on a profile you have created.

CareerSite. See Now Hiring.

CareerWeb *www.cweb.com*
Includes employer profiles, job fair listings, resume registration, JobMatch, work values tests, tips on resumes and internships, and of course, jobs. There is a primary database of jobs in all categories, plus a secondary database devoted specifically to health care jobs.

College Grad Job Hunter *www.collegegrad.com*
Geared toward the recent college grad, this site includes everything from resume preparation to interviewing tips and negotiating an offer. The number of job listings is not as high as some of the other sites, but those that are listed are geared toward entry-level candidates.

Contract Employment Weekly *www.ceweekly.com*
This online version of the periodical covers temporary and contract technical positions. Much of the information is not available unless you pay a subscription fee.

Cool Works   *www.coolworks.com*

Specializes in seasonal employment positions at national parks, resorts, camps, and ski areas. This site also contains information on volunteer positions. If you're yearning for a job "adventure," even a temporary one, this is the place to find it.

FedWorld Federal Job Search   *www.fedworld.gov/jobs/jobsearch.html*

Want to work for the federal government? Then this is the site you need to search. The number of jobs posted does not put this among the top sites, but it does include some interesting features, such as links to various government databases and even White House press releases and news about Supreme Court decisions.

Get a Job   *www.getajob.com*

While the Get a Job site does not list any specific jobs available, tit is definitely worth a visit for the links it provides to other career resources and Web sites, including "Work from Home" and "Teen Jobs."

Help Wanted   *www.helpwanted.com*

Includes a small but growing job database, a resume database, and a pretty good list of employment agencies and recruiters.

Hot Jobs   *http://hotjobs.yahoo.com*

Part of the comprehensive Yahoo! network, this Web site lists jobs in all categories, but is especially heavy on jobs in computer/technical, finance/accounting, and marketing/sales. This site also includes a resume database and tips on resume writing, as well as a nifty salary calculator for help in determining what certain job types should command in the way of financial compensation.

The Internet Job Locator   *www.joblocator.com*

No job listings here, but a nice, comprehensive list of links to other job-related Web sites.

JobBank USA   *www.jobbankusa.com*

Not only does this site have job and resume databases, it also contains links to other job hunting sites and services on the Web, including a "Work at Home" section.

Jobs.com   *www.jobs.com*

Another in the massive Monster.com network, this Web site is particularly user friendly. From the home page, you can easily access thousands of job listings in several ways: by state, city, country, or zip code; by keyword; or by job category.

Jobs.net   *www.jobs.net*

Not to be confused with the previous site, Jobs.net provides a comprehensive listing of available jobs by location, keyword, company, and category. There are special listings for entry-level positions as well as freelance and part-time jobs.

JobSource   *www.jobsource.com*

Similar to The Internet Job Locator, but with a focus on information for recent graduates, including links to other job search sites and career assistance features.

JOBTRAK. See Monstertrak.

JobWeb   *www.jobweb.com*

Owned and sponsored by the nonprofit National Association of Colleges and Employers, JobWeb contains much useful information and services aside from the usual job database, including links to more than 100 other job-hunting resources. Job listings on this site may be searched by specific employer, keywords, job function, or location.

MedSearch America. See Monster.

Monster   *www.monster.com*

This site is home to an extensive job database covering every major field. In addition to thousands of job listings, Monster features employer profiles, job-hunting and career advice, and links to other career sites.

The former JOBTRAK, which emphasizes entry-level jobs for recent grads, has been absorbed into Monster.com as Monstertrak.com (see below). Monster has also absorbed two other formerly independent career-related Web sites: The Online Career Center and MedSearch. If you click on the previous addresses for either site, you will automatically be taken to Monster.com. In the case of MedSearch, in particular, you will arrive at a special Web page, which focuses exclusively on listings for jobs in the health care industry.

Monstertrak   *www.monstertrak.com*

Formerly called JOBTRAK and now part of the comprehensive Monster.com network of job-related Web sites, this site is designed specifically for college students and alumni, offering job and resume databases, as well as information about career centers, career fairs, scholarships, and online degree programs. The job listings focus on entry-level positions and internships. Monstertrak has formed partnerships with more than 600 colleges, universities, and alumni centers nationwide. To view job listings from a particular campus, you must be a student or alumnus of that institution.

Now Hiring   *www.nowhiring.com*
Formerly known as CareerSite, the distinguishing feature of this site is that if you fill out the credentials form, the site will search the job listings for you and then notify you of any matches. Company profiles, job alerts and career resources are also available here.

The Online Career Center. See Monster.

Simply Hired   *www.simplyhired.com*
Simply Hired touts itself as "the world's largest search engine for jobs." The site claims to have 5 million job listings, all of which are pulled from job boards, company Web pages, online classifieds, and other similar data sources. One unique feature of Simply Hired is its "GLBT-friendly" search filter, which helps job seekers identify companies that have friendly policies in place with regard to gender identity and expression.

SnagAJob   *www.snagajob.com*
This Web site lists approximately 100,000 jobs, but beware—most of them are part-time and/or hourly. If you are looking for a temporary or interim job to generate income while you hunt for a full-time professional position, this might be a good site to check out.

TOPjobs   *www.topjobsusa.com*
In addition to thousands of job listings (TOPjobs boasts close to 950,000 jobs available), this site features an extensive employer profile database and a directory of recruiters.

TrueCareers   *www.truecareers.com*
Job listings are posted to this Web site in 17 categories, including entry-level. You can search the jobs by location, keyword, or industry type. The site also features career resources, including articles on resumes, interviewing, and market trends. If you officially register on this site as a job seeker, you will automatically be directed to CareerBuilder.com, where you can access additional jobs and resources.

Index